Public Policy Analytics

CHAPMAN & HALL/CRC DATA SCIENCE SERIES

Reflecting the interdisciplinary nature of the field, this book series brings together researchers, practitioners, and instructors from statistics, computer science, machine learning, and analytics. The series will publish cutting-edge research, industry applications, and textbooks in data science.

The inclusion of concrete examples, applications, and methods is highly encouraged. The scope of the series includes titles in the areas of machine learning, pattern recognition, predictive analytics, business analytics, Big Data, visualization, programming, software, learning analytics, data wrangling, interactive graphics, and reproducible research.

Published Titles

For more information about this series, please visit: https://www.routledge.com/Chapman--HallCRC-Data-Science-Series/book-series/CHDSS

Public Policy Analytics
Code and Context for Data Science in Government

Ken Steif
Ph.D

CRC Press
Taylor & Francis Group
Boca Raton London New York

CRC Press is an imprint of the
Taylor & Francis Group, an **informa** business

A CHAPMAN & HALL BOOK

First edition published 2022
by CRC Press
6000 Broken Sound Parkway NW, Suite 300, Boca Raton, FL 33487-2742

and by CRC Press
4 Park Square, Milton Park, Abingdon, Oxon OX14 4RN

© 2022 Ken Steif
CRC Press is an imprint of Taylor & Francis Group, an Informa business

Library of Congress Cataloging-in-Publication Data
Names: Steif, Ken, author.
Title: Public policy analytics: code and context for data science in government / Ken Steif.
Description: Boca Raton : CRC Press, 2021. |
Series: Chapman & Hall/CRC data science series | Includes bibliographical references and index.
Identifiers: LCCN 2021002049 | ISBN 9780367507619 (paperback) | ISBN 9780367516253 (hardback) | ISBN 9781003054658 (ebook)
Subjects: LCSH: United States--Politics and government--Data processing. | Public policy--Data processing.
Classification: LCC JK468.A8 S72 2021 | DDC 352.3/80285--dc23
LC record available at https://lccn.loc.gov/2021002049

ISBN: 978-0-367-51625-3 (hbk)
ISBN: 978-0-367-50761-9 (pbk)
ISBN: 978-1-003-05465-8 (ebk)

DOI: 10.1201/9781003054658

Typeset in Latin Modern font
by KnowledgeWorks Global Ltd.

Contents

About the Author

Ken Steif, Ph.D is the director or the Master of Urban Spatial Analytics and a Professor of Practice in the City Planning program, both at the University of Pennsylvania. He is also the founder of Urban Spatial LLC, a consultancy that builds data-driven solutions for clients primarily in the non-profit and public sectors. He lives in West Philly with his wife Diana and two boys, Emil and Malcolm. You can follow him on Twitter `@KenSteif`.

Preface

Welcome to *Public Policy Analytics: Code and Context for Data Science in Government*, a book published by CRC Press as part of its Data Science Series. The data for this book can be found online.[1]

The goal of this book is to make data science accessible to social scientists, and City Planners in particular. I hope to convince readers that a person with strong domain expertise plus intermediate data skills can have a greater impact in government than the sharpest computer scientist who has never studied economics, sociology, public health, political science, criminology, etc.

Public Policy Analytics was written to pass along the knowledge I have personally gained from so many gifted educators over the last 20 years. They are too many to name individually, but their impression on me has been so lasting and so monumental that somewhere along the line I decided to become an educator myself. This book is a reflection of all that these individuals have given to me.

I am incredibly grateful to my colleague Sydney Goldstein, without whom this book would not have been possible. Sydney was instrumental in helping me edit and compile the text. Additionally, she and I co-authored an initial version of Chapter 7 as a white paper. Dr. Tony Smith, a most cherished mentor and friend, edited nearly every machine learning chapter in this book. Dr. Maria Cuellar (Ch. 5), Michael Fichman (Intro), Matt Harris (review of functions), Dr. George Kikuchi (Ch. 5); and Dr. Jordan Purdy (Chs. 6 and 7), each generously provided their time and expertise in review. I thank them wholeheartedly. All errors are mine alone. Finally, this book is dedicated to my wife, Diana, and my sons Emil and Malcolm, who always keep me focused on love and positivity.

I hope both non-technical policymakers and budding public-sector data scientists find this book useful, and I thank you for taking a look.

Ken

Fall, 2020

West Philadelphia, PA.

---

[1] https://github.com/urbanSpatial/Public-Policy-Analytics-Landing

Introduction

How governments make decisions

Although many readers chose this book for an introduction to R, geospatial data science, and machine learning, my goal was to write a book about public-sector decision-making.

The typical methods-driven public policy book is about generating evidence that legislators can use to set budgets. This 'budgetary' decision-making receives the bulk of attention from academics, journalists, and policymakers - and for good reason. However, simply signing a promising bill into a law, does not guarantee success.

Once millions of dollars are budgeted for a program, a government agency decides how to allocate that money, to whom, how often, and for how long. Despite receiving far less attention than budgetary decision-making, this 'operational' decision-making is equally important. A good policy manifested as a poorly-designed program can be just as ineffective as a bad policy.

A program should maximize benefits and minimize costs. This is much more difficult in the public sector, than in the private sector. There are no shortages of CEOs and management professionals who bloviate ad nauseam on the need for government to embody private-sector ideals and leadership practices.

Optimizing the cost/benefit ratio is easier in business because the only relevant bottom line is profit. It matters little whether profit maximization has a negative effect on competitors, consumers, the environment, or other stakeholders. Optimizing the cost/benefit ratio in government is far more difficult because the bottom lines are many, and at times, ambiguous. Yes, there are economic bottom lines, but a 'good' decision in government must simultaneously optimize for economics, political cohesion, equity, and bureaucracy, to name a few.

Because the bottom lines in government are so nuanced, it is often very difficult to understand how decisions are made. In my experience, there are four typical approaches:

Ad hoc: *'Why do we do it this way?'*

'I don't know.'

Decision-making without precedent is rare but not unheard of. Ad hoc decision-making is most common when decisions are made by individuals who are free to act autonomously in the absence of a top-down, centralized decision-making apparatus. An example might be an inspector, guided by a loose set of top-down directives on what to inspect and when. While an experienced inspector may make more good decisions than bad ones, the decisions of an inexperienced inspector may have significant economic and social costs.

Political: *'Why do we do it this way?'*

'Because I can't afford to upset the elected official who sets my agency's budget every year.'

Government is political by nature, and thus decisions may serve certain groups over others. If say, property developers capture a disproportional amount of political capital, then there is a higher likelihood that government decisions will go in their favor. The result is decision-making incentives that may not optimize for critical bottom lines, like equity.

Institutional knowledge: *'Why do we do it this way?'*

'Well, because we have always done it that way.'

As government progressed from Tammany-style, political machine governance to a system of checks and balances in the mid-19th century, a set of incentives emerged designed to maximize efficiency, promote rational decision-making, and prevent corruption. The 'bureaucracy' that resulted is characterized by top-down organization, a clear division of labor, practical expertise, and a rigid set of rules. While the bureaucracy can be helpful, it may also disincentivize innovation.

For example, government data scientists often report difficulty in downloading open-source technology because IT managers argue it preempts their ability to prevent computer security mishaps. Thus, older, clunky, and expensive to maintain 'legacy computer systems' are often hard to pivot away from.

Similar dynamics may exist when individuals attempt to innovate from midway in the chain of command. Innovation is newness, and nothing in government is newer than an incoming administration - with new ideas, new processes, and new politics. Members of the old administration unable to work within the new paradigm are often dismissed. Given the potential for shifting political winds every four years, self-preservation may lead the career bureaucrat to avoid risk-taking. When all stakeholders (particularly senior leadership) stay in their own lane, organizational processes become entrenched and innovation stifled. Not only then does 'Because we have always done it that way' become a slogan, but it becomes a firewall.

Evidenced-based: *'Why do we do it this way?'*

'Because the data suggests this is the best approach.'

Evidenced-based public policy is a major theme of this book. One of the key indicators of an evidenced-based approach is whether operational decisions are made reactively or proactively. Cash-strapped agencies may not have the resources to be proactive, instead they work to put out fires in real time. The proactive decision-maker generalizes their knowledge and experience from the past to preempt fires before they start.

Civil servants are the best among us - vastly underpaid, they work hard to solve society's most complex problems. While most government agencies use data and evidence in one form or another, the analytics discussed in this book are expressly designed to enable proactive decision-making and, hopefully, more effective government programs.

When I discuss this work with policymakers, the initial focus is almost never on data science or technology. Instead, I try to learn how they currently make decisions. What are the inputs, outputs and consequences of those decisions? A more evidenced-based approach is only possible with answers to these questions. Thus, the foundation for successful public-sector data science is not statistics or computer science but domain expertise.

Context as the foundation

Each chapter of this book focuses on a 'use case'. For our purpose, a use case is a specific set of circumstances that drive the development of a technology solution. For example, the use case of the Uber app is to match a rider with a driver and get them both from point A to B. The use case of Zillow's Zestimate algorithm is to provide a home buyer with an estimate of home value even if that house has not sold recently.

The term 'use case' is more prevalent in technology than in social science. An anti-eviction effort for instance, is far more comprehensive than Uber's singular use case: A housing stability initiative seeks to decrease evictions by providing tenants with legal protections; enacting stricter landlord regulations; strengthening code enforcement; promoting affordable housing in neighborhoods of opportunity; bettering schools; creating safer streets; more intergenerational mobility, and so on and so forth.

A comprehensive effort like this, can however, be deconstructed into a series of individual programs and, further still, into a set of discrete use cases around service delivery and operational decision-making. Perhaps one use case utilizes housing and court data to predict landlords who are renting without a license. Another might be to develop a website that allows at-risk families to be linked with community legal services.

How can complex policy initiatives boil down to discrete technology use cases? Start with the context. Here is my framework for doing so:

1. *What is the policy?* In a nutshell, the policy is a set of guiding principles used to achieve a set of goals or outcomes. If the data scientist does not know the policy, then it will be difficult to design solutions to achieve policy goals. Interestingly, sometimes different policies can support the same policy goal, and often policies change dramatically with successive administrations, across geographic locales, and over time.

2. *What are the programs in place to achieve the policy goals?* Programs and policies are often confused as being the same. The program is the tool used to implement the policy to achieve the policy goals. Designing strong programs is incredibly difficult and failed programs may result from ill-conceived policies or from bad program design. Perhaps the designer did not consider unintended consequences or misunderstood the role of incentives. In my experience, good programs have strong cost/benefit ratios, meaning a marginal government investment generates a significant economic, social, public health, etc. return for citizens.

3. *Does a program work?* Some government programs are truly transformational and others, not so much. Program evaluation is the art and science of estimating the efficacy of a program for the purposes of budgetary decision-making. It is typically the domain of trained social scientists who understand programs so well that they can estimate the causal impact of the program on an outcome of interest.

4. *How is the program delivered?* This is operational decision-making, and the area where data scientists can have the greatest impact. The goal is to deliver resources when, where, and to whom they are most needed. Who is eligible for a program? Must participants actively sign up for the program or can they be targeted based on certain criteria? Can we learn from the experience of past program participants to intervene more effectively with future participants? Do citizens interact with the program by mail, by showing up in person, or through a web portal? How can data and technology help an agency improve the program at the margins? These are just a few of many important questions.

This context is required for data scientists to have impact in government. While it is possible to procure data science from private vendors, the need to scale across many customers means one solution often lacks local domain experience. These products have also been known to 'over promise and under-deliver' - especially when their sales pitches include terms like 'Smart Cities' and 'AI'.

Developing data science in-house is much harder but ensures that solutions are based on local knowledge. The best mechanism for growing this human capital is free and open source technology. Open source software and open data has been a great catalyst for public-sector innovation, but the next horizon is 'open analytics'. As governments collect similar data and have similar use cases, shared analytical tools will help data science *learning* scale more easily.

I hope this book helps jump-start the open analytics movement and helps position data science as a tool for operational decision-making. While many see data science as this shiny new object - I contend that it is really just a new take on Planning - something government does by default. Data science as a planning tool is where its real potential lies.

Data science as a planning tool

I relate data science to Planning in the context of strategic planning rather than traditional, 'comprehensive' plan-making. Both Planning and data science are interested in the effective allocation of limited resources. Both ask what resources are at hand? Which are lacking? And where can these resources go to mitigate risk and promote opportunity?[2]

As I mentioned, a good government program means a greater return on a marginal investment. Data science as a planning tool is an example of a marginal government investment, particularly as government already collects data and already has a mandate to plan, mitigate risk, etc.

Many chapters in this book are focused on predictive modeling via a set of methods referred to as machine learning. The goal of machine learning, as I see it, is to 'borrow the experience' of people or places from the recent past and test the extent to which that experience generalizes into the near future.

In this context, prediction is a powerful planning tool that can borrow from the overdose experience on these vacant lots to predict overdose *risk* on those vacant lots, and prediction can borrow the homelessness experience from these residents to predict homelessness risk for others.

When these risks are known, Planners can more effectively target their limited resources, like overdose prevention and housing programs.

It is hard to predict things, particularly in complex urban systems. As we will learn in Chapter 3, the goal is not to model all the complexity, but slice off use cases in more bounded systems with more simplistic interactions.

The algorithms in this book are judged by their 'usefulness' as Planning and decision-making tools. A useful tool has a greater cost/benefit than the 'business-as-usual' approach. While economic costs and benefits are important, social costs are far more critical. Much time is spent in the second half of the book 'opening the black box' of our algorithms to mitigate decisions that further disenfranchise or discriminate.

---

[2]Planners might recognize this as the SWOT (Strengths, Weaknesses, Opportunities and Threats) model of strategic planning

By the Conclusion, we will learn how these insights inform a new 'algorithmic governance' approach, built on the belief that algorithmic decision-making is just a new take on the traditional approach to program design and Planning.

Many Planning questions are place-based, and start with the word 'where'. This book focuses heavily on 'geospatial data science' - which is a new label for a discipline, quantitative geography, that goes back at least as far as the 1950s. Quantitative geography has a rich history, much of which relates directly to Planning.

Geospatial data science repurposes the tools of quantitative geography to support Planning that increasingly relies on large, real-time geospatial databases, predictive modeling, data visualization, analytical dashboards, and other emerging technologies.

Answering 'where' questions can inform placed-based decision-making - but doing so requires an understanding of how spatial data is different from non-spatial data, and how modeling spatial systems requires a unique understanding of why things locate where they do.

The importance of spatial thinking

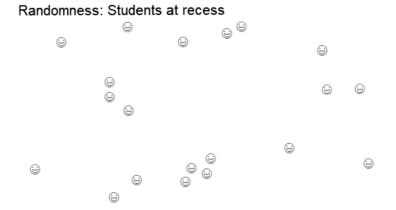

FIGURE 0.1 An example of a random spatial distribution.

Very infrequently are social science phenomena randomly distributed in space, like the visualization (Figure 0.1) of students roaming the recess blacktop.

Developers do not locate their next suburban shopping mall by throwing a dart at the map. Police do not randomly allocate patrols to neighborhoods. Civil engineers do not connect just any two places with a highway. Social scientists have spent decades understanding why people, businesses, and other entities locate where they do. Understanding why firms cluster can help cities grow the next Silicon Valley. Understanding why gentrifiers buy into certain neighborhoods can help cities plan affordable housing.

The best way to start understanding these dynamics is to simply map the 'spatial process' or spatial pattern in the outcome of interest. Let us look at some real and metaphorical examples of spatial processes below. Figure 0.2 illustrates the spatial configuration of students in a lecture hall. Why are the students located at a uniform distance from one another?

This spatial process is called 'dispersion'. A decision was made by the room's designer that no more than 60 students can be in the room and all chairs will be located at a fixed distance.

As illustrated in Figure 0.2, the location of fire stations provides a real-world example of dispersion. Fire stations are distributed to efficiently minimize response times and to ensure that fire service areas do not overlap.

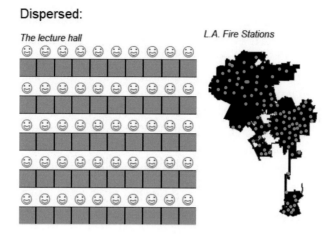

FIGURE 0.2 An example of a dispersed spatial distribution.

A third spatial process is clustering. The students in Figure 0.3 have chosen to sit with their friends at long tables in a lunchroom. This configuration is the result of students self-selecting into lunchtime cliques. _Reported_ burglaries are a real-world example of clustering - a spatial process discussed at length in Chapter 5.

Most spatial processes of interest to policymakers exhibit clustering. Tech companies cluster to take advantage of labor market efficiencies. Gentrifiers cluster to capitalize on emerging amenities. Disease clusters because vulnerable populations live among one another.

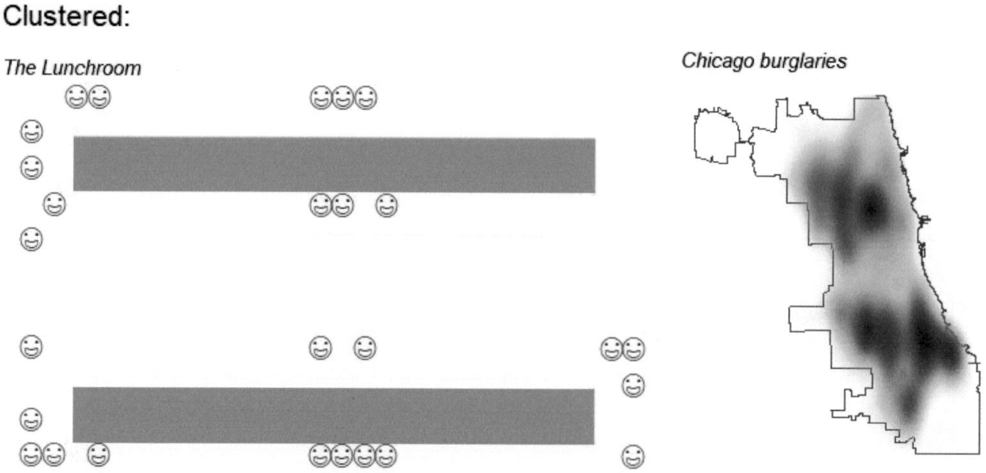

FIGURE 0.3 An example of a clustered spatial distribution.

The lecture hall designer chose to disperse students, while in the lunchroom, students self-selected into clusters. One way to think about these spatial processes is that the former is driven by an external decision imposed on the system, while the latter involves decisions imposed on the system from within.

The most difficult spatial phenomena typically feature both forms of decision-making. Take segregation for example. Segregation results from the external decisions of institutions to force certain people to live in certain places. It may also occur because members of one race self-select into neighborhoods with others of their same race. A thorough understanding of both spatial dynamics is required to fully understand segregation.

The classroom in Figure 0.4 is an example of multiple spatial processes. At a more global scale, an external decision was made to disperse the tables and thus the students at equal intervals. The students then can self-select into table clusters of their choosing.

Many spatial phenomena involve multiple scales of spatial interaction. The Boston home price map illustrates how home prices cluster across neighborhoods but also vary within neighborhoods. Chapters 3 and 4 explore the spatial process in home prices to help predict prices across space.

In a word, it is *scale* that makes the understanding of spatial process so difficult, and scale is the most difficult challenge to overcome in spatial analysis. Scale problems persist in how arbitrary units like census tracts are used to summarize an underlying population; in how one measures exposure from a community to nearby risk factors; and most importantly, in how a certain dynamic in one community generalizes to community contexts elsewhere.

Multiple Scales:

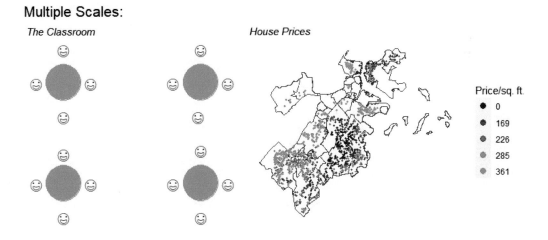

FIGURE 0.4 An example of multiple spatial scales.

These different spatial processes of clustering, randomness, and dispersion are well known to geographers. The famous First Law of Geography states that, although all things are related, nearer things are more related than farther things.[3] More of a statistical inevitability than a law, this 'spatial autocorrelation' suggests, for instance, that the elevation five feet from you is more like the elevation under your feet, than the elevation five miles away. The same can be said for crime, home prices, and the income of your neighbors. The more the analyst understands the scale in which nearer things are related, the more useful their analytics are for decision-making.

---

[3]Tobler, W. R. (1970). A computer movie simulating urban growth in the Detroit region. Economic geography, 46(sup1), 234-240.

Learning objectives

This book is as concerned with data science context as it is with data science code. I hope it appeals both to budding public-sector data scientists as well as policymakers looking to learn more about this technology. If you are reading the print version of this book and would like to run the code, the online 'Bookdown' makes it easy to copy and paste code from your browser into R.

Material for this book was originally written for graduate students in the Master of Urban Spatial Analytics program at the University of Pennsylvania - a program I direct. Most of my students come in with at least some technical experience - mostly in spatial analysis, but many have no experience writing R code. My goal is not to teach them coding per se, but how to take the code I give them (and have given you) and hack it together to create something new. I have found this format works well for teaching data science to social science students, so long as readers are interested in solving the underlying problems that motivate each chapter.

This book is written in R, which is a free and open source programming language with millions of users worldwide. R has fostered a huge community of impassioned individuals who are equally as interested in developing code for their own uses as they are in sharing it with others. As a result, a free and open source R package exists for almost any analytical pursuit. The reason to code data science, rather than mouse click it, is reproducibility - to write the code once such that it can be replicated in the future with ease.

Because R is open source and community-driven, it is constantly being updated and improved. Inevitably, the code in this book will become dated (likely as soon as it is published), and while I will try to update the text over time, you may have to rely on the internet for quick fixes.

There are many books and resources that you can use to supplement your learning. Google is smart enough to understand R-related error questions and will likely pass you along to websites like Stackoverflow. There are two supplemental books that I can recommend as well. The first is *R for Data Science* by Hadley Wickham and Garrett Grolemund, which provides a thorough introduction to the `tidyverse` approach to R programming.[4] The second is *Geocomputation with R* by Lovelace, Nowosad, and Muenchow.[5]

Chapters 1 and 2 of this book focus on descriptive data science. Chapter 1 introduces R in the context of exploratory spatial analysis, developing a series of transit indicators to communicate complex metrics to non-technical decision-makers. Chapter 2 continues introducing the R workflow, as well as geoprocessing to help Planners in Lancaster County, Pennsylvania, choose a town suitable for new development rights.

Chapters 3 through 8 convey predictive data science. Chapters 3 and 4 introduce geospatial machine learning, providing a framework for assessing the accuracy and generalizability of models across different spatial contexts. The goal is to forecast home prices, an algorithm many counties now use to assess property taxes. Home prices exhibit a very nuanced spatial process, which makes it a fascinating first use case of geospatial machine learning.

Chapter 5 introduces geospatial risk prediction, demonstrating the perils of predictive policing. Data from Chicago is used to train a predictive model that predicts burglary risk for every location citywide. Predictions are evaluated for fairness, and we begin to discuss how selection bias is converted to algorithmic bias.

---

[4]https://r4ds.had.co.nz/
[5]https://bookdown.org/robinlovelace/geocompr/

Chapter 6 introduces person-based predictive models focusing on 'churn', the probability that a client will re-subscribe to a subsidy or service. This use case is incredibly important for agencies that allocate resources to individuals, households, or families.

Chapter 7 builds on Chapters 5 and 6 by providing a framework for assessing algorithmic fairness in person-level predictions. Using a classic example from the criminal justice field, the goal is to understand the extent to which a decision-making tool may have a disparate impact on a protected class, like race.

Chapter 8 aggregates much of what we have learned about geospatial machine learning to help forecast space/time rideshare demand in Chicago. This use case brings us right to the cusp of integrating 'big data' in forecasting models, which is the reasonable next step for the would-be public-sector data scientist.

Finally, the Conclusion connects the algorithmic themes of the book with traditional Planning practice, introducing the 'algorithmic governance' framework for integrating data science into government programs.

All of the data in the book are open data, much of which can be accessed directly from the web. In each chapter, code is provided for downloading these datasets from the web. Should the form or path of these datasets change, the code will no longer be useful, and readers should read in data from the book's Github repository.[6]

Assignments are associated with each chapter. The goal is to have readers replicate what they have learned on a new dataset and to communicate important themes and findings to non-technical decision-makers. If you are working on these assignments independently, I urge you to focus on data visualization and short, concise written narrative.

---

[6]https://github.com/urbanSpatial/Public-Policy-Analytics-Landing

1

Indicators for Transit-oriented Development

1.1 Why start with indicators?

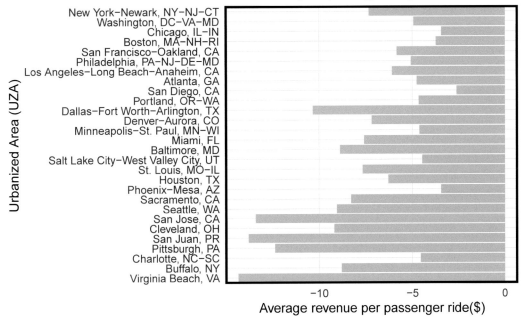

FIGURE 1.1 Revenue per passenger for passenger subway systems in the United States.

According to the Federal Transit Administration (FTA), not one of America's largest passenger subway systems saw fare revenues exceed operating expenses in 2015.[1]

This is an indicator - a stylized fact that gives simple insight into a complicated phenomena. Mastering indicators is critical for conveying nuanced context to non-technical audiences. Here are four suggestions on what makes a good indicator:

1. A *relatable* indicator is typically motivated by a pressing policy concern. "How is it possible that passenger rail in New York City has such widespread delays, service suspensions, and rider discontent?" A great indicator solicits interest from an audience.

---

[1] Federal Transit Administration. "NTD Data, 2015". https://www.transit.dot.gov/ntd/ntd-data

DOI: 10.1201/9781003054658-1

2. A *simple* indicator may be used as an exploratory tool in place of more complex statistics. Simplicity helps the audience understand the indicator's significance and keeps them engaged in the analysis.

3. A *relative* indicator draws a contrast. "How can New York City passenger rail, with the most trips, still lose more money than each of the next ten largest cities?" Contextualizing an indicator with a relevant comparison makes for greater impact.

4. A good indicator typically generates more questions than answers. Thus, a good indicator fits into a broader *narrative*, which helps motivate a more robust research agenda and ultimately, more applied analytics.

Simplicity is an indicator's strength, but it may also be its weakness. Most statistics make assumptions. You should be aware of these assumptions, how they affect your conclusions, and ultimately how the audience interprets your results.

In this first chapter, space/time indicators are built from U.S. Census data to explore transit-oriented development (TOD) potential in Philadelphia. Along the way, we will learn how assumptions can lead to incorrect policy conclusions.

TOD advocates for increased housing and amenity density around transit (rail, subway, bus, etc.). There are many benefits to promoting this density, but two examples are particularly noteworthy.

First, transit needs scale to exist. Transit demand is a function of density, and the more households, customers, and businesses around transit, the more efficient it is to operate a transit system. Efficiency means less maintenance, staffing, etc. Interestingly, Figure 1.1 suggests that most transit systems are remarkably inefficient despite being in cities with density of just about everything.

Second, TOD is important for land value capitalization, which is essential to both developers and governments. If renters and home buyers are willing to pay more to locate near transit amenities, it should be reflected in higher land values and property tax returns near stations.

In this chapter, we play the role of Transportation Planner for the City of Philadelphia and assess whether rents are higher in transit-rich areas relative to places without transit access. If residents value these locations, officials might consider changing the zoning code to allow increased density around transit.

As the analysis progresses, spatial data wrangling and visualization fundamentals are presented with the `tidyverse`, `sf`, and `ggplot2` packages. The `tidycensus` package is used to gather U.S. Census tract data. We begin by identifying some of the key assumptions made when working with geospatial census data.

1.1.1 Mapping and scale bias in areal aggregate data

Data visualization is a data scientist's strongest communication tool because a picture tells a thousand words. However, visualizations and maps in particular, can mislead. Figure 1.2 maps median household income for Philadelphia census tracts in 2000 and 2017. The narrative suggests that incomes in Center City (around City Hall) have increased. While this is likely true, the precise narrative is in part, driven by how colors are assigned to incomes on the map.

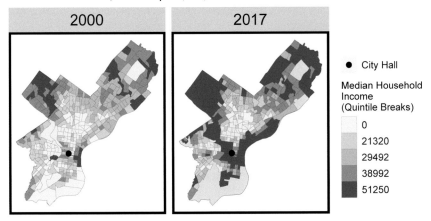

FIGURE 1.2 Median household income for Philadelphia census tracts in 2000 and 2017.

Figure 1.3 illustrates two different approaches. The top-most plots use `ggplot`'s default 'equal interval' breaks, while those on the bottom bin income into 5 quintile groups, which are intervals at the 1st, 20th, 40th, 60th, and 80th percentiles of the data.

Setting map breaks can alter the narrative of a map. Ultimately, breaks should 'hug the cliffs' of the distribution. Compared to the equal interval breaks, the quintile breaks map portrays a sharper contrast in incomes across the city.

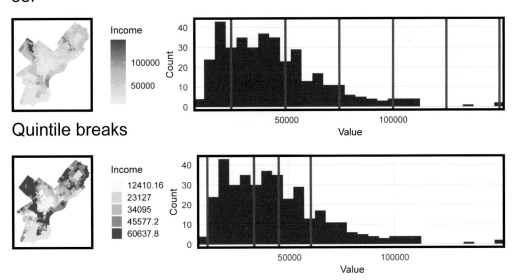

FIGURE 1.3 Two approaches for defining breaks (tract boundaries removed).

Census tract maps also introduce bias related to scale. To start, when summary statistics like mean or median are used to summarize individuals, results may be biased by the 'ecological fallacy'. For example, consider Figure 1.4, which visualizes three household income distributions in a tract.

One plot has a normal (i.e., bell curve) distribution with values close to the mean, one with much greater variance around the mean, and one skewed. These tracts are all very different, but they all share the same 'mean income'.

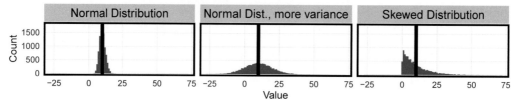

FIGURE 1.4 Three income distributions in a census tract with the same mean.

Figure 1.5 shows these differences geographically, drawing two of the above household income distributions across the same census tract. The normal distribution seems relatively homogeneous while the skewed distribution, appears like a mixed-income community.

The ecological fallacy is made worse if we assume a census tract polygon is akin to a neighborhood - an area of social, economic, and built environment homogeneity. Remember, the census uses tracts to count people, not to reference social phenomena. When counting occurs inside *arbitrarily* drawn aggregate units like tracts, another source of bias emerges. This kind of scale bias is known as the modifiable areal unit problem (MAUP).[2]

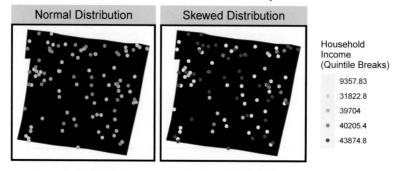

FIGURE 1.5 Maps of two income distributions with the same mean.

For example, Figure 1.6 locates houses in one corner of a tract, assuming that the remaining area is a park, perhaps. Again, we can see how representing this area with a single summary statistic may be problematic.

Scale bias is an important consideration when creating and interpreting indicators. We will continue to make scale assumptions throughout the remainder of this chapter, and in every other spatial chapter throughout the book. With experience, you will find it possible to create analytics that are useful despite scale bias.

---

[2]Openshaw, Stan and S. Openshaw. "The modifiable areal unit problem." Geo Abstracts, University of East Anglia, 1984.

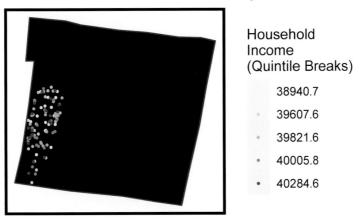

FIGURE 1.6 Houses clustered in one part of the census tract.

1.2   Set up

The code blocks below include the libraries, options, and functions needed for the analysis. The `tidyverse` library enables data wrangling and visualization; `tidycensus` allows access to the Census API; `sf` wrangles and processes spatial data; and `kableExtra` helps create tables.

```
library(tidyverse)
library(tidycensus)
library(sf)
library(kableExtra)

options(scipen=999)
options(tigris_class = "sf")

root.dir =
  paste0("https://raw.githubusercontent.com/urbanSpatial",
         "/Public-Policy-Analytics-Landing/master/DATA/")
source(
  paste0("https://raw.githubusercontent.com/urbanSpatial/",
         "Public-Policy-Analytics-Landing/master/functions.r"))
```

Two global `options` are set to first tell R not to use scientific notation (`scipen`) and second, `tigris_class` tells `tidycensus` to download census geometries in the `sf` or Simple Feature format. Finally, the functions used throughout this book are read in from a source file. This chapter uses the `mapTheme` and `plotTheme` to standardize the formatting of maps and plots, as well as the `qBr` and `q5` functions to create quintile map breaks.

palette5 is a color palette comprised of a list of hex codes. The operation c 'combines' a set of values into a list. There are a variety of websites like ColorBrewer that can help you explore color ramps for maps.[3]

```
palette5 <- c("#f0f9e8","#bae4bc","#7bccc4","#43a2ca","#0868ac")
```

1.2.1 Downloading and wrangling census data

The tidycensus package provides an excellent interface for querying census data in R. Table 1.1 shows a set of variables, variable codes, and the Short_name we will use for this analysis. For a list of the 2000 Census variables, use View(load_variables(2000, "sf3", cache = TRUE)).

Variable	Census_code_in_2000	Census_code_in_2017	Short_name
Total Population	P001001	B25026_001E	TotalPop
Number of white residents	P006002	B02001_002E	NumberWhites
Total: Female: 18 to 24 years: Bachelor's degree	PCT025050	B15001_050E	TotalFemaleBachelors
Total: Male: 18 to 24 years: Bachelor's degree	PCT025009	B15001_009E	TotalMaleBacheors
Median Household Income	P053001	B19013_001E	MedHHInc
Median contract rent	H056001	B25058_001E	MedRent
Total living in poverty	P092001	B06012_002E	TotalPoverty

TABLE 1.1 Data dictionary

Before querying the Census API, you will need your own Census API key, which can be downloaded for free.[4] Once acquired, input the key with census_api_key("myKey...").

The get_decennial function downloads tract data for the variables in Table 1.1. year is set to 2000 and state and county are set to Pennsylvania and Philadelphia, respectively. Setting geometry to true (T) ensures tract geometries are downloaded with the data.

st_transform is used to project the data from decimal degrees to feet. 'Projection' is the mathematical process by which the Earth is 'flattened' onto a plane, like a map. It is preferable to work in coordinate systems projected in feet or meters, where distance can be measured reliably.

In this chapter, the tidycensus is used to query and return census data directly into R. At the time of publication, however, the census has disabled the year 2000 endpoint/data.[5] Instead, the code that follows downloads an equivalent data frame called tracts00. A data frame is the most common way to store data in R. The code block at the end of this section demonstrates a tidycensus call to return 2017 data.

class(tracts00) shows that tracts00 is a unique type of data frame as it is also a Simple Features or sf object with polygon geometries for each census tract.

```
tracts00 <-
  st_read(file.path(root.dir,"/Chapter1/PHL_CT00.geojson")) %>%
  st_transform('ESRI:102728')
```

---

[3]http://colorbrewer2.org

[4]Request a Census API Key http://api.census.gov/data/key_signup.html

[5]When the service is again live, the change will be reflected in this book's online version

`tracts00[1:3,]` is an example of matrix notation and can be used to reference rows and columns of a data frame. This tells R to return the first three rows and all of the columns from the `tracts00` data frame. `tracts00[1:3,1]` returns the first three rows and the first column. In both instances, the `geometry` field is also returned. A specific set of columns can be returned by specifying a list, like so - `tracts00[1:3,c(1:3,5)]`. The first three rows are returned along with the first through third columns and column five.

`GEOID` is a unique identifier the census gives for each geography nationwide. '42' is the state of Pennsylvania; '101' is Philadelphia County; and the remaining digits identify a census tract.

Note the header information that outputs as well, including the `geometry type`, in this case, polygons; the layer's spatial extent, or bounding box, `bbox`; and the coordinate system, `CRS`. Google the CRS and find it on spatialreference.org to reveal its code, `102728`. This parameter is passed to `st_transform` to project the layer into feet.

The seven variables downloaded are structured in a strange way. You may be most familiar with data in 'wide' form, where each row represents a census tract and each column, a variable. This data is formatted in 'long' form, which provides some interesting advantages.

`table(tracts00$variable)` returns a frequency count of rows associated with each `variable`. Note the `$` operator, which points to a specific column in a data frame. The output shows seven variables have been downloaded, each consisting of 381 rows, suggesting there are 381 census tracts in Philadelphia. In this long-form, 381 tracts across seven variables are 'stacked' atop one another for a total 2,667 rows.

As an intro to mapping with `sf` layers, the code below creates a new data frame, `totalPop00`, including only Total Population in 2000, P001001. The `tracts00` data frame is 'piped' into the `filter` function using the `%>%` operator. `filter` performs a subset by evaluating a specific query, in this case, looking for any row where the `variable` field equals P001001. The result is set equal to (`<-`) the `sf` data frame, `totalPop00`.

```
totalPop00 <-
  tracts00 %>%
  filter(variable == "P001001")
```

`nrow(totalPop00)` tells us that the data frame has 381 rows. `names(totalPop00)` returns the data frame's column names. Finally, `head(totalPop00)` returns just the first six rows and all the columns.

A `geometry` field is included in a `sf` layer, and the `sf` package has some quick and useful plotting functions. `plot` is the base R plotting function, but when called with an `sf` layer, a map of each variable is returned. Matrix notation can be used to map a single variable, such as, `plot(totalPop00[,4])`

```
plot(totalPop00)
```

`ggplot2` is a powerful tool for designing maps and visualization. A `ggplot` is constructed from a series of 'geoms' or geometric objects. Many different geoms[6] exist, but `geom_sf` is used to map a Simple Features data frame.

---

[6]https://ggplot2.tidyverse.org/reference/#section-layer-geoms

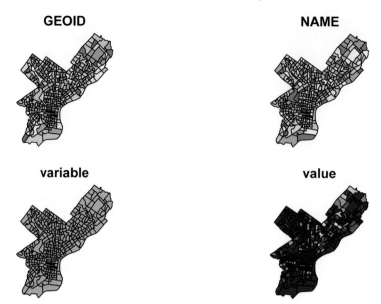

FIGURE 1.7 Using `plot` for sf objects.

The code block that follows and Figure 1.8 illustrate incrementally, how nuance can be added to a `ggplot`. Here, plot `A` maps `totalPop00`, using the `aes` or aesthetic parameter to `fill` the tract polygons by the `value` field.

Plot `B` converts `value` to 5 quintile categories using the `q5` function. These 5 categories are of class `factor`. Try `q5(totalPop00$value)`.

Plot `C` adds fill color and legend improvements using the `scale_fill_manual` function. Many different scale types are possible.[7] `values` is set to a list of colors, `palette5`. `labels` is set to the values of the associated quintiles (try `qBr(totalPop00, "value")`). Finally, a legend `name` is added. `\n` inserts a hard return.

Plot `D` inserts a title using the `labs` parameter, as well as a `mapTheme`.

```
A <-
  ggplot() +
  geom_sf(data = totalPop00, aes(fill = value))

B <-
  ggplot() +
  geom_sf(data = totalPop00, aes(fill = q5(value)))

C <-
  ggplot() +
  geom_sf(data = totalPop00, aes(fill = q5(value))) +
  scale_fill_manual(values = palette5,
                    labels = qBr(totalPop00, "value"),
                    name = "Popluation\n(Quintile Breaks)")
```

---

[7]https://ggplot2.tidyverse.org/reference/#section-scales

```
D <-
  ggplot() +
  geom_sf(data = totalPop00, aes(fill = q5(value))) +
  scale_fill_manual(values = palette5,
                    labels = qBr(totalPop00, "value"),
                    name = "Popluation\n(Quintile Breaks)") +
  labs(title = "Total Population",
       subtitle = "Philadelphia; 2000") +
  mapTheme()
```

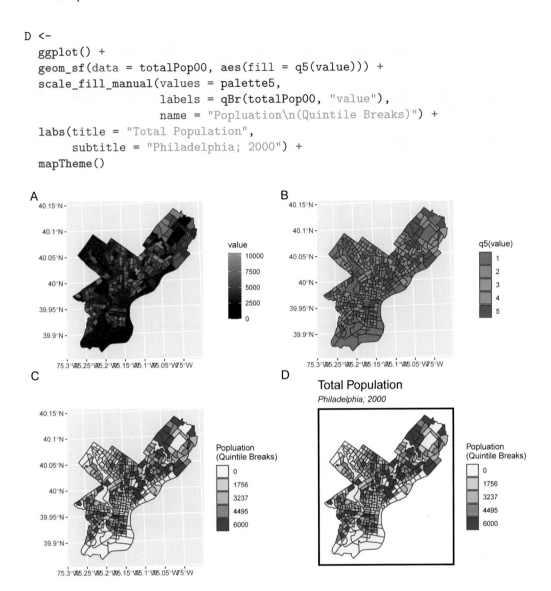

FIGURE 1.8 Styling ggplots.

To demonstrate how to calculate new variables, the raw census data is converted to rates. `tracts00` is converted from long to the more common wide-form using the `spread` function. The `select` function drops one of the tract identifiers, and `rename` is used to rename the variables.

Note the wide-form output now shows 381 rows, one for each unique tract. This is likely a more familiar format for most readers.

```
tracts00 <-
  dplyr::select(tracts00, -NAME) %>%
  spread(variable, value) %>%
  dplyr::select(-geometry) %>%
  rename(
```

```
      TotalPop = P001001, Whites = P006002,
      MaleBachelors = PCT025009, FemaleBachelors = PCT025050,
      MedHHInc = P053001, MedRent = H056001,
      TotalPoverty = P092001)
```

```
st_drop_geometry(tracts00)[1:3,1:6]
```

```
##        GEOID MedRent TotalPop Whites MedHHInc TotalPoverty
## 1 42101000100     858     2576   2095    48886         1739
## 2 42101000200     339     1355    176     8349          505
## 3 42101000300     660     2577   1893    40625         1189
```

Next, `mutate` is used to create the new rate variables; then extraneous columns are dropped using `select`. The `ifelse` prevents divide by 0 errors.

```
tracts00 <-
  tracts00 %>%
  mutate(
    pctWhite = ifelse(TotalPop > 0, Whites / TotalPop,0),
    pctBachelors =
      ifelse(TotalPop > 0, ((FemaleBachelors + MaleBachelors) /
                              TotalPop), 0),
    pctPoverty = ifelse(TotalPop > 0, TotalPoverty / TotalPop, 0),
    year = "2000") %>%
  dplyr::select(
    -Whites,-FemaleBachelors,-MaleBachelors,-TotalPoverty)
```

`tracts00` is now a complete dataset for the year 2000, but the TOD study requires data in the future as well. To download the 2017 American Community Survey or ACS data (`get_acs`), the following code block uses the pipe, `%>%`, to enable a more concise workflow.

The 2017 variable names are different from 2000, and the 2017 equivalent `value` field is called `estimate`. Setting `output="wide"`, automatically downloads the data into wide-form. `mutate` calculates rates. Finally, the `select` function is used with `starts_with` to remove all the original census codes (which happen to begin with B).

```
tracts17 <-
  get_acs(
    geography = "tract", variables =
      c("B25026_001E","B02001_002E","B15001_050E",
        "B15001_009E","B19013_001E","B25058_001E",
        "B06012_002E"),
    year=2017, state=42, county=101,
    geometry=T, output="wide") %>%
  st_transform('ESRI:102728') %>%
  rename(
    TotalPop = B25026_001E, Whites = B02001_002E,
    FemaleBachelors = B15001_050E, MaleBachelors = B15001_009E,
    MedHHInc = B19013_001E, MedRent = B25058_001E,
    TotalPoverty = B06012_002E) %>%
  dplyr::select(-NAME, -starts_with("B")) %>%
```

```
mutate(
  pctWhite = ifelse(TotalPop > 0, Whites / TotalPop,0),
  pctBachelors = ifelse(TotalPop > 0,
    ((FemaleBachelors + MaleBachelors) / TotalPop),0),
  pctPoverty = ifelse(TotalPop > 0,TotalPoverty / TotalPop, 0),
  year = "2017") %>%
dplyr::select(
  -Whites, -FemaleBachelors, -MaleBachelors, -TotalPoverty)
```

The last step then is to combine the 2000 and 2017 tracts together, stacking both layers atop one another with `rbind`. `allTracts` is now a complete time/space dataset.

```
allTracts <- rbind(tracts00,tracts17)
```

1.2.2 Wrangling transit open data

The next task is to relate the census tracts to subway stops, in space. Subway stations are downloaded directly into R from the SEPTA open data site.[8] Philadelphia has two subway lines, the El or elevated subway which runs east to west down Market Street, and the Broad Street Line, which runs north to south on Broad Street.

The following code downloads and binds together El and Broad Street station locations into a single layer, `septaStops`. `st_read` downloads the data in geojson form (with geometries) from the web. A `Line` field is generated and selected along with the `Station` field. Lastly, the data is projected into the same coordinate system as `tracts00`.

```
septaStops <-
  rbind(
    st_read(
      paste0("https://opendata.arcgis.com/datasets/",
             "8c6e2575c8ad46eb887e6bb35825e1a6_0.geojson")) %>%
    mutate(Line = "El") %>%
    select(Station, Line),
      st_read(
        paste0("https://opendata.arcgis.com/datasets/",
               "2e9037fd5bef406488ffe5bb67d21312_0.geojson")) %>%
      mutate(Line ="Broad_St") %>%
      select(Station, Line)) %>%
    st_transform(st_crs(tracts00))
```

`septaStops` are mapped in Figure 1.9 to illustrate a `ggplot` map overlay. The first `geom_sf` plots a Philadelphia basemap using `st_union` to 'dissolve' tract boundaries into a city boundary. The second `geom_sf` maps `septaStops`, assigning `colour` to the `Line` attribute. `show.legend` ensures the legend displays points. Note that a `data` parameter is specified for each `geom_sf`.

---

[8]SEPTA is 'Southeastern Pennsylvania Transit Authority', and is the transit provider for Philadelphia. SEPTA Open Data. http://septaopendata-septa.opendata.arcgis.com/search

Above, `scale_fill_manual` was used to `fill` the `totalPop00` tract *polygons* with color. In this case, `septaStops` *points* are coloured using `scale_colour_manual`.

```
ggplot() +
  geom_sf(data=st_union(tracts00)) +
  geom_sf(data=septaStops, aes(colour = Line),
          show.legend = "point") +
  scale_colour_manual(values = c("orange","blue")) +
  labs(title="SEPTA Stops", subtitle="Philadelphia, PA") +
  mapTheme()
```

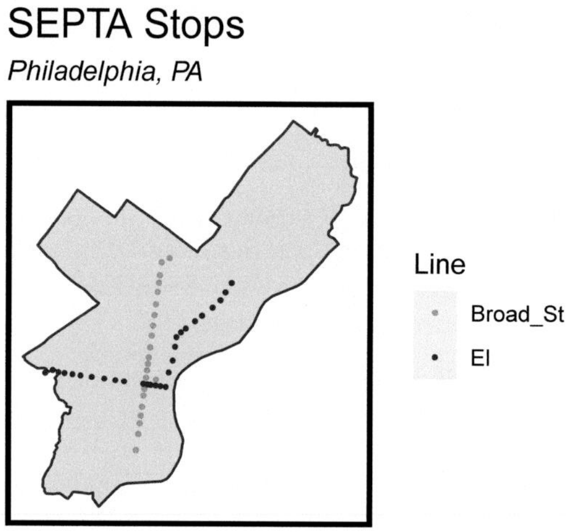

FIGURE 1.9 Overlaying multiple sf objects with ggplot.

1.2.3   Relating tracts and subway stops in space

To understand whether `TOD` tracts are valued more than `non-TOD` tracts, a methodology is needed to assign tracts to one of these two groups. Three overlay techniques are demonstrated to find tracts *close* to subway stations. Defining 'close' provides another important lesson on spatial scale.

Human beings have a very instinctual understanding of closeness. You may be willing to ride a bike three miles to work every day, but getting up to fetch the remote control from across the room is a noticeable burden. It's fine for near and far to be subjective in the real world, but here, spatial relationships must be defined explicitly. In the following code, close is defined as tracts within a half mile (2,640 ft.) of stations.

`st_buffer` generates polygon 'buffers' with boundaries exactly half mile from the stations. A long-form layer stacks two sets of station buffers, dissolving (`st_union`) the second set into one large polygon. 2640 is understood as feet because `septaBuffers` is projected in feet. Note the two `Legend` items and that the `st_union` output is converted to an `sf` layer with `st_sf`.

The resulting 'small multiple' map in Figure 1.10 is only possible when data is organized in long-form. `facet_wrap` is used to create the small multiple map, ensuring both are perfectly aligned.

```
septaBuffers <-
  rbind(
    st_buffer(septaStops, 2640) %>%
      mutate(Legend = "Buffer") %>%
      dplyr::select(Legend),
    st_union(st_buffer(septaStops, 2640)) %>%
      st_sf() %>%
      mutate(Legend = "Unioned Buffer"))

ggplot() +
  geom_sf(data=septaBuffers) +
  geom_sf(data=septaStops, show.legend = "point") +
  facet_wrap(~Legend) +
  mapTheme()
```

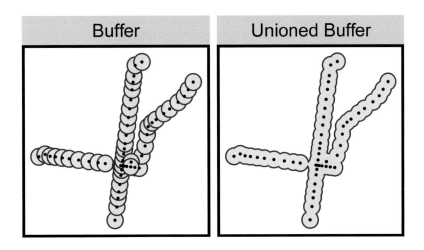

FIGURE 1.10 Creating a small multiple map using long-form data.

Now to select tracts that fall inside of the buffer. The `Unioned Buffer` is used because it enables a cleaner overlay. Below, three different approaches for selecting tracts that are with 0.5 miles of subway stations are considered.

1. Intersection or `Clip` - Relate tracts and the buffer using the latter to 'cookie cutter' the former.
2. `Spatial Selection` - Select all tracts that intersect or touch the buffer.
3. `Select by Centroids` - Select all the tract *centroids* that intersect the buffer.

A centroid is the gravitational center of a polygon. The centroid for a circle is the point at which you can balance it on your finger. Interestingly, very irregular shapes may have centroids outside of a polygon's boundary as Figure 1.11 illustrates.

In the code block below, the `buffer` object pulls out just the `Unioned Buffer`. The first approach, `clip` uses `st_intersection` to cookie cutter the tracts. `TotalPop` is selected, and a `Legend` is created. The second approach, `selection` uses matrix notation to select all `tracts00` that touch the `buffer`.

Shapes and their centroids

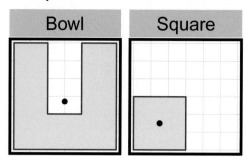

FIGURE 1.11 Two examples of polygon centroids.

The third approach, `selectCentroids` is more complicated. Run each line separately to see how it works. A spatial selection is used again, but this time, `st_centroid` returns tract centroid points instead of polygons. A polygon output is needed, so `st_drop_geometry` converts the `sf` to a data frame and `left_join` joins it back to the original `tracts00`, complete with the polygon geometries. `st_sf` then converts the data frame to `sf` with polygon geometries. Joining two tables together requires a unique identifier, in this case `GEOID`.

```
buffer <- filter(septaBuffers, Legend=="Unioned Buffer")

clip <-
  st_intersection(buffer, tracts00) %>%
    dplyr::select(TotalPop) %>%
    mutate(Selection_Type = "Clip")

selection <-
  tracts00[buffer,] %>%
    dplyr::select(TotalPop) %>%
    mutate(Selection_Type = "Spatial Selection")

selectCentroids <-
  st_centroid(tracts00)[buffer,] %>%
    st_drop_geometry() %>%
    left_join(dplyr::select(tracts00, GEOID)) %>%
    st_sf() %>%
    dplyr::select(TotalPop) %>%
    mutate(Selection_Type = "Select by Centroids")
```

Can you create the small multiple map in Figure 1.12? To do so, `rbind` the three selection types together and use `facet_wrap` to return three maps. Remember, `st_union(tracts00)` creates a basemap. What are the apparent differences across the selection criteria?

`Clip` is the worst choice as changing the geometries exasperates ecological fallacy and MAUP bias. `Spatial Selection` is better, but a tract is included even if only a sliver of its area touches the `buffer`. This approach selects perhaps too many tracts.

`Select by Centroids` is my choice because it captures a concise set of tracts without altering geometries. While well-reasoned, it is still subjective, and each choice will ultimately lead to different results. Such is the impact of scale problems in spatial analysis.

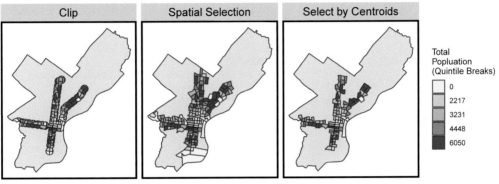

Total population within 1/2 mi. of subways

3 Spatial selection techniques

FIGURE 1.12 Examples of spatial selection techniques.

1.3 Developing TOD indicators

1.3.1 TOD indicator maps

Let us now explore the hypothesis that if residents value TOD, then rents should be higher in areas close to transit relative to places at distance.

The following code block replicates the select by centroid approach to return `allTracts` within and beyond the 0.5 mile `buffer` (the TOD and Non-TOD groups, respectively). The second spatial selection uses `st_disjoint` to select centroids that *do not* intersect the `buffer` and are thus beyond a half mile. `mutate` is used to adjust 2000 rents for inflation.

```
allTracts.group <-
  rbind(
    st_centroid(allTracts)[buffer,] %>%
      st_drop_geometry() %>%
      left_join(allTracts) %>%
      st_sf() %>%
      mutate(TOD = "TOD"),
    st_centroid(allTracts)[buffer, op = st_disjoint] %>%
      st_drop_geometry() %>%
      left_join(allTracts) %>%
      st_sf() %>%
```

```
        mutate(TOD = "Non-TOD")) %>%
  mutate(
    MedRent.inf = ifelse(year=="2000", MedRent*1.42, MedRent))
```

The small multiple map on the left in Figure 1.13 visualizes both the `year` and `TOD` groups. The small multiple map on the right in Figure 1.13 then maps inflation-adjusted rent for 2000 and 2017. Can you re-create the right image in Figure 1.13 using three `geom_sf` layers? The first is a basemap; the second maps rents using `fill = q5(MedRent.inf)`, removing tract boundaries by setting `colour=NA`; and the third overlays `buffer`, setting `colour = "red"` and `fill = NA`.

The map suggests that although rents increased dramatically in Philadelphia's central business district, many areas close to transit did not see significant rent increases.

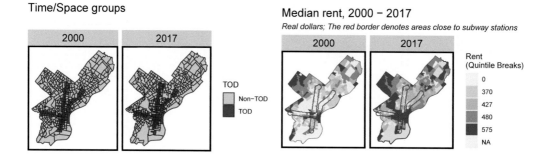

FIGURE 1.13 TOD indicator maps.

1.3.2   TOD indicator tables

Tables are often the least compelling approach for presenting data, but they can be useful. Table 1.2 shows the average difference for variables across `year` and `TOD_Group`.

The `tidyverse` package makes summary statistics easy. `group_by` defines the grouping variables, and `summarize` calculates the across-group means. `na.rm = T` removes any missing or `NA` values from the calculation. Without their removal, the calculation would return `NA`. The result is TOD by year group means.

A clean table is then generated using the `kable` function. Is this the best format for comparing across space and time?

```
allTracts.Summary <-
  st_drop_geometry(allTracts.group) %>%
    group_by(year, TOD) %>%
    summarize(Rent = mean(MedRent, na.rm = T),
              Population = mean(TotalPop, na.rm = T),
              Percent_White = mean(pctWhite, na.rm = T),
              Percent_Bach = mean(pctBachelors, na.rm = T),
              Percent_Poverty = mean(pctPoverty, na.rm = T)) %>%
  kable() %>%
  kable_styling()
```

year	TOD	Rent	Population	Percent_White	Percent_Bach	Percent_Poverty
2000	Non-TOD	470.5458	3966.789	0.4695256	0.0096146	0.3735100
2000	TOD	469.8247	4030.742	0.3848745	0.0161826	0.4031254
2017	Non-TOD	821.1642	4073.547	0.4396967	0.0116228	0.2373258
2017	TOD	913.3750	3658.500	0.4803197	0.0288166	0.3080936

TABLE 1.2 Variable averages for TOD and non-TOD census tracts by year.

How about an approach with variables as rows and the groups as columns? The `year` and `TOD` fields are 'spliced' together into a `year.TOD` field with the `unite` function. `gather` converts the data tolong-form using `year.TOD` as the grouping variable. `mutate` can `round` the `Value` field, and `spread` transposes the rows and columns allowing for comparisons across both group types.

Is Table 1.3 better? What can you conclude about our hypothesis?

```
allTracts.Summary %>%
  unite(year.TOD, year, TOD, sep = ": ", remove = T) %>%
  gather(Variable, Value, -year.TOD) %>%
  mutate(Value = round(Value, 2)) %>%
  spread(year.TOD, Value) %>%
  kable() %>%
    kable_styling()
```

Variable	2000: Non-TOD	2000: TOD	2017: Non-TOD	2017: TOD
Percent_Bach	0.01	0.02	0.01	0.03
Percent_Poverty	0.37	0.40	0.24	0.31
Percent_White	0.47	0.38	0.44	0.48
Population	3966.79	4030.74	4073.55	3658.50
Rent	470.55	469.82	821.16	913.38

TABLE 1.3 TOD indicator table reformatted.

1.3.3 TOD indicator plots

The best way to visualize group differences is with a grouped bar plot. Figure 1.14 is created by moving the data into long-form with `gather`. Explore how the minus sign works inside `gather`.

In the plotting code, `year` is defined on the x-axis, with each bar color filled by `TOD`. `geom_bar` defines a bar plot with two critical parameters. `stat` tells `ggplot` that a y-axis `Value` is provided, and `position` ensures the bars are side-by-side. What happens when the `position` parameter is removed?

`facet_wrap` is used to create small multiple plots across `Variables`, and `scales = "free"` allows the y-axis to vary with the scale of each variable (percentages vs. dollars).

```
allTracts.Summary %>%
  gather(Variable, Value, -year, -TOD) %>%
  ggplot(aes(year, Value, fill = TOD)) +
    geom_bar(stat = "identity", position = "dodge") +
    facet_wrap(~Variable, scales = "free", ncol=5) +
    scale_fill_manual(values = c("#bae4bc", "#0868ac")) +
    labs(title = "Indicator differences across time and space") +
    plotTheme() + theme(legend.position="bottom")
```

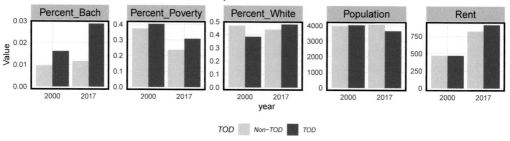

FIGURE 1.14 Group differences for TOD and non-TOD census tracts.

What do these indicators tell us about TOD in Philadelphia? Between 2000 and 2017, the city became significantly more educated and less impoverished while rents increased dramatically. In 2000, there was almost no difference in rents between TOD and non-TOD tracts, but in 2017, that difference increased to more than $100. It appears that residents increasingly are willing to pay more for transit access.

This is not the end of the story, however. Thus far, our analysis has ignored a key question - *what is the relevant spatial process*? The Introduction discusses how the spatial process or pattern relates to decision-making. Residents may be willing to pay more for transit, but perhaps there are other reasons behind rent increases?

It turns out that some TOD areas also happen to be in Center City, Philadelphia's central business district. Living in and around Center City affords access to many other amenities beyond transit. Could omitting this critical spatial process from our analysis bias our results?

Let's find out by creating three housing submarkets, one for each of the two subway lines and a third, Center City area, where the two subway lines intersect.

1.4   Capturing three submarkets of interest

In this section, three new submarkets are created. The `centerCity` submarket is created where the unioned El and Broad Street Line buffers intersect (`st_intersection`).

The `el` and `broad.st` submarket areas are created a bit differently. `st_difference` is used to *erase* any portion of the unioned El and Broad Street Line buffers areas that intersect `centerCity`. The three buffers are then bound into one layer, and the result is mapped.

```
centerCity <-
  st_intersection(
    st_buffer(filter(septaStops, Line == "El"), 2640) %>%
      st_union(),
    st_buffer(filter(septaStops, Line == "Broad_St"), 2640) %>%
      st_union()) %>%
    st_sf() %>%
    mutate(Submarket = "Center City")

el <-
  st_buffer(filter(septaStops, Line == "El"), 2640) %>%
  st_union() %>%
  st_sf() %>%
  st_difference(centerCity) %>%
  mutate(Submarket = "El")

broad.st <-
  st_buffer(filter(septaStops, Line == "Broad_St"), 2640) %>%
  st_union() %>%
  st_sf() %>%
  st_difference(centerCity) %>%
  mutate(Submarket = "Broad Street")

threeMarkets <- rbind(el, broad.st, centerCity)
```

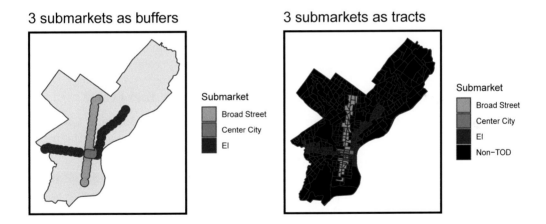

FIGURE 1.15 Visualizing the three submarkets.

allTracts is then related to the threeMarkets. A spatial join (st_join) is used to 'stamp' each tract centroid with the submarket it falls into. Note a spatial selection will not work here because there are now three submarket groups instead of one unioned buffer.

The spatial join result then takes the polygon geometries with a left_join to allTracts. Any tract that is not overlayed by one of threeMarkets receives NA. The mutate then converts NA to a Non-TOD submarket with replace_na. st_sf finally converts the output with polygon geometries to an sf data frame, which can be mapped as Figure 1.15 above.

```
allTracts.threeMarkets <-
  st_join(st_centroid(allTracts), threeMarkets) %>%
  st_drop_geometry() %>%
  left_join(allTracts) %>%
  mutate(Submarket = replace_na(Submarket, "Non-TOD")) %>%
  st_sf()
```

Finally, as before, rent is adjusted for inflation and a grouped bar plot is created.

It was previously estimated that Philadelphians were willing to pay an additional $100 on average, to rent in tracts with transit access. However, now that the Center City effect has been controlled for, it seems these differences are negligible. It is now clear that rents in Center City may have been driving these results.

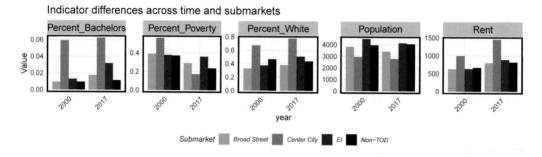

FIGURE 1.16 Group differences for three submarkets.

1.5 Conclusion: Are Philadelphians willing to pay for TOD?

Are Philadelphians willing to pay a premium to live in transit-rich areas? I hate to tell you this, but not enough has been done to fully answer this question - which is one of the two main takeaways of this chapter.

It is critical to understand how omitted variables affect the relevant spatial process and ultimately, the results of an analysis. We suggested that the Center City effect played a role. Another way to think about the Center City effect is in the context of decision-making:

It could be that households are willing to pay more for transit amenities, or that they pay more for other amenities in neighborhoods that happen to also be transit-rich. These selection dynamics will play a massive role in our analytics later in the book.

The second takeaway from this chapter is that although indicators enable the data scientist to simplify complex ideas, those ideas must be *interpreted* responsibly. This means acknowledging important assumptions in the data.

How useful are the indicators we've created? They are *relatable*. Philadelphia is gentrifying, and there is a need to add new housing supply in areas with transit access. These indicators, built from census data, calculated from means, and visualized as maps and bar plots are *simple*. Comparisons made across time and submarket, make them *relative*. The final reason these indicators are useful is that they have clearly generated more questions than answers. Should Philadelphia wish to learn more about how renters value transit, these results suggest a more thorough study is needed.

1.6   Assignment - Study TOD in your city

Recreate this analysis in a city of your choosing and prepare a policy brief for local city council representatives. Do households value transit-rich neighborhoods compared to others? How certain can you be about your conclusions given some of the spatial biases we've discussed? You must choose a city with open transit station data and crime data.

Prepare an accessible (non-technical) R markdown document with the following deliverables. Provide a **brief** motivation at the beginning, annotate each visualization appropriately, and then provide brief policy-relevant conclusions. Please show all code blocks. Here are the specific deliverables:

1. Show your data wrangling work.
2. Four small-multiple (2000 and 2017+) visualizations comparing four selected census variables across time and space (TOD vs. non-TOD).
3. One grouped bar plot making these same comparisons.
4. One table making these same comparisons.
5. Create two graduated symbol maps of population and rent within 0.5 mile of each *transit station*. Google for more information, but a graduate symbol map represents quantities for each transit station proportionally.
6. Create a `geom_line` plot that shows mean rent as a function of distance to subway stations (Figure 1.17). To do this you will need to use the `multipleRingBuffer` function in the `functions.R` script read in above.
7. Download and wrangle point-level crime data (pick a crime type). What is the relationship between crime, transit access, and rents?

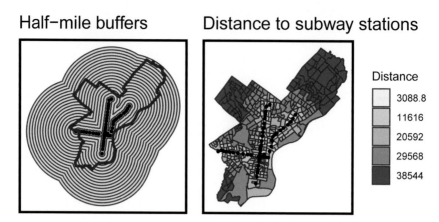

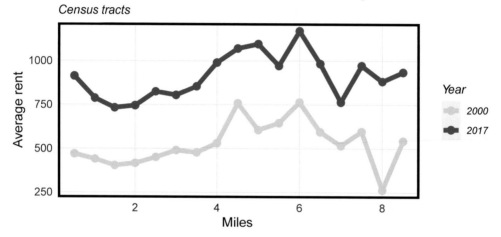

FIGURE 1.17 TOD assignment visuals.

Below is an example of how the `multipleRingsBuffer` tool works. The first parameter of `st_join` are tract centroids. The second parameter is the buffer tool, drawing buffers in half-mile intervals, out to a nine-mile distance.

```
allTracts.rings <-
  st_join(
    st_centroid(dplyr::select(allTracts, GEOID, year)),
    multipleRingBuffer(st_union(septaStops), 47520, 2640)) %>%
  st_drop_geometry() %>%
  left_join(dplyr::select(allTracts, GEOID, MedRent, year),
          by=c("GEOID"="GEOID", "year"="year")) %>%
  st_sf() %>%
  mutate(distance = distance / 5280) #convert to miles
```

2

Expanding the Urban Growth Boundary

2.1 Introduction - Lancaster development

Cheap housing, cheap gas, and a preference for 'country living' have lured American families to the suburbs for decades, but at what cost?

Development patterns that promote lengthy car commutes and oversized 'McMansions' are generally not sustainable. We know that sprawl generates air and water pollution and degrades the quality of ecosystem services - but what about economic competitiveness?

Lancaster County, Pennsylvania, a lush, rolling agricultural county 60 miles west of Philadelphia, has been wrestling with sprawl for more than three decades, as new development swallows up the farms that help drive the local economy. The rate of farm workers in Lancaster is nearly three times the rate statewide.[1] According to the 2017 Census of Agriculture, agricultural commodity sale totals were estimated at more than $1 billion dollars in Lancaster, making it the 55th highest-grossing county nationally (top 2%) and the highest in Pennsylvania.[2]

Lancaster's farmland is quite valuable, but increasingly, that land is being paved over in favor of suburban housing. Figure 2.1 visualizes the rate of suburban expansion in Lancaster since 1990. Over the last 30 years, Between 1990 and 2018, Lancaster's population grew 17% while developed land increased 140% - a clear indicator of sprawl.

---

[1] Referring to the 'Location Quotient' - Lancaster County Profile - January, 2020; PA. Dept of Labor and Industry; https://www.workstats.dli.pa.gov/Documents/County%20Profiles/Lancaster%20County.pdf

[2] National Agricultural Statistics Service, Quick Stats. https://quickstats.nass.usda.gov

DOI: 10.1201/9781003054658-2

Land Cover Change – Lancaster, PA: 1990 – 2018
Author's estimations via supervised classification. Source: USGS

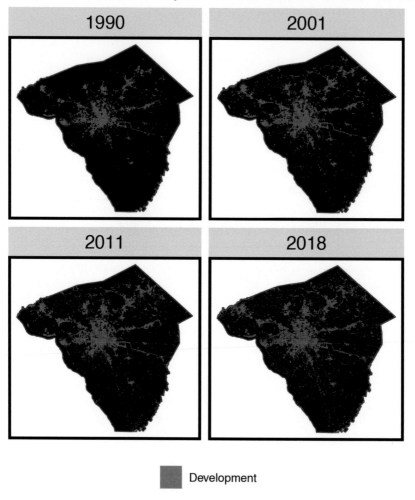

FIGURE 2.1 Development change in Lancaster, PA over time.

What does the relationship between Lancaster development and population growth teach us about sprawl? Figure 2.2a plots census tract population (y-axis) by acres of developed land (x-axis) by decade. Note the decreasing line slopes. In 1990, one-acre of development is associated with ~2 people, but by 2018, despite an overall population increase, the figure halved to ~1 person per acre.

Figure 2.2b visualizes the same relationship but with *housing units*. Here the trend is similar. In 1990, a one acre increase in development was associated with ~2/3 of a housing unit - already at a very low density. Again, by 2018, despite population increases, that figure fell by half.

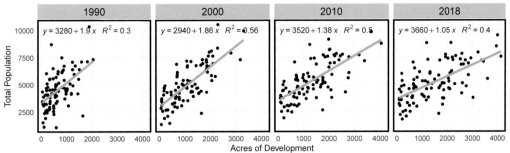

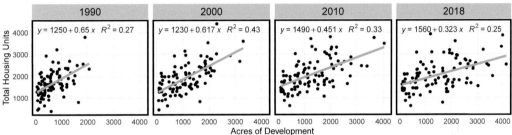

FIGURE 2.2 The relationship between housing and population growth.

To stem the sprawl, savvy Lancaster Planners in the 1990s worked with politicians, conservationists, and other stakeholders to develop a set of Urban Growth Areas (UGA) (Figure 2.3) to encourage development *inside* the urban core while discouraging development *outside* on outlying farmland. To what extent has the UGA succeeded to date?

Figure 2.3 plots development change inside and outside the UGA boundary between 1990 and 2018. Areas inside the UGA are developing much faster - which is the purpose of the UGA. However, the UGA represents just 8.6% of the total area of the county, and as it fills, the development trend flattens. On an acreage basis, development outside of the UGA has skyrocketed from more than 60,000 acres in 1990 to nearly 145,000 acres in 2018. This suggests the UGA is not sufficiently containing sprawl.

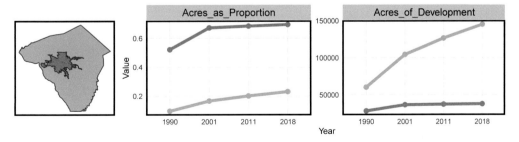

FIGURE 2.3 Differences in urban development inside and outside the UGA.

One reasonable policy solution might be to increase development restrictions outside the UGA, while strategically expanding the existing UGA to promote infill development. In this chapter, we will develop a simple economic model to identify towns best suited for expanding its growth area.

In the previous chapter's discussion of the modifiable areal unit problem (MAUP), we discussed how boundaries can be a liability for the spatial analyst. In this chapter, however, boundaries are an asset, leveraged for their discontinuous nature to understand their affect on development.

The next section introduces the economic model used to identify towns suitable for UGA expansion. In Section 2.2, analytics are created to delineate areas inside and outside of the UGA. Section 2.3 uses the result as an input to the economic model. Section 2.4 concludes.

2.1.1   The bid-rent model

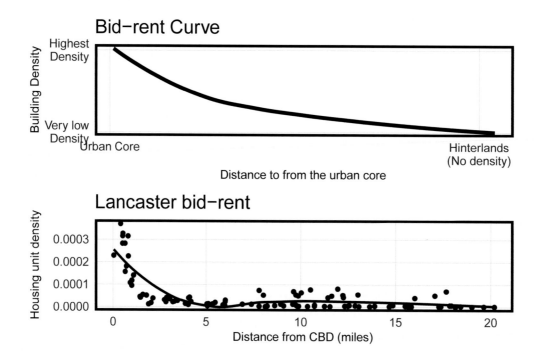

FIGURE 2.4 Visualizing the bid-rent curve.

The bid-rent model of urban land markets is used to understand the spatial pattern of density, price, and land uses in market-oriented cities.[3] Illustrated in the top panel of Figure 2.4, the model suggests that as distance from the City Center increases, building density decreases. Building density is closely correlated to population density, and it also reflects locational demand.

---

[3]See Alonso (1964), Location and Land Use: Toward a General Theory of LandRent, Harvard University Press, Cambridge and any other urban economic text for more information

As demand for a place increases, firms and households are willing to pay a premium, even for marginally less space. Like all 'models', bid-rent is a simple abstraction of reality, but this simplicity can provide important insight into the problem at hand.

The bottom panel of Figure 2.4 shows the bid-rent curve for Lancaster County with housing unit density on the y-axis. Compared to the theoretical curve, density in Lancaster flattens dramatically at the five-mile mark continuing flat out to the county boundary. As we'll learn below, this sharp drop-off pattern is heavily influenced by the UGA.

For contrast, Figure 2.5 visualizes bid-rent curves for eight cities/metro areas throughout the United States. In most dense, post-industrial cities like New York, Philadelphia, and San Francisco, the bid-rent curve decreases exponentially out from the urban core. In more sprawling metro areas like Houston and Indianapolis, the downward curve is more linear and flat.

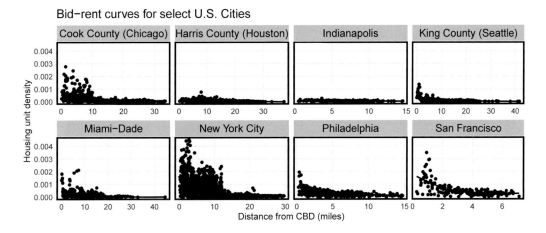

FIGURE 2.5 Examples of bid-rent curves across the United States.

How can bid-rent help us understand where to expand the UGA? Let's take a look at a map of the fictitious 'Ken County', its UGA, and the three towns within (Figure 2.6). Assume Emil City is the urban core and contains higher-density development compared to Dianaville and New Baby Town.

In the map below, two polygons are drawn at 1/8-mile radial distance out from and in from the UGA, respectively. These buffers are drawn to delineate areas just outside and just inside the UGA, and can be used to calculate differences in housing unit density across the boundary. Comparing these densities on either side of the UGA in a bid-rent context can help identify in which Ken County town to expand the UGA boundary.

Ken County − UGA buffers & towns

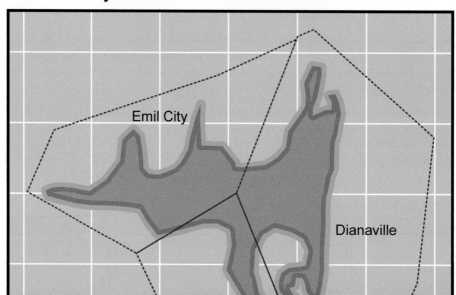

FIGURE 2.6 UGA and towns inside the fictitious Ken County.

Let's visualize bid-rent curves in Emil City and Dianaville in Figure 2.7. Emil City is the urban core and while density is greatest within the UGA, areas outside are also relatively high density. Conversely, inside Dianaville's UGA there is some density, but just outside, density falls dramatically.

Currently, density and land value just outside the UGA are artificially low because land use regulations make it difficult to develop. If that restriction were to suddenly be lifted, however, potential building density and land values would likely *rise* to meet those just inside the UGA. Assuming the optimal town for UGA expansion is the one with the maximum economic impact, Dianaville would be the choice.

Which is the optimal town in Lancaster County? Let's find out.

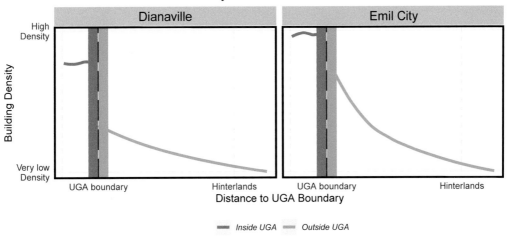

FIGURE 2.7 Bid-rent curves for the towns in Ken County.

2.1.2 Set up Lancaster data

Begin by loading the requisite libraries, turning off scientific notation, and reading in the `mapTheme` and `plotTheme`.

```
options(scipen=999)

library(tidyverse)
library(sf)
library(gridExtra)
library(grid)
library(kableExtra)

root.dir =
  paste0("https://raw.githubusercontent.com/urbanSpatial",
         "/Public-Policy-Analytics-Landing/master/DATA/")
source(
  paste0("https://raw.githubusercontent.com/urbanSpatial/",
         "Public-Policy-Analytics-Landing/master/functions.r"))
```

The data for this analysis is read in, including:

1. `studyAreaTowns` - A polygon layer of town polygons inside of the Lancaster County study area. Note that there is a `MUNI` or municipal town name for each town polygon.
2. `uga` - A polygon layer of the spatial extent of Lancaster County's Urban Growth Area.
3. `lancCounty` - A polygon layer of the spatial extent of Lancaster County.
4. `buildings` - A polygon layer of the footprint for all buildings in the study area.
5. `greenSpace` - A polygon layer showing areas classified as non-developed land cover as classified by the USGS.

```
lancCounty <- st_read(file.path(
  root.dir,"/Chapter2/LancasterCountyBoundary.geojson")) %>%
  st_transform('ESRI:102728')

uga <- st_read(file.path(
  root.dir,"/Chapter2/Urban_Growth_Boundary.geojson")) %>%
  st_transform('ESRI:102728')

studyAreaTowns <- st_read(file.path(
  root.dir,"/Chapter2/StudyAreaTowns.geojson")) %>%
  st_transform('ESRI:102728')

buildings <- st_read(file.path(
  root.dir,"/Chapter2/LancasterCountyBuildings.geojson")) %>%
  st_transform('ESRI:102728')

greenSpace <- st_read(file.path(
  root.dir,"/Chapter2/LancasterGreenSpace.geojson")) %>%
  st_transform('ESRI:102728')
```

2.2   Identifying areas inside and outside of the Urban Growth Area

In this section, a polygon layer is produced where each unit is assigned 1) the town it is in and 2) whether it is 1/8th-mile inside the UGA or 1/8th-mile outside. This layer is created from just two inputs: `studyAreaTowns`, which delineates the 14 towns in Lancaster County, and `uga`, the boundary of the Urban Growth Area. Figure 2.8 visualizes those boundaries.

Towns and Urban Growth Area, Lancaster

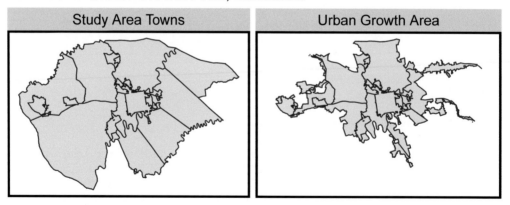

FIGURE 2.8 Small multiple map of study area features.

The `uga` layer is used to find areas 1/8th-mile inside and outside of the UGA. To make this easier, the following code block dissolves away (`st_union`) the towns, leaving just the

UGA boundary. The `st_buffer` is a quick way to remove some of the extraneous slivers that otherwise appear in the middle of the UGA.

```
uga_union <-
  st_union(uga) %>%
  st_buffer(1) %>%
  st_sf()
```

Next, steps are taken to find areas 1/8th-mile inside and outside the UGA. Here is the process:

1. `st_buffer` is used to find areas 1/8th-mile *outside* of the `uga_union`. This results in a polygon larger than the original `uga_union`.
2. `st_difference` is then used to erase the original extent of `uga_union`, leaving only the 1/8th-mile `outsideBuffer`.
3. To get areas 1/8th-mile *inside* of the `uga_union`, a negative parameter is input to `st_buffer` to shrink the diameter of `uga_union`.
4. `st_difference` is used again to erase part of the geometry. This time however, the placement of the . means that the negative buffer polygon cookie cutters the larger `uga_union` leaving just the area 1/8th-mile `insideBuffer`.

Note the `Legend` mutated for each buffer denoting its position inside or outside, and the creation of `bothBuffers`.

```
outsideBuffer <-
  st_buffer(uga_union, 660) %>%
  st_difference(uga_union) %>%
  mutate(Legend = "Outside")

insideBuffer <-
  st_buffer(uga_union, dist = -660) %>%
  st_difference(uga_union, .) %>%
  mutate(Legend = "Inside")

bothBuffers <- rbind(insideBuffer, outsideBuffer)
```

Finally, `bothBuffers` are plotted in Figure 2.9.

```
ggplot() +
  geom_sf(data = bothBuffers, aes(fill = Legend)) +
  scale_fill_manual(values = c("#F8766D", "#00BFC4")) +
  labs(title = "1/8-mi. buffer inside and outside UGA") +
  mapTheme()
```

1/8−mi. buffer inside and outside UGA

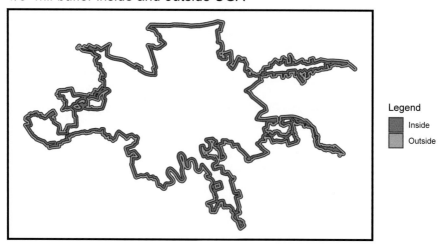

FIGURE 2.9 Mapping the UGA buffer.

2.2.1   Associate each inside/outside buffer with its respective town.

Additional wrangling associates a town with each buffer. `table(st_is_valid(studyAreaTowns))` will likely tell you that there is a broken geometry in this layer. In the following code block, `st_make_valid` corrects the issue.

The goal is for the intersection to yield an `Inside` feature and an `Outisde` feature for each town. Two towns only show up on one side of the boundary and are thus removed. `arrange(buffersAndTowns, MUNI) %>% print(n=25)` shows the remaining features.

```
buffersAndTowns <-
  st_intersection(st_make_valid(studyAreaTowns), bothBuffers) %>%
  filter(MUNI != "MOUNTVILLE BOROUGH" &
         MUNI != "MILLERSVILLE BOROUGH")
```

Finally, the map in Figure 2.10 can be produced which shows for each town, areas inside and outside the UGA. I have purposely mislabeled this map and omitted a legend. Can you build a better data visualization than this?

Inside/Outside the UGA by town

Comparable shades of the same color represent inside/outside the UGA by town

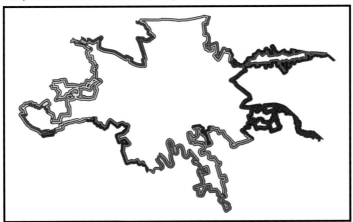

FIGURE 2.10 Visualizing areas inside and outside the UGA for each town.

2.2.2 Building density by town and by inside/outside the UGA

The bid-rent model suggests that the town best suited for UGA expansion has the greatest infill potential, defined as the difference in building density on either side of the UGB. In this section, building density is calculated inside/outside the UGA by town, and the difference is taken.

To do so, each building must know its town and its place `Inside` or `Outside` the UGA. These relationships are calculated below.

The first code block that follows converts the `building` polygon layer to point centroids (`st_centroid`). A `counter` field is set to 1, and will be used to sum the number of `buildingsCentroids` that fall into each town by inside/outside polygon.

The second code block uses `aggregate` to spatially join `buildingCentroids` to `buffersAndTowns`, taking the `sum` of `counter`, to get the count of buildings. `cbind` marries the spatial join to the original `buffersAndTowns` layer; `mutate` replaces `NA` with 0 for polygons with no buildings, and `Area` is calculated (`st_area`).

```
buildingCentroids <-
  st_centroid(buildings) %>%
  mutate(counter = 1) %>%
  dplyr::select(counter)


buffersAndTowns_Buildings <-
  aggregate(buildingCentroids, buffersAndTowns, sum) %>%
  cbind(buffersAndTowns) %>%
  mutate(counter = replace_na(counter, 0),
         Area = as.numeric(st_area(.)))
```

The resulting data is grouped and summarized to get the sum of buildings and area for each town by inside/outside polygon. `Building_Density` is then calculated. Check out the `buffersAndTowns_Buildings_Summarize` layer to see the result.

```
buffersAndTowns_Buildings_Summarize <-
  buffersAndTowns_Buildings %>%
  group_by(MUNI, Legend) %>%
    summarize(Building_Count = sum(counter),
              Area = sum(Area)) %>%
    mutate(Building_Density = Building_Count / Area)
```

The following code block calculates the inside/outside density difference by town. Note this requires the data be moved to wide form with `spread`. The resulting `Building_Difference` is sorted in descending order, and the results can be used with other metrics to plan UGA expansion. Section 2.3 provides additional context for these differences.

Which towns seem like good candidates for UGA expansion?

```
buildingDifferenceTable <-
  st_drop_geometry(buffersAndTowns_Buildings_Summarize) %>%
    dplyr::select(MUNI, Legend, Building_Density) %>%
    spread(Legend, Building_Density) %>%
      mutate(Building_Difference = Inside - Outside) %>%
      arrange(desc(Building_Difference))
```

2.2.3   Visualize buildings inside and outside the UGA

For a more precise look at a single town, the map below shows buildings inside and outside West Hempfield Township's UGA, and a cutout map situating the town within the larger county.

The first step to create this map is to classify West Hempfield buildings by whether they are inside or outside the UGA. Start by intersecting the UGA and the West Hemptfield township to find areas in the UGA and the town (`uga_WH`).

`buildings_WH` is a layer of buildings labeled by their location `Inside UGA` and `Outside UGA`. This layer is created by first using a spatial selection to find all the `buildings` *within* the `uga_WH` polygon. To find buildings *without* (i.e., outside) the UGA, a spatial selection finds all `buildings` in West Hempfield, which is then passed to another spatial selection to remove (`st_disjoint`) all buildings **not** in West Hempfield's UGA. This leaves buildings in West Hempfield but not in its UGA.

```
westHempfield <-
  filter(studyAreaTowns, MUNI == "WEST HEMPFIELD TOWNSHIP")

uga_WH <-
  st_intersection(uga, westHempfield) %>%
  st_union() %>%
  st_sf()
```

```
buildings_WH <-
  rbind(
    buildings[uga_WH,] %>%                    #Within
      mutate(Legend = "Inside UGA"),
    buildings[westHempfield,] %>%             #Without
      .[uga_WH, , op = st_disjoint] %>%
      mutate(Legend = "Outside UGA"))
```

Can you re-create the map in Figure 2.11? There are two maps that need to be created - one for West Hempfield and one for the cutout.

The West Hempfield map contains three `geom_sf` calls that 1) plot the boundary of `westHempfield`; 2) plot the `st_intersection` of `greenSpace` and `westHempfield` to find all the green space in town; and 3) plot `buildings_WH` colored by the Inside/Outside `Legend`.

The cutout includes two `geom_sf` calls that 1) plot all `studyAreaTowns` in grey and 2) plot `WestHempfield` in black.

The two `ggplot` layers are then `print` in succession. The second line adds the cutout map and specifies where on the plot it should be located.

```
print(WestHempfield_BuildingsPlot)
print(studyAreaCutoutMap, vp=viewport(.32, .715, .35, .5))
```

Buildings on either side of the
Urban Growth Area

West Hempfield Township, Lancaster County, PA; Green space included

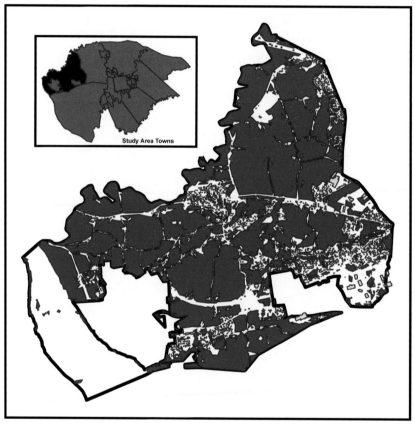

Inside UGA   Outside UGA

FIGURE 2.11 Development inside and outside the UGA for West Hempfield Township

2.3   Return to Lancaster's bid-rent

Section 2.1.1 suggested that development restrictions just outside of the UGA keeps building density artificially low, and if those restrictions were lifted, a short-term increase to building density (and land values) might be expected just outside.

In this section, we visualize density as a function of distance to the UGA, much like a bid-rent curve. These plots should provide visual evidence of a sharp discontinuity in density at the UGA boundary.

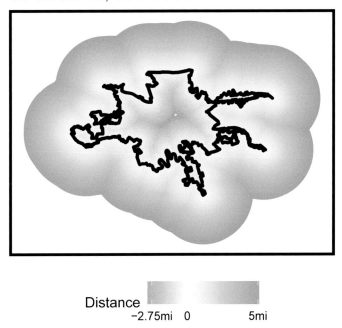

FIGURE 2.12 Visualizing the multiple ring buffer for Lancaster's UGA.

Figure 2.7 calculated housing unit density from aggregated census tract data, but here, building density is calculated with the actual `building_centroids`, as it was in Section 2.2.2. Instead of calculating densities on either immediate side of the UGA, it is calculated at multiple distance intervals using the `multipleRing` buffer tool.

The `multipleRing` function iteratively draws buffers at successive intervals inside and outside the UGA. The following code block uses the function twice - drawing negative buffers first and positive buffers second, both at 1/8-mile intervals. Note that the negative buffer can only extend so far into the interior of the UGA - in this case, 2.75 miles (14,250 ft).

The map plots the multiple-ring buffer without buffer boundaries. `scale_fill_gradient2` is used to create the dual color gradient that diverges at `Distance == 0`.

```
multipleRing <-
  rbind(
    multipleRingBuffer(uga_union, -14520, -660) %>%
    mutate(Legend = "Inside the UGA"),
      multipleRingBuffer(uga_union, 26400, 660) %>%
      mutate(Legend = "Outside the UGA"))
```

Figures 2.13 and 2.14 visualize the bid-rent curve for the study area and by town, respectively. To calculate these plots, the code in Section 2.2.2 is extended. As before, each building must know its location Inside or Outside the UGA; the studyAreaTown in which it is located; and now, its distance to/from the uga.

First, buildingCentroids is intersected with the multipleRing buffer. As before, aggregate spatial joins buildingCentroids to the RingsAndTowns polygons, calculating the sum of buildings for each. Area is calculated and ring/town polygons with no buildings have NA changed to 0.

```
RingsAndTowns <-
  st_intersection(multipleRing, st_make_valid(studyAreaTowns))

buildings.in.RingsAndTowns <-
  aggregate(buildingCentroids,
            RingsAndTowns, sum) %>%
  cbind(RingsAndTowns) %>%
  dplyr::select(-geometry.1) %>%
  mutate(counter = replace_na(counter, 0),
         Area = as.numeric(st_area(.)))
```

Figure 2.13 plots building density as a function to and from the UGA. To create this plot, the sf layer is converted to a data frame with st_drop_geometry. The data is grouped by the distance interval and inside/outside and Building_Density is calculated.

geom_vline is used to create the vertical line at the UGA and the line break is created by setting colour = Legend in the aes parameter of ggplot. geom_smooth(method="loess", se=F) fits a 'local regression' (loess) line to the scatterplot relationship between distance and Building_Density.

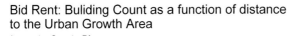

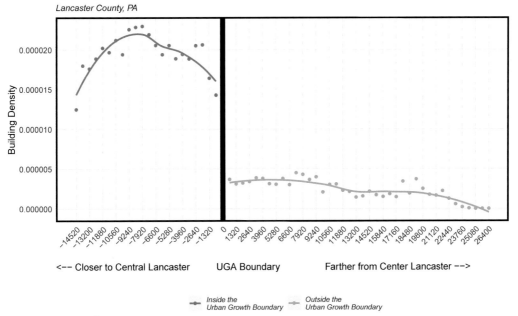

FIGURE 2.13 Bid-rent curve for Lancaster County.

This 'boundary discontinuity' plot highlights how the bid-rent conditions change on either immediate side of the UGA. How does it look for each town?

Figure 2.14 is created below in the same way that Figure 2.13 is created but with the addition of MUNI in the group_by, as well as facet_wrap. Some towns are completely within the UGA, and thus have no Building_Density outside. These plots again help reveal towns likely suitable for UGA expansion.

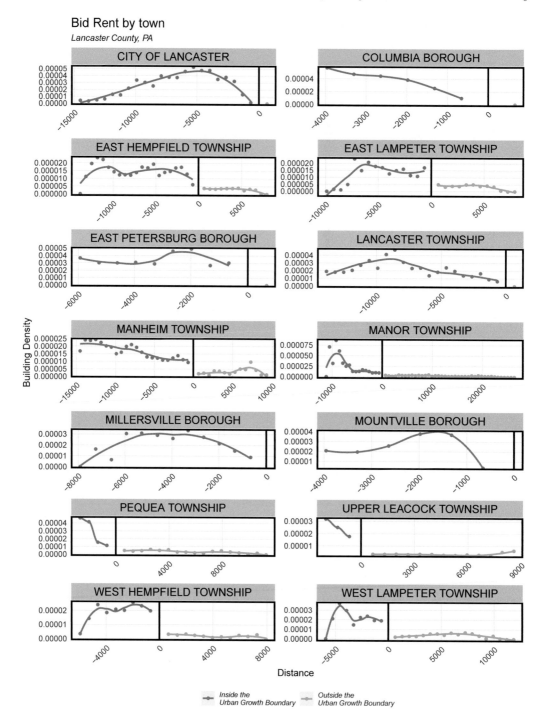

FIGURE 2.14 Bid-rent curves for each town in the study area.

2.4   Conclusion - On boundaries

Boundaries are a ubiquitous feature of the American landscape. States, counties, school districts, Congressional districts, and municipalities are all delineated by exacting boundaries that divide the landscape into neighborhoods, enclaves, political regimes, and economies. Boundaries dictate the haves and have-nots; who pays more taxes and who pays less; who can access resources, and who cannot. Boundaries dictate the allocation of resources across space.

At times, boundaries are drawn to prevent phenomena from spilling out across space. In this chapter, the concern was with suburban sprawl spilling out onto hinter farmlands and hurting Lancaster County's agrarian economy. To make room for more development, the bid-rent model was used to identify towns suitable for UGA expansion. Our assumption was that once expanded, building density, land values, and real estate prices just outside the UGA would adjust to those just inside.

Thus far, the reader has learned a series of analytical and visualization strategies for working with geospatial data. These methods will be invaluable as we move into more complex data science in the chapters to follow.

2.5   Assignment - Boundaries in your community

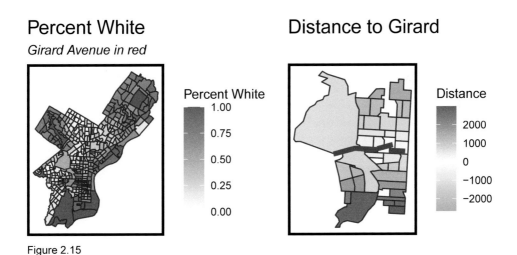

Figure 2.15

FIGURE 2.15 Girard Avenue in Philadelphia is a soft boundary between two neighborhoods.

At the periphery of an Urban Growth Area is a hard boundary, a wall, with a different legal regime on either side. Interestingly, cities and regions are divided by many soft boundaries as well, with appreciably different conditions on either side, but not because of any legal mandate. Many historical inequities partitioned America into economic and racial enclaves, the results of which are still evident today.

What soft boundaries exist in your community and how do they separate the communities on either side? In this assignment, you will wrangle together a significant street, avenue or other soft boundary of your choosing and create discontinuity plots similar to Figure 2.15.

Take Philadelphia's Girard Avenue (Figure 2.15), a clear dividing line between gentrified neighborhoods to the south (adjacent to Center City), and those to the north, which have been slower to change.

The following code block calculates distance from each tract to the Girard Avenue line. `tract.centroids.NS` stamps `tract.centroids` with their location in either a North or South-side buffer. Note that these are one-sided buffers (`singleSide = TRUE`). `tract.centroids.distance` column binds (`cbind`) together the resulting data frame with a column measuring distance to `girard`.

The `dist2Line` function from the `geosphere` package, takes two inputs. The first is a matrix of `tract.centroids` projected into decimal degrees (`4326`). The second is the `girard` avenue line, also in decimal degrees. `dist2Line` does not take an `sf`, however, but a layer converted to the older R geospatial standard `sp`, with `as_Spatial`. Finally, `mutate` sets all distances north of Girard negative to enable the plots in Figure 2.16. As always, run each line separately to understand the process.

```
tract.centroids.NS <-
  st_intersection(tract.centroids,
    rbind(
      st_buffer(girard, 10000, singleSide = TRUE) %>%
        mutate(Side = "South"),
      st_buffer(girard, -10000, singleSide = TRUE) %>%
        mutate(Side = "North")))


tract.centroids.distance <-
  cbind(
    tract.centroids.NS,
    dist2Line(
      st_coordinates(st_transform(tract.centroids.NS, 4326)),
      as_Spatial(st_transform(girard, 4326)))) %>%
  mutate(
    distance = ifelse(Side == "North", distance * -1, distance))
```

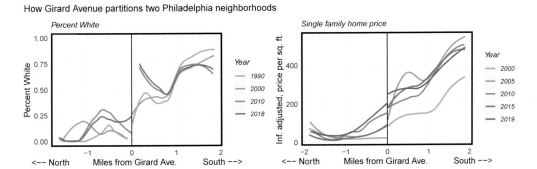

FIGURE 2.16 Boundary discontinuity in race and home prices, Girard Avenue.

The resulting discontinuity plots (Figure 2.16) for both `Percent_White` and single-family house price show significant differences at the Girard Avenue boundary, and these differences seem to increase with time. The deliverables for this assignment include:

1. Wrangle street (line) data, Census and other open data for your study area. Buffer the street line and use it to subset tracts/data from the larger city. Measure the distance from a tract centroid or other outcome to the boundary line with `geosphere::dist2Line`.

2. Choose two census outcomes and two other point-level outcomes from local open data, such as crime, home prices, construction permits, etc. Develop maps and discontinuity plots to show across-boundary differences.

3. Write a short research brief asking, 'How does the such-and-such-boundary partition my community?' Motivate your analysis; provide some historical context in your community; present your maps and plots; and conclude.

4. Bonus: After you have finished this book and have a better understanding of fixed-effect regression, estimate a regression of say, house price as a function of a boundary-side fixed effect and year. Interact or multiply the side and year variables. What is the interpretation of the resulting estimate?

3

Intro to Geospatial Machine Learning, Part 1

3.1 Machine learning as a planning

The descriptive analytics in the first two chapters provide context to non-technical decision-makers. The predictive analytics in this and subsequent chapters help convert those insights into actionable intelligence.

Prediction is not new to Planners. Throughout history, Planners have made ill-fated forecasts into an uncertain future. The 1925 Plan for Cincinnati is one such example. Cincinnati, delighted with the prosperity it had achieved up to 1925, set out to plan for the next hundred years by understanding future demand for land, housing, employment, and more.

Population forecasting, the author wrote, is the 'obvious...basis upon which scientific city planning must be formulated'. Rebuilt from the actual plan, Figure 3.1 visualizes the city's dubious population forecast, which made the assumption that historical growth would continue or 'generalize' long into the future.[1] In reality, a great depression, suburbanization, and deindustrialization caused the city's population to fall nearly 70% below its 1950 peak. So much for the 'the plan'.

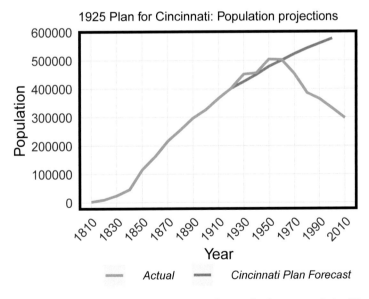

FIGURE 3.1 Population projection versus actual population growth in Cincinnati.

---

[1] *1925 Plan for Cincinnati*, Chapter 1, "Community Development", https://web.archive.org/web/201604 07123222/http://www.plancincinnati.org/documents/1925_Plan/Chapter_1_Community_Development .pdf

DOI: 10.1201/9781003054658-3

To reasonably assume Cincinnati's past would generalize to its future, Planners would have had to understand how complex systems like housing markets, labor markets, credit markets, immigration, politics, and technology all interrelate. If those systems were understood, Planners would know which levers to pull to bring health, happiness, and prosperity to all.

We are far from such an understanding. Thus, our goal will be to make predictions in more bounded systems, where recent experiences more reasonably *generalize* to the near future. We will 'borrow' experiences from observed data, and test whether they can be used to predict outcomes where and when they are unknown. Throughout the remainder of the book, we will learn that generalizability is the most important concept for applying machine learning in government.

3.1.1   Accuracy and generalizability

This chapter focuses on home price prediction, which is a common use case in cities that use data to assess property taxes. The goal is to *train* a model from recent transactions, the 'training set', and test whether that model generalizes to properties that have not recently sold. This is comparable to the *Zestimate* algorithm that Zillow uses to estimate home prices.

One way to evaluate such a model is to judge its *accuracy*, defined as the difference between predicted and observed home prices. Another, more nuanced criteria is *generalizability*, which has two different meanings:

Imagine training an age-prediction robot on data from 1,000 people, including you and me. It is far less impressive for the robot to predict my age compared to a random person, because it was trained in part, on my data. Thus, a generalizable model is one that accurately predicts on *new* data - like every house that hasn't sold in recent years.[2]

Now imagine the age-prediction robot was trained on data from a retirement community and tasked to predict in a middle school. The robot might be accurate for seniors but would likely fail for young adults. Thus, a generalizable model is also one that predicts with comparable accuracy across different groups - like houses in different neighborhoods. As we will learn, a predictive model lacking accuracy and generalizability will not be a useful decision-making tool.

3.1.2   The machine learning process

Curiosity, creativity, and problem-solving are the key to useful data science solutions, but organization ensures a reproducible workflow. The below framework highlights the major steps in the predictive modeling process:

Data wrangling: The first step is to compile the required data into one dataset, often from multiple sources. This includes the outcome of interest (the 'dependent variable') and the 'features' needed to predict that outcome. Data wrangling often involves data cleaning, which is both arduous and critical. If mistakes are made at the data wrangling stage, all the downstream work may be for naught.

---

[2]This definition of generalizability should be familiar to social scientists who look for 'external validity' - meaning their conclusions can be applied in settings outside of the current study.

Exploratory analysis: Exploratory analysis, like the indicators we have already discussed, is critical for understanding the system of interest. Exploratory analysis investigates both the underlying spatial process in the outcome of interest as well as trends and correlations between the outcome and the predictive features.

Feature engineering: Feature engineering is the difference between a good machine learning model and a great one. Features are the variables used to predict the outcome of interest by mining the data for predictive insight. Social scientists refer to these as 'independent variables', but features are a bit different.

Social scientists fear that transforming a variable (i.e., changing its context without a good theoretical reason) may muddle the interpretation of a statistical result. In prediction, interpretation is not as important as accuracy and generalizability, so transformation or feature engineering becomes imperative.

The first key to strong feature engineering is experience with feature engineering. While we practice here, many transformation and 'dimensionality reduction' techniques are beyond the scope of this book, but critical to machine learning. The second key is domain expertise. It may seem that reducing machine learning success to accuracy and generalizability negates the importance of context. In fact, the more the data scientist understands the problem, the better she will be at parameterizing the underlying system.

Geospatial feature engineering is about measuring 'exposure' from an outcome, like a house sale, to the locational phenomena that can help predict it, like crime. We will spend a great deal of time discussing this.

Feature selection: While hundreds of features may be engineered for a single project, often only a concise set is included in a model. Many features may be correlated with each other, a phenomenon known as 'colinearity', and feature selection is the process of whittling features down to a parsimonious set.

Model estimation and validation: A statistical model is an abstraction of reality that produces 'estimates', not facts. There are many different models, some more simple than others. In this book, the focus is on Linear and Generalized Linear regression models because they are more transparent and computationally more efficient. Once one is familiar with the machine learning framework however, more advanced algorithms can be substituted.

3.1.3 The hedonic model

The hedonic model is a theoretical framework for predicting home prices by deconstructing house price into the value of its constituent parts, like an additional bedroom, the presence of a pool, or the amount of local crime.[3]

For our purposes, home prices can be deconstructed into three constituent parts - 1) physical characteristics, like the number of bedrooms; 2) public services/(dis)amenities, like crime; and 3) the spatial process of prices - namely that house prices cluster at the neighborhood, city, and regional scales. The regression model developed in Section 3.3 omits the spatial process, which is then added in Chapter 4. Pay close attention to how this omission leads to a less accurate and generalizable model.

---

[3]There are some key assumptions of the hedonic model, including that all buyers and sellers have access to the same market information, and that all buyers share the same preferences for goods like school quality. The model can also be used for goods other than housing. See Greenstone, M. (2017). The continuing impact of Sherwin Rosen's "Hedonic prices and implicit markets: product differentiation in pure competition". Journal of Political Economy, 125(6), 1891-1902.

In this chapter, key concepts like colinearity and feature engineering are returned to at different stages throughout. While this makes for a less linear narrative, a focus on these skills is necessary to prepare us for the more nuanced use cases that lie ahead. In the next section, data is wrangled, followed by an introduction to feature engineering. Ordinary least squares regression is introduced, and models are validated in the context of cross-validation.

3.2 Data wrangling - Home price and crime data

Libraries and functions are loaded in the code block below.

```
library(tidyverse)
library(sf)
library(spdep)
library(caret)
library(ckanr)
library(FNN)
library(grid)
library(gridExtra)
library(ggcorrplot)

root.dir =
  paste0("https://raw.githubusercontent.com/urbanSpatial/",
         "Public-Policy-Analytics-Landing/master/DATA/")

source(
  paste0("https://raw.githubusercontent.com/urbanSpatial/",
         "Public-Policy-Analytics-Landing/master/functions.r"))

palette5 <- c("#25CB10","#5AB60C","#8FA108","#C48C04","#FA7800")
```

Our model will be trained on home price data from Boston, Massachusetts. The following code block downloads a neighborhoods geojson from the Boston open data site; reads in the home sale price data as a csv; converts to an sf layer (`st_as_sf`); and projects.

```
nhoods <-
  st_read(
    paste0("http://bostonopendata-boston.opendata.arcgis.com/",
      "datasets/3525b0ee6e6b427f9aab5d0a1d0a1a28_0.geojson")) %>%
  st_transform('ESRI:102286')

boston <-
  read.csv(file.path(root.dir,
           "/Chapter3_4/bostonHousePriceData_clean.csv"))

boston.sf <-
  boston %>%
  st_as_sf(coords = c("Longitude", "Latitude"), crs = 4326,
```

```
            agr = "constant") %>%
  st_transform('ESRI:102286')
```

Sale prices are then mapped in quintile breaks using the `nhoods` base map. What do you notice about the spatial process of home prices? Are they randomly distributed throughout the city or do they seem clustered? Why do you think prices are spatially distributed the way they are?

```
ggplot() +
  geom_sf(data = nhoods, fill = "grey40") +
  geom_sf(data = boston.sf, aes(colour = q5(PricePerSq)),
          show.legend = "point", size = .75) +
  scale_colour_manual(values = palette5,
                      labels=qBr(boston,"PricePerSq"),
                      name="Quintile\nBreaks") +
  labs(title="Price Per Square Foot, Boston") +
  mapTheme()
```

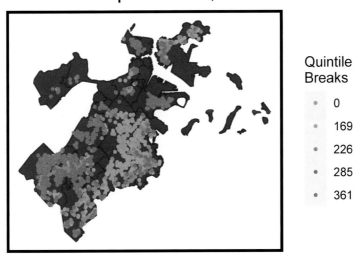

FIGURE 3.2 Visualizing price per square foot for home sales in Boston.

`names(boston.sf)` suggests the data includes many parcel and building-specific features, but no neighborhood characteristics. The Analyze Boston open data site has many datasets that could be engineered into useful features.[4]

The site runs on the Comprehensive Knowledge Archive Network or CKAN open data framework, which includes an API on 'Crime Incident Reports.'[5] For a glimpse into the API, paste the commented out query in the code block below in to your browser.

---

[4]https://data.boston.gov/

[5]Analyze Boston - Crime Incident Reports - https://data.boston.gov/dataset/crime-incident-reports-august-2015-to-date-source-new-system.

The R package, `ckanr`, can talk directly to open data APIs built on CKAN technology, like Analyze Boston. In the next code block, `resource_id` corresponds to the Incidents dataset and returns the first row and several select fields of the `records` table. Note for this resource, the maximum number of rows the API will return is 100, but a function can be created to return all the data incrementally.

```
ds_search(resource_id = '12cb3883-56f5-47de-afa5-3b1cf61b257b',
          url = "https://data.boston.gov/",
          as = "table")$records[1,c(2,7,11,13)]
```

To keep it simple, a downloaded and wrangled crime dataset has been provided as `bostonCrimes.csv`, which can be read in with `read.csv`. `length(unique(bostonCrimes$OFFENSE_CODE_GROUP))` tells us there are 64 unique offenses in the data. Below, the five most frequent incident types are output.

```
group_by(bostonCrimes, OFFENSE_CODE_GROUP) %>%
  summarize(count = n()) %>%
  arrange(-count) %>% top_n(5)
```

```
## # A tibble: 5 x 2
##   OFFENSE_CODE_GROUP              count
##   <chr>                          <int>
## 1 Motor Vehicle Accident Response 23717
## 2 Larceny                        16869
## 3 Drug Violation                 15815
## 4 Other                          12797
## 5 Medical Assistance             12626
```

For now, the code block below subsets `Aggravated Assault` crimes with XY coordinates. Note the `st_as_sf` function converts a data frame of coordinates to `sf`, and that the original crs of `bostonCrimes.sf` is in decimal degrees (4326). Map the points or visualize assault hotspots with the `stat_density2d` function like in Figure 3.3, as follows.

```
bostonCrimes.sf <-
  bostonCrimes %>%
    filter(OFFENSE_CODE_GROUP == "Aggravated Assault",
           Lat > -1) %>%
    dplyr::select(Lat, Long) %>%
    na.omit() %>%
    st_as_sf(coords = c("Long", "Lat"), crs = 4326,
             agr = "constant") %>%
    st_transform('ESRI:102286') %>%
    distinct()

ggplot() + geom_sf(data = nhoods, fill = "grey40") +
  stat_density2d(data = data.frame(
                     st_coordinates(bostonCrimes.sf)),
                 aes(X, Y, fill = ..level.., alpha = ..level..),
                 size = 0.01, bins = 40, geom = 'polygon') +
  scale_fill_gradient(low = "#25CB10", high = "#FA7800",
                      breaks=c(0.000000003,0.00000003),
                      labels=c("Minimum","Maximum"),
                      name = "Density") +
```

```
scale_alpha(range = c(0.00, 0.35), guide = FALSE) +
labs(title = "Density of Aggravated Assaults, Boston") +
mapTheme()
```

Density of Aggravated Assaults, Boston

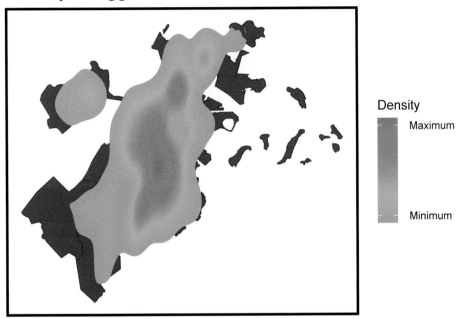

FIGURE 3.3 Mapping aggravated assault density in Boston.

3.2.1   Feature engineering - Measuring exposure to crime

Of a potential home purchase, many buyers ask, "Is there a lot of crime in this neighborhood?" What is 'a lot', how should one define 'neighborhood', and what is a good indicator of crime? Any set of choices will suffer from both 'measurement error' and scale bias, and different buyers in different neighborhoods will value crime exposure differently. Feature engineering is the art and science of defining these relationships in a model, and below, three possible approaches are discussed as follows.

The first is to sum crime incidents for an arbitrary areal unit, like census tract. This is the least optimal as it introduces scale bias related to the modifiable areal unit problem (Section 1.1.1).

The second is to sum crimes within a fixed buffer distance of each home sale observation. This approach implies that the scale relationship between crime and home prices is uniform citywide, which is not likely true.

The code block below creates a new feature, `crimes.Buffer`, that uses a spatial join (`aggregate`) to count crimes within a 1/8-mile buffer of each home sale observation. `pull` converts the output from an `sf` layer to a numeric vector.

```
boston.sf$crimes.Buffer =
    st_buffer(boston.sf, 660) %>%
    aggregate(mutate(bostonCrimes.sf, counter = 1),., sum) %>%
    pull(counter)
```

A third method calculates the 'average nearest neighbor distance' from each home sale to its *k* nearest neighbor crimes. Figure 3.4 provides an example when k=4. The average nearest neighbor distance for the 'close' and 'far' groups is 15 and 34, respectively, suggesting the close group is 'more exposed' to crime than the far group.

How is this approach advantageous over a fixed buffer? There are still scale biases in assuming one parameter of *k* is the 'correct' one. In my experience, however, this approach allows for a model to capitalize on very small continuous variations in distance.

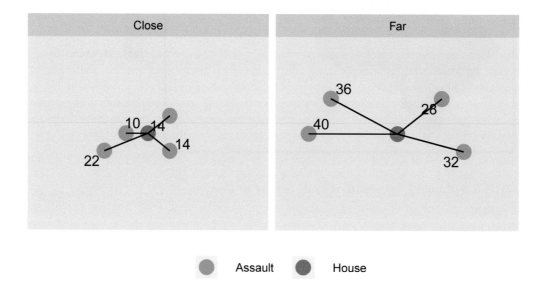

FIGURE 3.4 An example of calculating nearest neighbor distances at different spatial scales.

The `function.R` file includes the function, `nn_function` for calculating average nearest neighbor distance. The function takes three parameters - coordinates of the point layer we wish to `measureFrom`; coordinates of the point layer we wish to `measureTo`; and the number of k nearest neighbors.

It is easier to understand how the `nn_function` works if the reader is willing to run through it line-by-line. The logic is as follows:

1. The `get.knnx` function creates a matrix of nearest neighbor distances, `nn.dist`, from each `measureFrom` point to k `measureTo` points.
2. The `nn.dist` matrix is converted into a data frame.
3. `rownames_to_column` creates a unique field denoting each unique `measureFrom` point.

4. `gather` converts from wide to long form.
5. `arrange` sorts the `measureFrom` field ascending.
6. `group_by` each `measureFrom` point and use `summarize` to take the mean `pointDistance`.
7. Convert `thisPoint` to numeric, sort ascending again, then remove `thisPoint`.
8. `pull` the average nearest neighbor distance.

The `nn_function` is embedded in `mutate` to create five new features in `boston.sf` with up to five k nearest neighbors. `st_c` (shorthand for `st_coordinates`) converts the data frame to a matrix of XY coordinates. `boston.sf` and `bostonCrimes.sf` are also converted to shorthand to limit the size of the below code block. This section has provided a short introduction in geospatial feature engineering. In the next section, each of these features are correlated with house price.

```
st_c <- st_coordinates
b.sf <- boston.sf
bc.sf <- bostonCrimes.sf

boston.sf <-
  boston.sf %>%
    mutate(
      crime_nn1 = nn_function(st_c(b.sf), st_c(bc.sf), 1),
      crime_nn2 = nn_function(st_c(b.sf), st_c(bc.sf), 2),
      crime_nn3 = nn_function(st_c(b.sf), st_c(bc.sf), 3),
      crime_nn4 = nn_function(st_c(b.sf), st_c(bc.sf), 4),
      crime_nn5 = nn_function(st_c(b.sf), st_c(bc.sf), 5))
```

3.2.2   Exploratory analysis - Correlation

```
st_drop_geometry(boston.sf) %>%
  mutate(Age = 2015 - YR_BUILT) %>%
  dplyr::select(SalePrice, LivingArea, Age, GROSS_AREA) %>%
  filter(SalePrice <= 1000000, Age < 500) %>%
  gather(Variable, Value, -SalePrice) %>%
    ggplot(aes(Value, SalePrice)) +
      geom_point(size = .5) + geom_smooth(method = "lm", se=F,
                                colour = "#FA7800") +
      facet_wrap(~Variable, ncol = 3, scales = "free") +
      labs(title="Price as a function of continuous variables") +
      plotTheme()
```

Correlation is an important form of exploratory analysis, identifying features that may be useful for predicting `SalePrice`. In this section, correlation is visualized, and in the next, correlation is estimated.

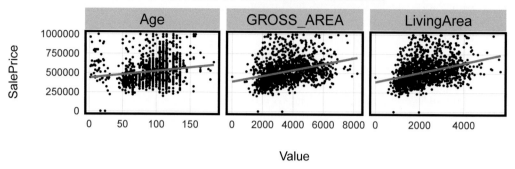

FIGURE 3.5 The relationship between sale price and continuous housing variables.

In Figure 3.5, `SalePrice` is plotted as a function of three numeric features, `Age` (a feature created from `YR_BUILT`), `LivingArea`, and `GROSS_AREA`. Is home sale price related to these features? A 'least squares' line is drawn through the point cloud and the more the point cloud 'hugs' the line, the greater the correlation. In the code block below, the least squares line is generated with `geom_smooth(method = "lm")`.

These plots suggest a correlation exists. In all cases, the regression line slopes upward from left to right, meaning that on average, as age and house size increase, so does price. Correlation can also be described by the slope of the line as well. The greater the slope, the greater the feature's effect on price.

Many features in the `boston.sf` dataset are not numeric but categorical, making correlation more complex. Slope cannot be calculated when the x-axis is categorical. Instead, a significant *difference* in *mean* price is hypothesized across each category. For example, Figure 3.6 outputs bar plots for three categorical features, using `geom_bar` to calculate `mean SalePrice` by category.

```
boston %>%
  dplyr::select(SalePrice, Style, OWN_OCC, NUM_FLOORS) %>%
  mutate(NUM_FLOORS = as.factor(NUM_FLOORS)) %>%
  filter(SalePrice <= 1000000) %>%
  gather(Variable, Value, -SalePrice) %>%
  ggplot(aes(Value, SalePrice)) +
    geom_bar(position = "dodge", stat = "summary",
             fun.y = "mean") +
    facet_wrap(~Variable, ncol = 1, scales = "free") +
    labs(title="Price as a function of\ncategorical variables",
         y = "Mean_Price") +
    plotTheme() + theme(axis.text.x = element_text(angle = 45,
                                                    hjust = 1))
```

`OWN_OCC` or 'owner-occupied', describes likely rental properties. Note that there is no difference on average, between owner and non-owner-occupied home sales. This is a good indicator that `OWN_OCC` may not be a good predictor of `SalePrice`. Conversely, there appears a significant premium associated with the `Victorian` architectural `Style`. Section 3.2.2 discusses why feature engineering like recoding `Style` into fewer categories, or converting `NUM_FLOORS`

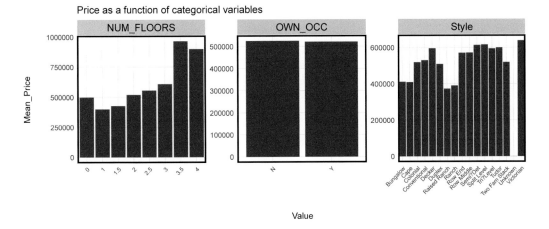

FIGURE 3.6 Testing the relationship between sales prices and categorical housing variables.

from numeric to categorical, could lead to a significant improvement in a predictive model.

Finally, the relationship between `SalePrice` and crime exposure is visualized in Figure 3.7 for the six crime features. Figure 3.7 subsets with `dplyr::select(starts_with("crime")`. `filter` is used to remove sales less than $1000 and greater than $1 million.

These points do not 'hug' the line like the scatterplots in Figure 3.5, suggesting little correlation between crime and price. However, the plots consider just two variables (i.e., 'bivariate'), while a regression is able to account for multiple features simultaneously (i.e., multivariate). We will see how the multivariate regression makes crime a significant predictor.

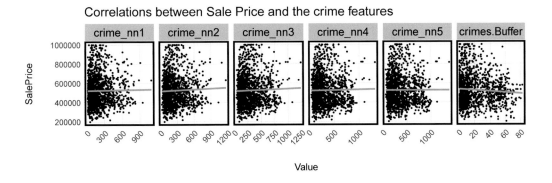

FIGURE 3.7 Visualizing the relationship between sale price and crime.

A correlation matrix is another way to visualize correlation across numeric variables. In the following code block, `cor` and `cor_pmat`, calculate bivariate correlation and statistical significance, respectively. These statistics are explained below. In Figure 3.8, the darker the shade of orange or green, the stronger the correlation. The `SalePrice` row shows correlations relevant to our model, but this plot also shows features that may be colinear, like `LivingArea` and `GROSS_AREA`.

Correlation analysis is a critical component of the machine learning workflow, but exploratory analysis goes beyond just correlation. Keep in mind that good exploratory analysis adds valuable context, particularly for non-technical audiences. Next, statistical correlation and regression is introduced.

```
numericVars <-
  select_if(st_drop_geometry(boston.sf), is.numeric) %>% na.omit()

ggcorrplot(
  round(cor(numericVars), 1),
  p.mat = cor_pmat(numericVars),
  colors = c("#25CB10", "white", "#FA7800"),
  type="lower",
  insig = "blank") +
    labs(title = "Correlation across numeric variables")
```

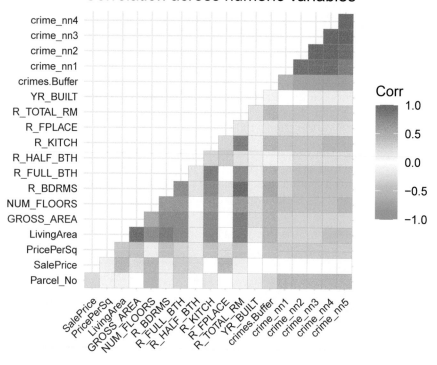

FIGURE 3.8 Visualizing correlation.

3.3   Introduction to ordinary least squares regression

This section gives a quick and applied introduction to regression that may not satisfy readers looking for a mathematical framework. The applied approach is designed for those primarily interested in interpretation and communication.

The purpose of Linear regression or ordinary least squares regression (OLS), is to predict the SalePrice of house i, as a function of several components, as illustrated in the equation offered in this section. The first is the 'intercept', β_0, which is the predicted value of SalePrice if nothing was known about any other features. Next, the regression 'coefficient', β_1, is interpreted as the average change in SalePrice given a unit increase in X. X is a feature, such as the living area of a house.

Finally, ε_i, is the error term or residual, which represents all the variation in SalePrice not explained by X. The goal is to account for all the systematic variation in SalePrice, such that anything leftover (ε_i) is just random noise. Consider the regression equation below can be used to explore the constituent parts of home prices as discussed in the hedonic model.

Of all the nuances of the regression model, one of the most important is the idea that regression models look for predictive 'signals' at the mean. This is very intuitive so long as a predictive feature does not vary substantially from its mean. For example, regressing home price and crime exposure assumes that the average relationship (the spatial process) is comparable for all neighborhoods. This is a significant assumption and one that will be discussed in the next chapter.

$$SalePrice_i = \beta_0 + \beta_1 X_i + \varepsilon_i$$

Let us now try to understand how a regression is estimated starting with the Pearson correlation coefficient, r. Correlation was visualized above, and here it is tested empirically. An r of 0 suggests no correlation between the two variables; -1 indicates a strong negative relationship; and 1, a strong positive relationship. The results of the cor.test below describe a marginal ($r = 0.36$) but statistically significant ($p < 0.001$) positive correlation between SalePrice and LivingArea.

```
cor.test(boston$LivingArea, boston$SalePrice, method = "pearson")
```

In correlation and regression, the slope of the linear relationship between SalePrice and LivingArea, β_1, is calculated with a 'least squares' line fit to the data by minimizing the squared difference between the observed SalePrice and the predicted SalePrice. The algebra used to fit this line is relatively uncomplicated and provides the slope and y-intercept.

One very special characteristic of this line is that it represents the prediction. Figure 3.9 visualizes the observed relationship between SalePrice and LivingArea in green along with the resulting sale price regression prediction, in orange. Note that these predictions fit perfectly on the least squares line. Two larger points are shown for the *same observation* to illustrate the error or residual between predicted and observed SalePrice.

The large residual difference (or error), ε_i, between the orange and green points, suggests that while LivingArea is a good predictor, other features are needed to make a more robust prediction.

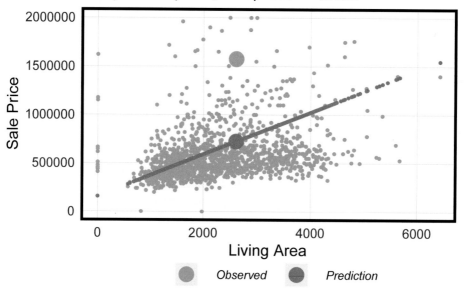

FIGURE 3.9 The observed relationship between sales price and living area is plotted in green and sale price prediction is visualized in orange.

3.3.1   Our first regression model

In R, OLS regression is performed with the lm or 'linear model' function. The dependent variable SalePrice, is modeled as a function of (~) LivingArea and output as an lm object called livingReg. The summary function is used to see the results of the regression.

```
livingReg <- lm(SalePrice ~ LivingArea, data = boston)

summary(livingReg)
```

	SalePrice
LivingArea	216.539*** (14.466)
Constant	157,968.300*** (35,855.590)
N	1,485
R^2	0.131
Adjusted R^2	0.131
Residual Std. Error	563,811.900 (df = 1483)
F Statistic	224.077*** (df = 1; 1483)

$^*p < .1;\ ^{**}p < .05;\ ^{***}p < .01$

TABLE 3.1 livingReg

The actual `summary` looks different from the regression output above. The `Intercept` or 'Constant' is the value of `SalePrice` if living area was 0. In many instances, including this one, the `Intercept` interpretation is not particularly useful.

The estimated coefficient for `LivingArea`, is 216.54. The interpretation is that, "On average, a one foot increase in living area is associated with a \$216.54 increase in sale price". Note that the coefficient is on the scale of the dependent variable, dollars.

The `Std. Error` refers to the standard error of the coefficient and is a measure of precision. The best way to interpret the standard error is in the context of the coefficient. If the standard errors are large relative to the coefficient, then the coefficient may not be reliable.

The p-value is a more direct way to measure if the coefficient is reliable and is a standard measure of statistical significance.[6] It is a hypothesis test based on the 'null hypothesis' that there is *no* relationship between `SalePrice` and `LivingArea`. If the p-value is, say, 0.05, then there is 5% probability that the null hypothesis was mistakenly rejected. In other words, we can be 95% confident that our coefficient estimation is reliable, and thus a useful predictor of `SalePrice`.[7] In the regression summary, the p-values are labeled with asterisks (*) and referenced with a legend at the bottom of the output.

The final component of the regression summary is (Adjusted) R^2 - a common regression 'goodness of fit' indicator that describes how well the features explain the outcome. R^2 runs from 0 to 1 and is defined as the proportion of variation in the dependent variable, `SalePrice`, that is explained by the linear combination of the features. R^2 is interpreted on a percentage basis, so in this model, `LivingArea` explains roughly 13% of the variation in price.[8]

The 'proportion of variation' interpretation is useful for comparing across models. R^2 is also linear, so a model with an R^2 of 0.80 accounts for twice as much variation as a model with an R^2 of 0.40. Despite its interpretability, below we will learn other goodness of fit indicators better suited for prediction.

To understand how regression is used to predict, consider how coefficients relate to the regression equation. In the equation that follows, the β_1 has been substituted for the estimated coefficient. Substitute X in the equation below, for the `LivingArea` of any Boston house, and a price prediction can be calculated.

$$SalePrice_i = 157968 + 216.54X_i + \varepsilon_i$$

Assuming a house with the mean living area, 2,262 square feet, the equation would yield the following prediction:

$$647781.50 = 157968 + (216.54 * 2262) + \varepsilon_i$$

---

[6]I provide a very remedial definition of p-value. Interestingly, many statisticians struggle to define it. For more on this, see: Aschwanden, Christie (2015). Not even scientists can easily explain p-values. FiveThirtyEight. http://fivethirtyeight.com/features/not-even-scientists-can-easily-explain-p-values/

[7]A p-value of 0.05 is the typical threshold of statistical significance, but the appropriate threshold of p depends on the context for the test. Strong statistical significance is indicative of a strong predictive feature, but features with p-values greater than 0.05 may also help predict. The only way to know is to assess model accuracy and generalizability with and without a given feature.

[8]Interestingly, the Pearson correlation, r, for `LivingArea` was estimated to be 0.36. Squaring that value gives the R^2 estimated for this regression.

The error for this model, ε_i, is high given that only 13% of the variation in `SalePrice` has been explained. These errors are explored in detail in Section 3.4, but for now, more features are added to reduce the error and improve the model.[9] `lm` does not take `sf` layers as an input, so geometries are dropped from `boston.sf`. Only certain variables are `selected` for the model, which is useful syntax for quickly adding and subtracting features.

```
reg1 <- lm(SalePrice ~ ., data =
               st_drop_geometry(boston.sf) %>%
               dplyr::select(SalePrice, LivingArea, Style,
                       GROSS_AREA, R_TOTAL_RM, NUM_FLOORS,
                       R_BDRMS, R_FULL_BTH, R_HALF_BTH,
                       R_KITCH, R_AC, R_FPLACE))
summary(reg1)
```

These additional features now explain 56% of the variation in price, a significant improvement over `livingReg`. Many more coefficients are now estimated, including the architectural `Style` feature, which R automatically converts to many categorical features (Table 3.2). These 'dummy variables' or 'fixed effects' as they are called, hypothesize a statistically significant *difference* in price across each `Style` category relative to a *reference* category - Bungalow (`levels(boston.sf$Style)`). More intuition for fixed effects is provided in the next chapter.

3.3.2 More feature engineering and colinearity

Before going forward, this section further emphasizes two critical concepts, feature engineering and colinearity. Beginning with feature engineering, `reg1` estimates the effect of `NUM_FLOORS` encoded as a continuous feature. `table(boston$NUM_FLOORS)` shows that houses have between 0 and 5 floors, and some have half floors. What happens when this feature is re-engineered as categorical? The below `mutate` does just this with `case_when`, a more nuanced `ifelse`.

```
boston.sf <-
  boston.sf %>%
  mutate(NUM_FLOORS.cat = case_when(
          NUM_FLOORS >= 0 & NUM_FLOORS < 3  ~ "Up to 2 Floors",
          NUM_FLOORS >= 3 & NUM_FLOORS < 4  ~ "3 Floors",
          NUM_FLOORS > 4                    ~ "4+ Floors"))
```

The newly recoded `NUM_FLOORS.cat` feature is input into `reg2` below. In the results (not pictured), R automatically removed `3 Floors` as the reference. The remaining two groups are statistically significant. More importantly, judging from the increase in Adjusted R^2, this marginal amount of feature engineering added significant predictive power to the model.

---

[9]When 2+ features are added to the regression, the two-dimensional scatterplot now becomes an n-dimensional 'scatter-cloud'. The least squares approach still seeks to minimize the errors between the predicted fit and observed values.

	SalePrice
LivingArea	609.346*** (48.076)
StyleCape	−140, 506.900* (79, 096.260)
StyleColonial	−343, 096.200*** (78, 518.600)
StyleConventional	−261, 936.800*** (84, 123.070)
StyleDecker	−365, 755.900*** (102, 531.300)
StyleDuplex	−183, 868.500 (128, 816.900)
StyleRaised Ranch	−390, 167.100*** (109, 706.600)
StyleRanch	−92, 823.330 (95, 704.750)
StyleRow End	−68, 636.710 (98, 864.510)
StyleRow Middle	172, 722.600* (100, 981.400)
StyleSemi?Det	−274, 146.000*** (96, 970.880)
StyleSplit Level	−232, 288.100 (168, 146.100)
StyleTri?Level	−803, 632.100** (408, 127.000)
StyleTudor	−394, 103.100 (408, 553.700)
StyleTwo Fam Stack	−147, 538.200* (84, 835.410)
StyleUnknown	−656, 090.500** (291, 530.300)
StyleVictorian	−507, 379.700*** (130, 751.100)
GROSS_AREA	−206.257*** (29.108)
R_TOTAL_RM	−19, 589.190** (8, 268.468)
NUM_FLOORS	163, 990.700*** (38, 373.070)
R_BDRMS	−33, 713.420*** (11, 174.750)
R_FULL_BTH	179, 093.600*** (23, 072.960)
R_HALF_BTH	85, 186.150*** (22, 298.990)
R_KITCH	−257, 206.200*** (33, 090.900)
R_ACD	−203, 205.700 (401, 281.500)
R_ACN	−108, 018.900*** (35, 149.110)
R_ACU	487, 882.600*** (127, 385.500)
R_FPLACE	172, 366.200*** (16, 240.410)
Constant	294, 677.700*** (90, 767.260)
N	1,485
R^2	0.571
Adjusted R^2	0.563
Residual Std. Error	399,781.200 (df = 1456)
F Statistic	69.260*** (df = 28; 1456)

*p < .1; **p < .05; ***p < .01

TABLE 3.2 Regression 1

```
reg2 <- lm(SalePrice ~ ., data =
           st_drop_geometry(boston.sf) %>%
           dplyr::select(SalePrice, LivingArea, Style,
                         GROSS_AREA, R_TOTAL_RM,
                         NUM_FLOORS.cat, R_BDRMS,
                         R_FULL_BTH, R_HALF_BTH, R_KITCH,
                         R_AC, R_FPLACE))
```

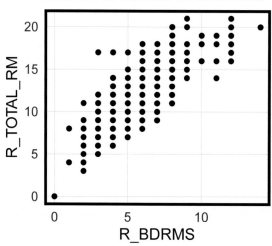

FIGURE 3.10 The colinear relationship between number of rooms and number of bedrooms.

More now on colinearity, as Figure 3.10 indicates a strong (and obvious) correlation between total number of rooms, R_TOTAL_RM, and number of bedrooms R_BDRMS. In reg2, R_BDRMS is significant, but R_TOTAL_RM is not. These two features are 'colinear', or correlated with one another, so if both are input into the regression, one is insignificant. In such an instance, retain the feature that leads to a more accurate and generalizable model.

As the crime features are also colinear, only one should be entered in the model. Try iteratively entering each of the crime features into the regression in addition to reg2. crimes.Buffer seems to have the greatest predictive impact. A model (not pictured) suggests that conditional on the other features, an additional crime within the 1/8th-mile buffer is associated with an average price decrease of -$4,390.82.

Although the correlation plots in Figure 3.7 suggested little correlation between crime and price, once other variables are controlled for in a multivariate regression, crime becomes significant.

Thus far, our most accurate model (with crimes.buffer) explains just 64% of the variation in SalePrice. In Chapter 4, new geospatial features are added to increase the model's predictive power. In the final section of this chapter however, cross-validation and a new set of goodness of fit metrics are introduced.

3.4 Cross-validation and return to goodness of fit

Generalizability is the most important concept for the public-sector data scientist, defined in Section 3.1.1 as a model that can 1) predict accurately on new data and 2) predict accurately across different group contexts, like neighborhoods. In this section, the first definition is explored.

Note that R^2 judges model accuracy on the data used to train the model. Like the age prediction robot, this is not an impressive feat. A higher bar is set below by randomly splitting `boston.sf` into `boston.training` and `boston.test` datasets, *training* a model on the former and *testing* on the latter. New goodness of fit indicators are introduced, and we will see how validation on new data is a better way to gauge accuracy and generalizability. This ultimately helps dictate how useful a model is for decision-making.

3.4.1 Accuracy - Mean absolute error

Below, the `createDataPartition` function randomly splits `boston.sf` into a 60% `boston.training` dataset and a 40% `boston.test` dataset.[10] Note that the air conditioning feature, `R_AC`, contains three possible categories, and D appears just once in the data (`table(boston.sf$R_AC)`). The D observations must be moved into the training set or removed altogether, otherwise, no β coefficient would be estimated, and the model would fail to `predict`. The parameter y balances factors for three such categories across training and test sets.

Another model is then estimated on the training set, `reg.training`.

```
inTrain <- createDataPartition(
              y = paste(boston.sf$NUM_FLOORS.cat,
                        boston.sf$Style, boston.sf$R_AC),
              p = .60, list = FALSE)
boston.training <- boston.sf[inTrain,]
boston.test <- boston.sf[-inTrain,]

reg.training <- lm(SalePrice ~ ., data =
                   st_drop_geometry(boston.training) %>%
                   dplyr::select(SalePrice, LivingArea, Style,
                                 GROSS_AREA, NUM_FLOORS.cat,
                                 R_BDRMS, R_FULL_BTH,
                                 R_HALF_BTH, R_KITCH, R_AC,
                                 R_FPLACE, crimes.Buffer))
```

Three new fields are created in `boston.test`. `SalePrice.Predict` is the sale price prediction calculated using `reg.training` to `predict` onto `boston.test`. The `SalePrice.Error` and `SalePrice.AbsError` calculate differences in predicted and observed prices. Absolute values (abs) may be suitable if over or under-predictions are less of a concern. `SalePrice.APE`

---

[10]As `createDataPartition` randomly partitions the data, the reader's partition (and results) will be different from the one presented here.

is the 'absolute percent error' - the difference between predicted and observed prices on a percentage basis. Any sale with a price greater than $5 million is removed from `boston.test`.

Keep in mind, these statistics reflect how well the model predicts for data it has never seen before. Relative to R^2, which tests goodness of fit on the training data, this is a more reliable validation approach.

```
boston.test <-
  boston.test %>%
  mutate(SalePrice.Predict = predict(reg.training, boston.test),
         SalePrice.Error = SalePrice.Predict - SalePrice,
         SalePrice.AbsError = abs(SalePrice.Predict - SalePrice),
         SalePrice.APE = (abs(SalePrice.Predict - SalePrice)) /
                          SalePrice.Predict)%>%
  filter(SalePrice < 5000000)
```

Now that measures of error are attributed to each sale, some basic summary statistics describe goodness of fit. First, mean absolute error (MAE) is calculated. The error is not trivial given the mean `SalePrice` for `boston.test` is $609,530.

```
mean(boston.test$SalePrice.AbsError, na.rm = T)
```

```
## [1] 169980.9
```

Next, Mean Absolute Percent Error is calculated by taking the mean `SalePrice.APE`. The 'MAPE' confirms our suspicion, suggesting the model errs by 32%.

```
mean(boston.test$SalePrice.APE, na.rm = T)
```

```
## [1] 0.3192212
```

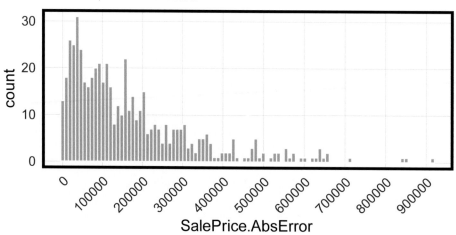

FIGURE 3.11 The distribution of prediction errors shows high, outlying errors.

Data visualizations are also useful for diagnosing models. The `geom_histogram` in Figure 3.11 reveals some very high, outlying errors. In this plot, `scale_x_continuous` ensures x-axis labels at $100k intervals.

Perhaps the most useful visualization is the left-most of Figure 3.12, which plots `SalePrice` as a function of `SalePrice.Predict`. The orange line represents a perfect fit and the green line represents the average predicted fit. If the model were perfectly fit, the green and orange lines would overlap. The deviation suggests that across the range of prices, model predictions are slightly higher than observed prices, on average.

That is not the entire story, however. The right-most panel in Figure 3.12 is the same as the left, but divides prices into three groups to show that the extent of over-prediction is much higher for lower-priced sales. A good machine learner will use diagnostic plots like these to understand what additional features may be helpful for improving the model. Here the lesson is more features are needed to account for lower prices.

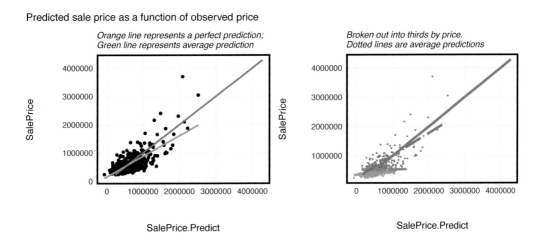

FIGURE 3.12 Visualizing predicted sale price as a function of observed price.

3.4.2 Generalizability - Cross-validation

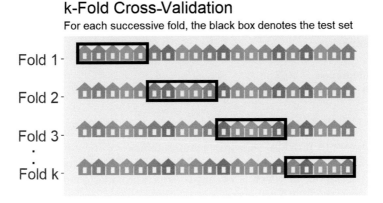

FIGURE 3.13 Explaining k-fold cross-validation.

Predicting for a single hold-out test set is a good way to gauge performance on new data, but testing on many holdouts is even better. Enter cross-validation.

Cross-validation ensures that the goodness of fit results for a single hold-out is not a fluke. While there are many forms of cross-validation, Figure 3.13 visualizes an algorithm called 'k-fold' cross-validation, which works as such:

1. Partition the `boston.sf` data frame into k equal-sized subsets (also known as 'folds').
2. For a given fold, train on a subset of observations, predict on a test set, and measure goodness of fit.
3. Average goodness of fit across all k folds.

The `caret` package and the `train` function is used for cross-validating. Below, a parameter called `fitControl` is set to specify the number of k-fold partitions - in this case 100. In the following code, `set.seed` ensures reproducible folds. An object `reg.cv`, is estimated using the same regression as specified in `reg.training`.

```
fitControl <- trainControl(method = "cv", number = 100)
set.seed(825)

reg.cv <-
  train(SalePrice ~ ., data = st_drop_geometry(boston.sf) %>%
                          dplyr::select(SalePrice,
                          LivingArea, Style, GROSS_AREA,
                          NUM_FLOORS.cat, R_BDRMS,
                          R_FULL_BTH, R_HALF_BTH, R_KITCH,
                          R_AC, R_FPLACE, crimes.Buffer),
      method = "lm", trControl = fitControl, na.action = na.pass)

reg.cv

## Linear Regression
##
## 1485 samples
##    11 predictor
##
## No pre-processing
## Resampling: Cross-Validated (100 fold)
## Summary of sample sizes: 1471, 1469, 1470, 1471, 1471, 1469, ...
## Resampling results:
##
##   RMSE       Rsquared    MAE
##   272949.7   0.4866642   181828.1
##
## Tuning parameter 'intercept' was held constant at a value of TRUE
```

The cross-validation output provides very important goodness of fit information. The value of each metric is actually the *mean* value across *all* folds. The `train` function returns many objects (`names(reg.cv)`), one of which is `resample` which provides goodness of fit for each of the 100 folds. Below, the first 5 are output.

```
reg.cv$resample[1:5,]
```

```
##          RMSE   Rsquared        MAE Resample
## 1 183082.9 0.4978145 138100.8  Fold001
## 2 580261.8 0.9449456 299042.0  Fold002
## 3 314298.3 0.1778472 217442.4  Fold003
## 4 441588.1 0.7750248 250324.4  Fold004
## 5 193053.7 0.4765171 138188.8  Fold005
```

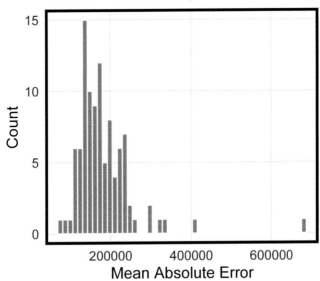

FIGURE 3.14 Distribution of mean absolute error from 100-fold cross-validation.

`mean(reg.cv$resample[,3])` returns the mean for all 100 `MAE` observations, which should be exactly the same as the average MAE shown above.

If the model is generalizable to new data, we should expect comparable goodness of fit metrics across each fold. There are two ways to see if this is true. The first is simply by taking the standard deviation, `sd`, of the `MAE` across all folds. $74,391 suggests significant variation across folds. This variation can also be visualized with a histogram of across-fold `MAE`. If the model generalized well, the distribution of errors would cluster tightly together. Instead, this range of errors suggests the model predicts inconsistently, and would likely be unreliable for predicting houses that have not recently sold. This is an important connection for readers to make.

One reason the model may not generalize to new data is that it is simply not powerful enough, as indicated by the high MAE. Figure 3.15 below maps sale prices and absolute errors for `boston.test`. What do you notice about the errors? Do they look like random noise or are they systematically distributed across space? What is the spatial process behind these errors? These questions will be explored in the next chapter.

Test set sale prices

Test set absolute sale price errors

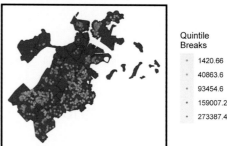

FIGURE 3.15 Mapping predicted sale price and sale price errors.

3.5   Conclusion - Our first model

In this chapter, geospatial machine learning was introduced by way of home price prediction, an important use case for local governments that use prediction to assess property taxes. The goal of geospatial machine learning is to 'borrow the experience' of places where data exists (the training set) and test whether that experience generalizes to new places (the test set). Accuracy and generalizability were introduced as two critical themes of prediction, and we will return to these frequently in the coming chapters.

If this chapter is your first exposure to regression, than I think it would be helpful to really understand key concepts before moving forward. Why is feature engineering so important? Why is identifying colinearity important? What does it mean for regression errors to be random noise? How does cross-validation help to understand generalizability?

Keep in mind that the three components of home prices that need to be modeled are internal/parcel characteristics, public services/amenities, and the spatial process of prices. Omitting the spatial process leads to errors that are clearly non-random across space. Chapter 4 will teach us how to account for this missing variation.

3.6   Assignment - Predict house prices

When I teach this module to my students, the homework is a three-week long home price predictive modeling competition. I give the students a training set of prices and tax parcel ids in a city, keeping a subset of prices hidden. Students then work in pairs to wrangle these data with other open datsets, and build models with minimal errors.

Cash prizes are awarded for the top two best-performing teams and a third prize for data visualization and R markdown presentation. Unless you are taking my class, I have no cash for you (sorry to say), but that should not stop you from replicating this analysis on any number of open home sale datasets across the country.

Your focus should not only be on developing an accurate and generalizable model but on presenting the workflow for a non-technical decision-maker.

4

Intro to Geospatial Machine Learning, Part 2

4.1 On the spatial process of home prices

Test set sale prices

Quintile
Breaks

- 254550
- 399200
- 480000
- 552250
- 670000

Sale price errors on the test set

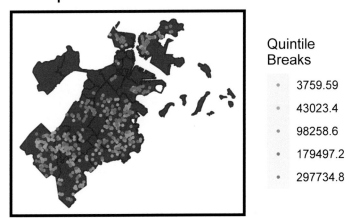

Quintile
Breaks

- 3759.59
- 43023.4
- 98258.6
- 179497.2
- 297734.8

FIGURE 4.1 Predicted sale price and sale price errors on the test set.

Recall the three components of the hedonic home price model - internal characteristics, like the number of bedrooms; neighborhood amenities/public services, like crime exposure; and the underlying spatial process of prices. Modeling the first two in the previous chapter still left nearly one third of the variation in price unexplained.

DOI: 10.1201/9781003054658-4

In this chapter, the spatial process is added, and we learn why generalizability across space is so important for geospatial machine learning. Let's start with the relevant spatial process in home prices.

To me, the most interesting housing market dynamic is that a systematic spatial pattern of house prices emerges from individual real estate transactions. The top-most map in Figure 4.1 illustrates this pattern. As discussed in the Introduction, these patterns result both from external and internal decision-making.

External decision-makers, like Planners, enact zoning regulations dictating what can be built, where, while internal decision-makers, like home buyers, bid on locations according to their preferences. Both preferences and zoning can be accounted for in the first two components of the hedonic model - so what is left unexplained in the error term?

First, imagine that all nearby houses have a backyard pool valued at $10k. If the pool was the only component left unaccounted for in the model, then each nearby house should exhibit regression errors (of $10k) that cluster in space.

Second, homes are 'appraised' by looking at 'comparable' houses, nearby. This means that these comparable houses, nearby are a 'price signal', and if that signal is left unaccounted for, regression errors will also cluster in space.[1]

The key to engineering features that account for this spatial process is understanding the *spatial scale* of comparable houses, nearby. This is challenging because, as Figure 4.1 illustrates, prices in Boston exhibit clustering at different spatial scales - both within *and* across neighborhoods.

The goal in this chapter is to engineer features that account for neighborhood-scale clustering. We will test for generalizability of model predictions with and without these features, and conclude by considering the implications of deploying a property tax assessment algorithm that does not generalize across space.

In the next section, clustering of home price and regression errors is explored, followed by the creation of a 'neighborhood fixed effect' feature. Models with and without this feature are then estimated and validated.

4.1.1   Set up and data wrangling

In this section, libraries are loaded; the final Chapter 3 dataset, including crime features, is read in and split into training and test sets. The `reg.training` model is estimated again, and goodness of fit metrics are calculated on the `boston.test` set.

```
library(tidyverse)
library(sf)
library(spdep)
library(caret)
library(ckanr)
library(grid)
library(gridExtra)
library(knitr)
library(kableExtra)
```

---

[1] The first issue is often referred to as the 'Spatial Error'. For a terrific discussion of both dynamics, see Anselin, L., & Rey, S. (1991). Properties of tests for spatial dependence in Linear regression models. Geographical analysis, 23(2), 112-131.

```
library(tidycensus)
library(scales)

palette5 <- c("#25CB10","#5AB60C","#8FA108","#C48C04","#FA7800")
```

The data and functions are loaded.

```
root.dir =
  paste0("https://raw.githubusercontent.com/urbanSpatial/",
         "Public-Policy-Analytics-Landing/master/DATA/")

boston.sf <-
  st_read(file.path(root.dir,
          "/Chapter3_4/boston_sf_Ch1_wrangled.geojson")) %>%
          st_set_crs('ESRI:102286')

nhoods <-
  st_read(
    paste0("http://bostonopendata-boston.opendata.arcgis.com/",
           "datasets/3525b0ee6e6b427f9aab5d0a1d0a1a28_0.geojson"
           )) %>% st_transform('ESRI:102286')
```

Here the data is split into training and test sets, modeled, and predictions are estimated for a Baseline Regression.

```
inTrain <- createDataPartition(
                y = paste(boston.sf$Name, boston.sf$NUM_FLOORS.cat,
                          boston.sf$Style, boston.sf$R_AC),
                p = .60, list = FALSE)
boston.training <- boston.sf[inTrain,]
boston.test <- boston.sf[-inTrain,]

reg.training <-
  lm(SalePrice ~ ., data = as.data.frame(boston.training) %>%
                      dplyr::select(SalePrice, LivingArea, Style,
                                    GROSS_AREA, NUM_FLOORS.cat,
                                    R_BDRMS, R_FULL_BTH,
                                    R_HALF_BTH, R_KITCH, R_AC,
                                    R_FPLACE, crimes.Buffer))

boston.test <-
  boston.test %>%
  mutate(Regression = "Baseline Regression",
         SalePrice.Predict = predict(reg.training, boston.test),
         SalePrice.Error = SalePrice.Predict - SalePrice,
         SalePrice.AbsError = abs(SalePrice.Predict - SalePrice),
         SalePrice.APE = (abs(SalePrice.Predict - SalePrice)) /
           SalePrice.Predict)%>%
  filter(SalePrice < 5000000)
```

4.2   Do prices and errors cluster? The spatial lag

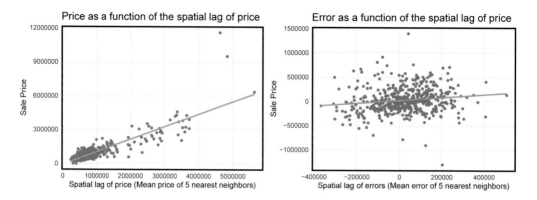

FIGURE 4.2 The spatial lag.

So we now understand that even if a regression perfectly accounts for internal characteristics and public services/amenities, it may still have errors that cluster in space. The best way to test for this is to simply map the errors, as Figure 4.1.

Clustering is also known as spatial autocorrelation - the idea that nearer things are more related than farther things. Let's consider a spatial autocorrelation test that correlates home prices with nearby home prices.

To do so, the following code block introduces new feature engineering that calculates for each home sale, the *average* sale price of its k nearest neighbors. In spatial analysis parlance, this is the 'spatial lag', and it is measured using a series of functions from the `spdep` package.

First, a data frame of `coords`, is created by taking the `st_coordinates` of `boston.sf`. The `knn2nb` function creates a `neighborList`, coding for each point, its 5 nearest neighbors. Next, a 'spatial weights matrix' is created, formally relating each sale price observation to those in the `neighborList`. Finally, the `lag.listw` function calculates a spatial lag of price, `boston.sf$lagPrice`, which is the average price of a home sale's 5 nearest neighbors. The leftmost panel of Figure 4.2 plots `SalePrice` as a function of `lagPrice`.

```
coords <- st_coordinates(boston.sf)

neighborList <- knn2nb(knearneigh(coords, 5))

spatialWeights <- nb2listw(neighborList, style="W")

boston.sf$lagPrice <- lag.listw(spatialWeights,
                                boston.sf$SalePrice)
```

The interpretation of this plot is that as price increases, so does the price of nearby houses. The correlation for this spatial lag relationship is 0.87 and is highly statistically significant. This is substantial evidence for clustering of home prices.

How about for model errors? The following code block replicates the spatial lag procedure for `SalePrice.Error`, calculating the lag directly in the `mutate` of ggplot. The relationship is visualized in right-most plot in Figure 4.2 and describes a marginal but significant correlation of 0.15. The interpretation is that as home price errors increase, so does nearby home price errors. That model errors are spatially autocorrelated suggests that critical spatial information has been omitted from the model. Let's now demonstrate a second approach for measuring spatial autocorrelation - Moran's *I*.

```
coords.test <-  st_coordinates(boston.test)

neighborList.test <- knn2nb(knearneigh(coords.test, 5))

spatialWeights.test <- nb2listw(neighborList.test, style="W")

boston.test %>%
  mutate(lagPriceError = lag.listw(spatialWeights.test,
                                   SalePrice.Error)) %>%
  ggplot(aes(lagPriceError, SalePrice.Error))
```

4.2.1   Do model errors cluster? - Moran's *I*

Moran's *I* is based on a null hypothesis that a given spatial process is randomly distributed. The statistic analyzes how local means deviate from the global mean. A positive *I* near 1, describes positive spatial autocorrelation, or clustering. An *I* near -1 suggests a spatial process where high and low prices/errors 'repel' one another, or are dispersed. Where positive and negative values are randomly distributed, the Moran's *I* statistic is near 0.

A statistically significant p-value overturns the null hypothesis to conclude a clustered spatial process. The Moran's *I* p-value is estimated by comparing the observed Moran's *I* to the *I* calculated from many random permutations of points, like so:

1. The point geometries of home sale observations remain fixed in space.
2. Values of `SalePrice.Error` are randomly assigned to observed home sale locations.
3. Moran's *I* is calculated for that permutation.
4. The process is repeated over *n* permutations creating a distribution of permuted Moran's *I* values, which is then sorted.
5. If the observed Moran's *I* value is greater than say, 95% of the permuted *I* values, then conclude that the observed spatial distribution of errors exhibit greater clustering than expected by random chance alone (a p-value of 0.05).

Figure 4.3 demonstrates Moran's *I* values for the three spatial processes. The `moran.mc` function (`mc` stands for 'Monte Carlo') is used for the random permutation approach. 999 random permutations of *I* are calculated plus 1 observed *I*, giving a total distribution of 1000 Moran's *I* observations.

The `Clustered` point process yields a middling *I* of 0.48, but a p-value of 0.001 suggests that the observed point process is more clustered than all 999 random permutations (1 / 999 = 0.001) and is statistically significant. In the `Random` case, the *I* is close to 0 at 0.0189, and the p-value is insignificant at 0.363. Here, about a third of the random permutations had

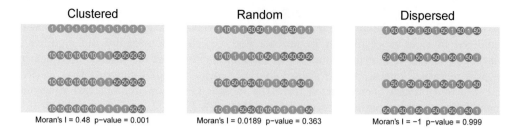

FIGURE 4.3 An example of Moran's I for clustered, random, and dispersed spatial processes.

higher Moran's I than the observed configuration. Finally, the `Dispersed` case has an I of -1 suggesting perfect dispersion of values. The p-value is 0.999, with all random permutations having Moran's I greater than the configuration pictured ($999/1000 = 0.999$).

The `moran.mc` function below calculates Moran's I for the `SalePrice.Error` in `boston.test`. Note the inclusion of the `spatialWeights.test` built above. The observed Moran's I of 0.08 seems marginal, but the p-value of 0.001 suggests model errors cluster more than what we might expect due to random chance alone.

In Figure 4.4, the frequency of all 999 randomly permutated I are plotted as a histogram with the Observed I indicated by the orange line. That the observed I is higher then all of the 999 randomly generated I's provides visual confirmation of spatial autocorrelation. Both the spatial lag and Moran's I test show that model errors exhibit spatial autocorrelation. Again, this suggests that variation in price likely related to the spatial process has been omitted from our current model.

In the next section, new geospatial features are created to account for some this spatial variation.

```
moranTest <- moran.mc(boston.test$SalePrice.Error,
                      spatialWeights.test, nsim = 999)

ggplot(as.data.frame(moranTest$res[c(1:999)]),
       aes(moranTest$res[c(1:999)])) +
  geom_histogram(binwidth = 0.01) +
  geom_vline(aes(xintercept = moranTest$statistic),
             colour = "#FA7800",size=1) +
  scale_x_continuous(limits = c(-1, 1)) +
  labs(title="Observed and permuted Moran's I",
       subtitle= "Observed Moran's I in orange",
       x="Moran's I",
       y="Count") +
  plotTheme()
```

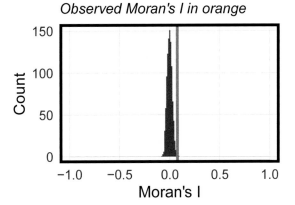

FIGURE 4.4 The distribution of 999 randomly permutated Moran's I with the observed Moran's I represented by the orange line.

4.3 Accounting for neighborhood

Now onto new geospatial features to help account for the spatial process at the neighborhood scale. To do so, a 'neighborhood fixed effect' feature is created.

Fixed effects were discussed in the previous chapter. These are categorical features, like architectural `Style`, that hypothesize statistically significant differences in price. `summary(reg.training)` shows that some of `Style` fixed effects are statistically significant and help to predict price. The same hypothesis can be extended to categorical, neighborhood fixed effects.

For some intuition, the following code block regresses `SalePrice` as a function of neighborhood fixed effects, `Name`. A table is created showing that for each neighborhood, the mean `SalePrice` and the `meanPrediction` for are identical. Thus, accounting for neighborhood effects accounts for the neighborhood mean of prices, and hopefully, some of the spatial process that was otherwise omitted from the model. Try to understand how `left_join` helps create Table 4.1.

```
left_join(
  st_drop_geometry(boston.test) %>%
    group_by(Name) %>%
    summarize(meanPrice = mean(SalePrice, na.rm = T)),
  mutate(boston.test, predict.fe =
                      predict(lm(SalePrice ~ Name,
                                 data = boston.test),
                      boston.test)) %>%
    st_drop_geometry %>%
    group_by(Name) %>%
      summarize(meanPrediction = mean(predict.fe))) %>%
      kable() %>% kable_styling()
```

Name	meanPrice	meanPrediction
Beacon Hill	2782500.0	2782500.0
Charlestown	979361.1	979361.1
Dorchester	514791.2	514791.2
East Boston	486074.0	486074.0
Hyde Park	415961.1	415961.1
Jamaica Plain	796536.3	796536.3
Mattapan	410210.5	410210.5
Mission Hill	1755000.0	1755000.0
Roslindale	483904.1	483904.1
Roxbury	484828.6	484828.6
South Boston	719065.0	719065.0
South End	2979500.0	2979500.0
West Roxbury	538281.8	538281.8

TABLE 4.1 Average sale price and predicted sale price for each neighborhood in Boston.

Let's see how much new predictive power these neighborhood effects generate by re-estimating the regression with the neighborhood `Name` feature. Note that `Name` was included in the `createDataPartition` function above to ensure that neighborhoods with few sale price observations are moved into the training set.

The code block below estimates `reg.nhood` and creates a data frame, `boston.test.nhood`, with all goodness of fit metrics.

```
reg.nhood <- lm(SalePrice ~ .,
               data = as.data.frame(boston.training) %>%
                   dplyr::select(Name, SalePrice, LivingArea,
                             Style, GROSS_AREA,
                             NUM_FLOORS.cat, R_BDRMS,
                             R_FULL_BTH, R_HALF_BTH,
                             R_KITCH, R_AC, R_FPLACE,
                             crimes.Buffer))


boston.test.nhood <-
  boston.test %>%
  mutate(Regression = "Neighborhood Effects",
         SalePrice.Predict = predict(reg.nhood, boston.test),
         SalePrice.Error = SalePrice.Predict - SalePrice,
         SalePrice.AbsError = abs(SalePrice.Predict - SalePrice),
         SalePrice.APE = (abs(SalePrice.Predict - SalePrice)) /
             SalePrice.Predict)%>%
  filter(SalePrice < 5000000)
```

4.3.1   Accuracy of the neighborhood model

How well do neighborhood fixed effects improve the model relative to the `Baseline Regression`? `summary(reg.nhood)` indicates that the neighborhood effects are very significant but have rendered the `Style` fixed effects insignificant, suggesting perhaps that architectural style and neighborhood are colinear. How might this make sense? The following code block binds error metrics from `bothRegresions`, calculating a `lagPriceError` for each.

```
bothRegressions <-
  rbind(
    dplyr::select(boston.test, starts_with("SalePrice"),
               Regression, Name) %>%
      mutate(lagPriceError =
               lag.listw(spatialWeights.test, SalePrice.Error)),
    dplyr::select(boston.test.nhood, starts_with("SalePrice"),
               Regression, Name) %>%
      mutate(lagPriceError =
               lag.listw(spatialWeights.test, SalePrice.Error)))
```

First, Table 4.2 is created describing the MAE and MAPE for `bothRegressions`. The `Neighborhood Effects` model is more accurate on both a dollars and percentage basis. Interestingly, the R^2 of `reg.nhood` is 0.92, which would be very high to a social scientist. To a data scientist however, a MAPE of 18% ($103,263 at the mean price) suggests this model still needs much improvement to be used in the real world.

```
st_drop_geometry(bothRegressions) %>%
  gather(Variable, Value, -Regression, -Name) %>%
  filter(Variable == "SalePrice.AbsError" |
         Variable == "SalePrice.APE") %>%
  group_by(Regression, Variable) %>%
    summarize(meanValue = mean(Value, na.rm = T)) %>%
    spread(Variable, meanValue) %>%
    kable()
```

Regression	SalePrice.AbsError	SalePrice.APE
Baseline Regression	192991.98	-0.1504314
Neighborhood Effects	98232.73	0.1775659

TABLE 4.2 MAE and MAPE for both regressions.

Next, predicted prices are plotted as a function of observed prices in Figure 4.5. Recall the orange line represents a would-be perfect fit, while the green line represents the predicted fit. The neighborhood effects model clearly fits the data better, and does so for all price levels, low, medium, and high. Note, for these plots, `Regression` is the grouping variable in `facet_wrap`.

The neighborhood effects added much predictive power, perhaps by explaining part of the spatial process. As such, we should now expect less clustering or spatial autocorrelation in model errors.

```
bothRegressions %>%
  dplyr::select(SalePrice.Predict, SalePrice, Regression) %>%
    ggplot(aes(SalePrice, SalePrice.Predict)) +
```

```
geom_point() +
stat_smooth(aes(SalePrice, SalePrice),
        method = "lm", se = FALSE, size = 1, colour="#FA7800") +
stat_smooth(aes(SalePrice.Predict, SalePrice),
        method = "lm", se = FALSE, size = 1, colour="#25CB10") +
facet_wrap(~Regression) +
labs(title="Predicted sale price as a function of observed price",
        subtitle="Orange line represents a perfect prediction;
        Green line represents prediction") +
plotTheme()
```

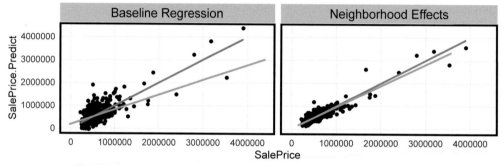

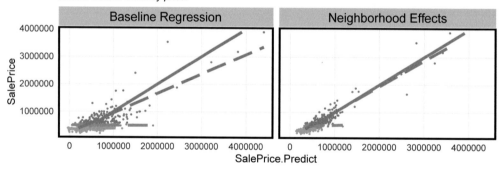

FIGURE 4.5 Model performance plots for both regressions.

4.3.2   Spatial autocorrelation in the neighborhood model

Model errors that cluster in space reflect a regression that has omitted the spatial process. Given that the neighborhood fixed effects improved model accuracy, we might expect errors to be less spatially autocorrelated.

To test this hypothesis, Figure 4.6 maps model errors across `bothRegressions`. Does it look like the errors from the `Neighborhood Effects` are more randomly distributed in space relative to the `Baseline`?

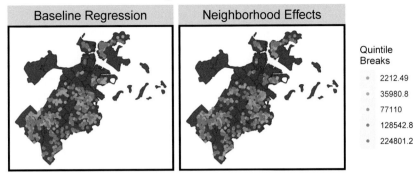

FIGURE 4.6 Mapping the sale price errors from the test set for both regressions.

The Moran's *I* for the `Baseline` and `Neighborhood Effects` regression errors are 0.08 and 0.04, respectively, and both are statistically significant.

Figure 4.7 plots price as a function of lagged model errors for both regressions. Note that range of errors is smaller for the `Neighborhood Effects` regression because it is more accurate. The correlations for the `Baseline` and `Neighborhood Effects` are 0.15 and 0.09, respectively, and are also statistically significant.

What does this all mean? We hypothesized that neighborhood effects could help account for the otherwise missing spatial process. Doing so, reduced errors by nearly half, but spatial autocorrelation remained. Why?

For one, the neighborhood fixed effect may be controlling for omitted public services/amenity features like schools, access to transit etc. Second, these features account the spatial process *across* neighborhoods. Is it possible that other spatial processes exist *within* neighborhoods? Can you think of some features that might help account for the spatial process at even smaller spatial scales?

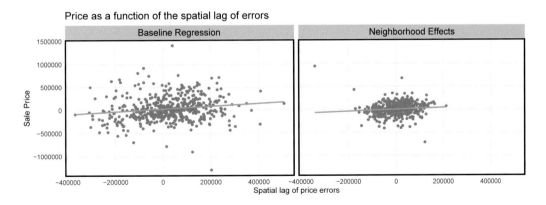

FIGURE 4.7 The relationship between price and the spatial lag of errors for both regressions.

4.3.3   Generalizability of the neighborhood model

Recall the two definitions of generalizability: First, the ability to predict accurately on new data - which was the focus of cross-validation in Chapter 3. Second, the ability to predict with comparable accuracy across different group contexts, like neighborhoods. Here, the focus will be on the latter. It is paramount that a geospatial predictive model generalize to different neighborhood contexts. If it does not then the algorithm may not be fair.

Generalizability across space is very challenging with OLS, because OLS focuses on relationships at the mean. A model trained on Boston will not perform well on Phoenix, for example, because the urban context (at the mean) varies so significantly. Similarly, a model trained on eight low-income neighborhoods and used to predict for a ninth wealthy neighborhood will also perform poorly.

Two approaches for testing across-neighborhood generalizability are demonstrated. The first simply maps mean absolute percent errors (MAPE) by neighborhood. The second gathers census data to test how well each model generalizes to different group contexts - like race and income.

Figure 4.8 maps the mean MAPE by `nhoods` for `bothRegressions`. Not only is the `Neighborhood Effects` model more accurate in general, but its accuracy is more consistent across neighborhoods. This consistency suggests the *Neighborhood Effects* model is more generalizable. Note the `left_join`, which attaches `mean.MAPE` to neighborhood geometries.

```
st_drop_geometry(bothRegressions) %>%
  group_by(Regression, Name) %>%
  summarize(mean.MAPE = mean(SalePrice.APE, na.rm = T)) %>%
  ungroup() %>%
  left_join(nhoods) %>%
  st_sf() %>%
  ggplot() +
    geom_sf(aes(fill = mean.MAPE)) +
    geom_sf(data = bothRegressions, colour ="black", size =.5) +
    facet_wrap(~Regression) +
    scale_fill_gradient(low = palette5[1], high = palette5[5],
                        name = "MAPE") +
    labs(title = "Mean test set MAPE by neighborhood") +
    mapTheme()
```

To test generalizability across urban contexts, `tidycensus` downloads census data to define a `raceContext` and an `incomeContext` (don't forget your `census_api_key`). `output = "wide"` brings in the data in wide form. Census tracts where at least 51% of residents are white receive a `Majority White` designation. Tracts with incomes greater than the citywide mean receive a `High Income` designation.

These designations are arbitrary and suffer from MAUP bias but are still useful for providing descriptive context of generalizability. Figure 4.9 maps `percentWhite` and `raceContext`. As these outcomes have different categorical labels, `facet_wrap` cannot be used to create a small multiple map. Instead `grid.arrange` binds both maps together over two columns (ncol=2).

Mean test set MAPE by neighborhood

FIGURE 4.8 Average mean absolute percent error for the test set across neighborhoods.

```
tracts17 <-
  get_acs(geography = "tract", variables =
          c("B01001_001E","B01001A_001E","B06011_001"),
          year = 2017, state=25, county=025,
          geometry=T, output = "wide") %>%
  st_transform('ESRI:102286')  %>%
  rename(TotalPop = B01001_001E,
         NumberWhites = B01001A_001E,
         Median_Income = B06011_001E) %>%
  mutate(percentWhite = NumberWhites / TotalPop,
         raceContext = ifelse(percentWhite >.5, "Majority White",
                                "Majority Non-White"),
         incomeContext = ifelse(Median_Income > 32322,
                                  "High Income", "Low Income"))

grid.arrange(ncol = 2,
  ggplot() + geom_sf(data = na.omit(tracts17),
                     aes(fill = raceContext)) +
    scale_fill_manual(values = c("#25CB10", "#FA7800"),
                       name="Race Context") +
    labs(title = "Race Context") +
    mapTheme() + theme(legend.position="bottom"),
  ggplot() + geom_sf(data = na.omit(tracts17),
                     aes(fill = incomeContext)) +
    scale_fill_manual(values = c("#25CB10", "#FA7800"),
                       name="Income Context") +
    labs(title = "Income Context") +
    mapTheme() + theme(legend.position="bottom"))
```

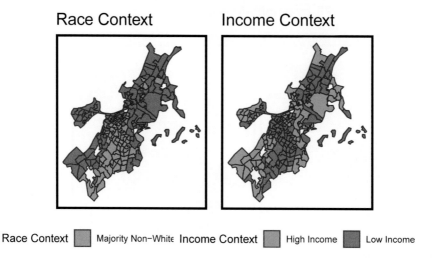

FIGURE 4.9 Demographic designations used to test model generalizability.

Figure 4.9 shows that Boston is very segregated with respect to both race and income. At least, we now observe that the data include a diverse set of neighborhood housing market 'experiences'. In the following code block, MAPE is calculated across `bothRegressions` and both neighborhood contexts. There is a significant difference in goodness of fit across the races, but the gap is closer for the `Neighborhood Effects` model. Table 4.3 is a function of the training/test split in your data.

```
st_join(bothRegressions, tracts17) %>%
  group_by(Regression, raceContext) %>%
  summarize(mean.MAPE = scales::percent(mean(SalePrice.APE,
                                              na.rm = T))) %>%
  st_drop_geometry() %>%
  spread(raceContext, mean.MAPE) %>%
  kable(caption = "Test set MAPE by neighborhood racial context")
```

Regression	Majority Non-White	Majority White
Baseline Regression	-74%	25%
Neighborhood Effects	19%	17%

TABLE 4.3 Test set MAPE by neighborhood racial context.

The same trend is evident for income, with the `Baseline Regression` exhibiting much higher error rate differences across income contexts. It is now clear how the inclusion of neighborhood effects makes the model more generalizable. What would be the consequences of deploying the `Baseline Regression` to assess property taxes?

What do you notice when calculating mean price *error* by group? `SalePrice.Error` is calculated by subtracting observed price from predicted, meaning that a positive price represents an over-prediction. If put into production, this algorithm would disproportionately over-assess and overtax poorer, minority neighborhoods. Such an outcome would be both grossly unfair and a political liability. This 'disparate impact' will be the focus in several chapters to come.

```
st_join(bothRegressions, tracts17) %>%
  filter(!is.na(incomeContext)) %>%
  group_by(Regression, incomeContext) %>%
  summarize(mean.MAPE = scales::percent(mean(SalePrice.APE,
                                             na.rm = T))) %>%
  st_drop_geometry() %>%
  spread(incomeContext, mean.MAPE) %>%
  kable(caption = "Test set MAPE by neighborhood income context")
```

Regression	High Income	Low Income
Baseline Regression	35%	-84%
Neighborhood Effects	16%	20%

TABLE 4.4 Test set MAPE by neighborhood income context.

4.4 Conclusion - Features at multiple scales

Chapter 3 introduced the geospatial machine learning framework, culminating in a model that did not account for the spatial process of home prices. In this chapter, new methods have been introduced for quantifying spatial autocorrelation. Neighborhood features were added to control for at least part of the spatial process.

These neighborhood 'fixed effects' increased the accuracy and generalizability of the model, but model errors remained clustered. What makes home prices so difficult to predict (and such a great first use case) is that prices cluster at different spatial scales. We successfully accounted for the neighborhood scale, but other spatial relationships exist at smaller scales.

Some readers will be drawn to the idea of location-based fixed effects and seek to engineer neighborhoods that better account for within and across price variation. This is a slippery slope. One reasonable approach may be to 'cluster' prices into a set of optimal neighborhoods, but quickly, one will realize that smaller neighborhoods are better - which is a slippery slope. Imagine the smallest neighborhood - a fixed effect for each house. The model would trend perfect, but fail if used to predict for a new property (for which no coefficient has been estimated).

This is referred to as 'overfitting'. The models in these two chapters lack accuracy and are 'underfit'. Conversely, a model with an R^2 of 1 or a MAPE of 0% are 'overfit' and would fail on new data. I have provided some tests to help, but no one statistic can conclude whether a model is under- or overfit. Accuracy and generalizability are trade-offs, and the best way to judge a model is by relating it to the decision-making process.

Finally, neighborhood controls created a more generalizable model, presumably because it successfully 'borrowed' a diverse set of housing market 'experiences' across different communities (i.e., low-income and wealthy). However, as we will learn in the next chapter, if the data gathering process itself does not generalize across space, it is unlikely the predictions generated from those data will generalize either. We will continue to see how generalizability is the most significant consideration in public-sector predictive modeling.

5

Geospatial Risk Modeling - Predictive Policing

5.1   New predictive policing tools

Of the few public-sector machine learning algorithms in use, few are as prevalent or as despised as the suite of algorithms commonly referred to as 'predictive policing'. There are several flavors of predictive policing from forecasting where crime will happen, who will commit crime, judicial response to crime, as well as investigative outcomes.

Policing has driven public-sector machine learning because law enforcement has significant planning and resource allocation questions. In 2017, the Chicago Police Department recorded 268,387 incidents or 735 incidents per day, on average. Nearly 12,000 sworn officers patrol a 228 square mile area. How should police commanders strategically allocate these officers in time and space?

As discussed in Section 1.3, data science is an ideal planning tool to ensure that the supply of a limited resource (i.e., policing), matches the demand for those resources (i.e., crime). For many years now, police departments have been all-in on using crime-related data for planning purposes.

New York City's CompStat program, which began in the mid-1990s, was set up to promote operational decision-making through the compilation of crime statistics and maps. A 1999 survey found that 11% of small- and 33% of large-sized police departments nationally implemented a CompStat program.[1] By 2013, 20% of surveyed police departments said they had at least one full-time sworn officer 'conducting research... using computerized records', and 38% reported at least one non-sworn full-time personnel.[2]

Emerging demand for this technology, a growing abundance of cloud services, and sophisticated machine learning algorithms have all given rise to several commercial predictive policing products. Several of these focus on placed-based predictions, including PredPol,[3] Risk Terrain Modeling,[4] and ShotSpotter Missions.[5]

Today, with growing awareness that Black Lives Matter and that policing resources in America are allocated, in part, by way of systematic racism, critics increasingly charge that predictive policing is harmful. Some cities like Santa Cruz, CA have banned the practice

---

[1] Weisburd, D., Mastrofski, S. D., Greenspan, R., & Willis, J. J. (2004). The growth of Compstat in American policing. Police Foundation Reports, 12.

[2] Law Enforcement Management and Administrative Statistics (LEMAS), 2013. United States Department of Justice. Office of Justice Programs. Bureau of Justice Statistics.

[3] https://www.predpol.com/

[4] https://www.riskterrainmodeling.com/

[5] https://www.shotspotter.com/missions/

outright,[6] while others like Pittsburgh are pivoting the technology to allocate social services instead of law enforcement.[7]

With this critique in mind, why include predictive policing in this book? First and foremost, this chapter provides important context for how to judge a 'useful' machine learning model in government (Section 0.3). Second, it provides an even more nuanced definition of model generalizability. Finally, it is the only open source tutorial on geospatial risk modeling that I am aware of. Whether or not these models proliferate (I don't see them going away any time soon), it will be helpful for stakeholders to gain a shared understanding of their inner-workings to prevent increased bias and unwarranted surveillance.

5.1.1   Generalizability in geospatial risk models

A geospatial risk model is a regression model, not unlike those covered in the previous two chapters. The dependent variable is the occurrence of discrete events like crime, fires, successful sales calls, locations of donut shops, etc.[8] Predictions from these models are interpreted as 'the forecasted risk/opportunity of that event occurring *here*'.

For crime, the hypothesis is that crime risk is a function of *exposure* to a series of geospatial risk and protective factors, such as blight or recreation centers, respectively. The assumption is that as exposure to risk factors increases, so does crime risk.

The goal is to borrow the experience from places where crime is observed and test whether that experience generalizes to places that may be at risk for crime, even if few events are reported. Crime is relatively rare, and observed crime likely discounts actual crime risk. Predictions from geospatial risk models can be thought of as *latent risk* - areas at risk even if a crime has not actually been reported there. By this definition, it is easy to see why such a forecast would be appealing for police.

Interestingly, a model that predicts crime risk equal to observed crime (a mean absolute error of 0) would not reveal any latent risk. As a resource allocation tool, this would not be any more useful than one which tells police to return to yesterday's crime scene. Thus, accuracy is not as critical for this use case, as it was in the last use case.

Generalizability, on the other hand, is incredibly important. Of the two definitions previously introduced, the second will be more important here. A generalizable geospatial risk prediction model is one that predicts risk with comparable accuracy across different neighborhoods. When crime is the outcome of interest, this is anything but straightforward.

Consider that home sale prices from Chapters 3 and 4, are pulled from a complete sample - any house that transacted shows up in the data. Not only is say, the location of every drug offense not a complete sample, but it is not likely a representative sample, either. For a drug offense event to appear in the data, it must be observed by law enforcement. Many

---

[6]Sturgill, Kristi (2020). Santa Cruz becomes the first U.S. city to ban predictive policing. Los Angeles Times. https://www.latimes.com/california/story/2020-06-26/santa-cruz-becomes-first-u-s-city-to-ban-predictive-policing

[7]Murray, A., Giammarise, K. (2020). Pittsburgh suspends policing program that used algorithms to predict crime 'hotspots'. https://www.post-gazette.com/news/crime-courts/2020/06/23/Pittsburgh-suspends-policing-police-program-algorithms-predict-predictive-hot-spots-crime-data/stories/202006230059

[8]For this use case, the dependent variable is the *count* of events, thus the predictions are also counts. Binary and continuous outcomes are also possible. Either way, the predictions generally speaking, can be interpreted as 'risk' or 'opportunity' of an event.

drug offenses go unobserved, and worse, officers may selectively choose to enforce drug crime more fervently in some communities than others.[9]

If selective enforcement is the result of an officer's preconceived or biased beliefs, then this 'selection bias' will be baked into the crime outcome. If a model fails to account for this bias, it will fall into the error term of the regression and lead to predictions that do not generalize across space.

One might assume that additional controls for race can help account for the selection bias, but the true nature of the bias is unknown. It may be entirely about race, partially so, or a confluence of factors; and likely some officers are more biased than others. Thus, without observing the explicit selection *criteria*, it is not possible to fully account for the selection bias.

For this reason, a model trained to predict drug offense risk, for instance, is almost certainly not useful. However, one trained to predict building fire risk may be. Fire departments cannot selectively choose which building fires to extinguish and which to let rage. Thus, all else equal, the building fire outcome (and ultimately the predictions) are more likely to generalize across space.

Selection bias may exist in the dependent variable, but it may also exist in the features as well. A second reason why these models may not generalize has to do with the exposure hypothesis.

The rationale for the exposure hypothesis can be traced in part to the broken windows theory, which posits a link between community 'disorder' and crime.[10] The theory is that features of the built environment, such as blight and disrepair, may signal a local tolerance for criminality. A host of built environment risk factors impact crime risk, but many of these suffer from selection bias.[11]

Perhaps graffiti is a signal that criminality is more locally accepted. The best source of address-level graffiti data comes from 311 open datasets.[12] Assume graffiti was equally distributed throughout the city, but only residents of certain neighborhoods (maybe those where graffiti was rare) chose to file 311 reports. If this reporting criteria is not observed in the model, model predictions would reflect this spatial selection bias and predictions would not generalize.

Operators of 'risk factors' like homeless shelters, laundromats, and check cashing outlets may select into certain neighborhoods based on market preferences. Spatial selection here may also be an issue. So why is this important and what role does broken windows and selection bias play in predictive policing?

5.1.2 From broken windows theory to broken windows policing

There is a wealth of important criminological and social science research on the efficacy of broken windows theory. While I am unqualified to critique these findings, I do think it is

---

[9]See Lum & Isaac (2016) for a terrific discussion of bias in recorded police data. Lum, K., & Isaac, W. (2016). To predict and serve?. Significance, 13(5), 14-19.

[10]Wilson, J. Q., & Kelling, G. L. (1982). Broken windows. Atlantic Monthly, 249(3), 29-38.

[11]Kennedy, L. W., Caplan, J. M., Piza, E. L., & Buccine-Schraeder, H. (2016). Vulnerability and exposure to crime: Applying risk terrain modeling to the study of assault in Chicago. Applied Spatial Analysis and Policy, 9(4), 529-548.

[12]311 systems are used by many cities to provide information to residents or collect non-emergency information. A 311 graffiti report could be passed along to a city department to dispatch an abatement crew for clean up.

useful to consider the consequences of developing a police allocation tool based on broken windows theory.

Racist place-based policies, like redlining and mortgage discrimination, corralled low-income minorities into segregated neighborhoods without the tools for economic empowerment.[13] Many of these communities are characterized by blight and disrepair. A risk model predicated on disrepair (broken windows) might only perpetuate these same racist place-based policies.

In other words, if the data inputs to a forecasting model are biased against communities of color, then the prediction outputs of that model will also be biased against those places. This bias compounds when risk predictions are converted to resource allocation. Surveillance increases, more crimes are 'reported', and more risk is predicted.

When a reasonable criminological theory is operationalized into an empirical model based on flawed data, the result is unuseful decision-making tool.

Because the lack of generalizability is driven in part by unobserved information like selection bias, despite our best efforts below, we still will not know the degree of bias baked in the risk predictions. While a different outcome, like fire, could have been chosen to demonstrate geospatial risk prediction, policing is the most ubiquitous example of the approach, and worth our focus.

In this chapter, a geospatial risk predictive model of burglary is created. We begin by wrangling burglary and risk factor data into geospatial features, correlating their exposure, and estimating models to predict burglary latent risk. These models are then validated in part, by comparing predictions to a standard, business-as-usual measure of geospatial crime risk.

5.1.3   Set up

Begin by loading the requisite packages and functions, including `mapTheme()`, which is used to standardized the map outputs created from the following code.

```
library(tidyverse)
library(sf)
library(RSocrata)
library(viridis)
library(spatstat)
library(raster)
library(spdep)
library(FNN)
library(grid)
library(gridExtra)
library(knitr)
library(kableExtra)
library(tidycensus)

root.dir =
  paste0("https://raw.githubusercontent.com/urbanSpatial",
         "/Public-Policy-Analytics-Landing/master/DATA/")
```

---

[13]A great contemporary recounting of this history is Rothstein, R. (2017). The Color of Law: A forgotten history of how our government segregated America. Liveright Publishing.

```
source(
  paste0("https://raw.githubusercontent.com/urbanSpatial/",
         "Public-Policy-Analytics-Landing/master/functions.r"))
```

5.2 Data wrangling: Creating the `fishnet`

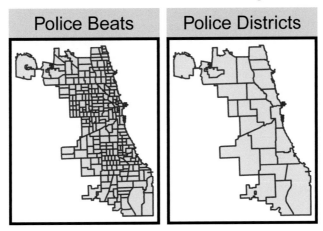

FIGURE 5.1 Police administrative areas at different scales.

What is the appropriate unit of analysis for predicting geospatial crime risk? No matter the answer, scale biases are likely (Chapter 1). The best place to start however, is with the resource allocation process. Many police departments divide the city into administrative areas in which some measure of decision-making autonomy is allowed. How useful would a patrol allocation algorithm be if predictions were made at the police beat or district scale as Figure 5.1?

Tens or hundreds of thousands of people live in a police district, so a single, district-wide risk prediction would not provide enough precision intelligence on where officers should patrol. In the following code, `policeDistricts` and `policeBeats` are downloaded.

```
policeDistricts <-
  st_read(paste0("https://data.cityofchicago.org/api/geospatial",
                 "/fthy-xz3r?method=export&format=GeoJSON")) %>%
  st_transform('ESRI:102271') %>%
  dplyr::select(District = dist_num)

policeBeats <-
  st_read(paste0("https://data.cityofchicago.org/api/geospatial/",
```

```
                "aerh-rz74?method=export&format=GeoJSON")) %>%
  st_transform('ESRI:102271') %>%
  dplyr::select(District = beat_num)

bothPoliceUnits <- rbind(
  mutate(policeDistricts, Legend = "Police Districts"),
  mutate(policeBeats, Legend = "Police Beats"))
```

Instead, consider crime risk not as a phenomenon that varies across administrative units, but one varying smoothly across the landscape, like elevation. Imagine that crime clusters in space, and that crime risk dissipates outward from these 'hotspots', like elevation dips from mountaintops to valleys. The best way to represent this spatial trend in a regression-ready form, is to aggregate point-level data into a lattice of grid cells.

This grid cell lattice is referred to as the `fishnet` and is visualized in Figure 5.2. The `fishnet` is created in the following code from a `chicagoBoundary` that omits O'Hare airport in the northwest of the city. `st_make_grid` is used to create a `fishnet` with 500 ft by 500 ft grid cells.[14]

```
chicagoBoundary <-
  st_read(file.path(root.dir,
                    "/Chapter5/chicagoBoundary.geojson")) %>%
  st_transform('ESRI:102271')

fishnet <-
  st_make_grid(chicagoBoundary, cellsize = 500) %>%
  st_sf() %>%
  mutate(uniqueID = rownames(.))
```

---

[14]500 ft may be a reasonable scale as perhaps it conforms to the size of a city block. It is also helpful to have a distribution of crime counts that follows a theoretical distribution (more on that in Section 5.5). Finally, 500 ft might limit the number of grid cells to be analyzed, and thus the overall computing time.

Fishnet in Chicago

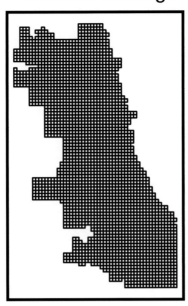

FIGURE 5.2 The 500 by 500 ft fishnet mapped.

Next, `burglaries` are downloaded from the Chicago Open Data site using the `RSocrata` package. Socrata is the creator of the open source platform that Chicago uses to share its data.

The following code block downloads the data and selects only 'forcible entry' burglaries. Some additional data wrangling removes extraneous characters from the`Location` field with `gsub`. The resulting field is then converted to `separate` fields of `X` and `Y` coordinates. Those fields are then made numeric, converted to simple features, projected, and duplicate geometries are removed with `distinct`. The density map in Figure 5.3 (`stat_density2d`) shows some clear burglary hotspots in Chicago.

```
burglaries <-
    read.socrata(paste0("https://data.cityofchicago.org/",
                        "Public-Safety/Crimes-2017/d62x-nvdr")) %>%
      filter(Primary.Type == "BURGLARY" &
                Description == "FORCIBLE ENTRY") %>%
      mutate(x = gsub("[()]", "", Location)) %>%
      separate(x,into= c("Y","X"), sep=",") %>%
      mutate(X = as.numeric(X),Y = as.numeric(Y)) %>%
      na.omit() %>%
      st_as_sf(coords = c("X","Y"), crs=4326, agr="constant") %>%
      st_transform('ESRI:102271') %>%
      distinct()
```

Burlaries, Chicago − 2017   Density of Burglaries

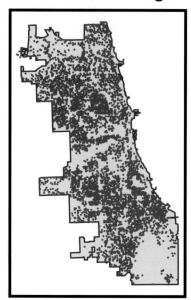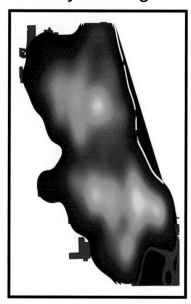

FIGURE 5.3 Visualizing burglaries as points and density.

5.2.1 Data wrangling: Joining burglaries to the `fishnet`

To get the count of burglaries by grid cell, first `mutate` a 'counter' field, `countBurglaries`, for each burglary event, and then spatial join (`aggregate`) burglary points to the `fishnet`, taking the sum of `countBurglaries`.

A grid cell with no burglaries receives `NA`, which is converted to 0 with `replace_na`. A random `uniqueID` is generated for each grid cell, as well as a random group `cvID`, used later for cross-validation later. Roughly 100 `cvIDs` are generated (`round(nrow(burglaries) / 100)`) to allow 100-fold cross-validation below.

Figure 5.4 maps the count of burglaries by grid cell, and the clustered spatial process of burglary begins to take shape. Notice the use of `scale_fill_viridis` from the `viridis` package, which automatically inputs the blue through yellow color ramp.

```
crime_net <-
  dplyr::select(burglaries) %>%
  mutate(countBurglaries = 1) %>%
  aggregate(., fishnet, sum) %>%
  mutate(countBurglaries = replace_na(countBurglaries, 0),
         uniqueID = rownames(.),
         cvID = sample(round(nrow(fishnet) / 24),
                       size=nrow(fishnet), replace = TRUE))

ggplot() +
  geom_sf(data = crime_net, aes(fill = countBurglaries)) +
  scale_fill_viridis() +
```

Count of Burglaires for the fishnet

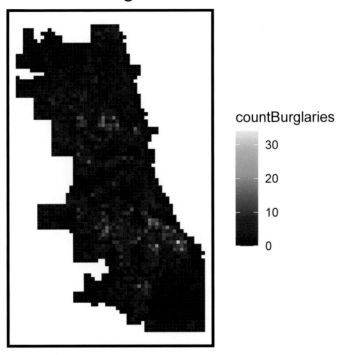

FIGURE 5.4 Aggregating burglaries to the fishnet.

```
labs(title = "Count of Burglaires by grid cell") +
mapTheme()
```

5.2.2   Wrangling risk factors

The crime_net includes counts of the dependent variable, burglary. Next, a small set of risk factor features are downloaded and wrangled to the fishnet. The very simple model created in this chapter is based on a limited set of features. A typical analysis would likely include many more.

Six risk factors are downloaded, including 311 reports of abandoned cars, streetlights out, graffiti remediation, sanitation complaints, and abandoned buildings, along with a neighborhood polygon layer and the location of retail stores that sell liquor to go.

Take note of the approach used to wrangle each dataset. Data is downloaded; year and coordinates are created; and the latter converted to sf. The data is then projected, and a Legend field is added to label the risk factor. This allows each to be rbind into one dataset below for small multiple mapping, as shown in Figure 5.5.

The graffiti code block is the first where we have seen the %in% operator, which enables filter to take inputs from a list rather than chaining together several 'or' (|) statements.

```
abandonCars <-
  read.socrata(paste0("https://data.cityofchicago.org/Service",
  "-Requests/311-Service-Requests-Abandoned-Vehicles/",
  "3c9v-pnva")) %>%
    mutate(year = substr(creation_date,1,4)) %>%
    filter(year == "2017") %>%
    dplyr::select(Y = latitude, X = longitude) %>%
    na.omit() %>%
    st_as_sf(coords = c("X","Y"), crs=4326, agr="constant") %>%
    st_transform(st_crs(fishnet)) %>%
    mutate(Legend = "Abandoned_Cars")

abandonBuildings <-
  read.socrata(paste0("https://data.cityofchicago.org/Service",
  "-Requests/311-Service-Requests-Vacant-and-Abandoned-Building/",
  "7nii-7srd")) %>%
    mutate(year=substr(date_service_request_was_received,1,4))%>%
    filter(year == "2017") %>%
    dplyr::select(Y = latitude, X = longitude) %>%
    na.omit() %>%
    st_as_sf(coords = c("X","Y"), crs=4326, agr="constant") %>%
    st_transform(st_crs(fishnet)) %>%
    mutate(Legend = "Abandoned_Buildings")

graffiti <-
  read.socrata(paste0("https://data.cityofchicago.org/Service",
  "-Requests/311-Service-Requests-Graffiti-Removal-Historical/",
  "hec5-y4x5")) %>%
    mutate(year = substr(creation_date,1,4)) %>%
    filter(year == "2017") %>%
    filter(where_is_the_graffiti_located_ %in%
            c("Front","Rear","Side")) %>%
    dplyr::select(Y = latitude, X = longitude) %>%
    na.omit() %>%
    st_as_sf(coords = c("X","Y"), crs=4326, agr="constant") %>%
    st_transform(st_crs(fishnet)) %>%
    mutate(Legend = "Graffiti")

streetLightsOut <-
  read.socrata(paste0("https://data.cityofchicago.org/Service",
  "-Requests/311-Service-Requests-Street-Lights-All-Out/",
  "zuxi-7xem")) %>%
    mutate(year = substr(creation_date,1,4)) %>%
    filter(year == "2017") %>%
    dplyr::select(Y = latitude, X = longitude) %>%
    na.omit() %>%
    st_as_sf(coords = c("X","Y"), crs=4326, agr="constant") %>%
    st_transform(st_crs(fishnet)) %>%
    mutate(Legend = "Street_Lights_Out")
```

```r
sanitation <-
  read.socrata(paste0("https://data.cityofchicago.org/Service",
  "-Requests/311-Service-Requests-Sanitation-Code-Complaints-Hi/",
  "me59-5fac")) %>%
    mutate(year = substr(creation_date,1,4)) %>%
    filter(year == "2017") %>%
    dplyr::select(Y = latitude, X = longitude) %>%
    na.omit() %>%
    st_as_sf(coords = c("X","Y"), crs=4326, agr="constant") %>%
    st_transform(st_crs(fishnet)) %>%
    mutate(Legend = "Sanitation")

liquorRetail <-
  read.socrata(paste0("https://data.cityofchicago.org/resource/",
  "nrmj-3kcf.json")) %>%
    filter(business_activity ==
            "Retail Sales of Packaged Liquor") %>%
    dplyr::select(Y = latitude, X = longitude) %>%
    na.omit() %>%
    st_as_sf(coords = c("X","Y"), crs=4326, agr="constant") %>%
    st_transform(st_crs(fishnet)) %>%
    mutate(Legend = "Liquor_Retail")

neighborhoods <-
  st_read(paste0("https://raw.githubusercontent.com/",
  "blackmad/neighborhoods/master/chicago.geojson")) %>%
  st_transform(st_crs(fishnet))
```

Risk Factors, points

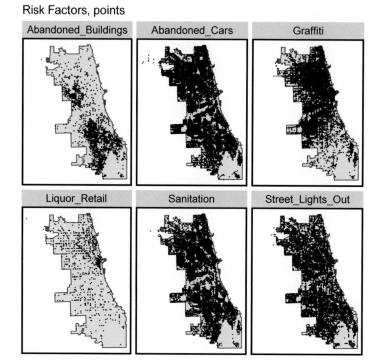

FIGURE 5.5 Mapping the location of six risk factors in Chicago.

5.3   Feature engineering - Count of risk factors by grid cell

We have already seen feature engineering strategies for measuring exposure, but grid cells are an added nuance. We start by joining a long form layer of crime events to the `vars_net` fishnet. First, the individual risk factor layers are bound. Next, the fishnet is spatially joined (`st_join`) *to each point*. The outcome is a large point data frame with a column for each fishnet `uniqueID`.

That output is then converted from a long-form layer of risk factor points with grid cell `uniqueID`s, to a wide-form layer of grid cells with risk factor columns. This is done by grouping on grid cell `uniqueID` and risk factor `Legend`, then summing the count of events. The `full_join` adds the fishnet geometries, and `spread` converts to wide form. `vars_net`, is now regression-ready.

```
vars_net <-
  rbind(abandonCars,streetLightsOut,abandonBuildings,
        liquorRetail, graffiti, sanitation) %>%
  st_join(., fishnet, join=st_within) %>%
  st_drop_geometry() %>%
  group_by(uniqueID, Legend) %>%
  summarize(count = n()) %>%
    full_join(fishnet) %>%
    spread(Legend, count, fill=0) %>%
```

```
st_sf() %>%
dplyr::select(-`<NA>`) %>%
na.omit() %>%
ungroup()
```

Now let's map each `vars_net` feature as a small multiple map. Each risk factor has a different range (min, max), and at this stage of `sf` development, `facet_wrap` is unable to calculate unique legends for each. Instead, a function is used to loop through the creation of individual risk factor maps and compile (i.e., `grid.arrange`) them into one small multiple plot (Figure 5.6).

`vars_net.long` is `vars_net` in long form; `vars` is a vector of `Variable` names; and `mapList` is an empty list. The loop says for each `Variable`, *i*, in `vars`, create a map by `filtering` for `Variable` *i* and adding it to `mapList`. Once all six risk factor maps have been created, `do.call` then loops through the `mapList` and arranges each map in the small multiple plot. Try to recreate this visualization with `facet_wrap` and notice the difference in legends.

These risk factors illustrate slightly different spatial processes. `Abandoned_Buildings` are mainly clustered in South Chicago, while `Abandoned_Cars` are mostly in the north. 311 complaints for graffiti tend to cluster along major thoroughfares and `Liquor_Retail` is heavily clustered in the Loop, Chicago's downtown. In Section 5.4.2, we'll test the correlation between these features and `burglaries`.

```
vars_net.long <-
  gather(vars_net, Variable, value, -geometry, -uniqueID)

vars <- unique(vars_net.long$Variable)
mapList <- list()

for(i in vars){
  mapList[[i]] <-
    ggplot() +
      geom_sf(data = filter(vars_net.long, Variable == i),
              aes(fill=value), colour=NA) +
      scale_fill_viridis(name="") +
      labs(title=i) +
      mapTheme()}

do.call(grid.arrange,c(mapList, ncol=3,
                  top="Risk Factors by Fishnet"))
```

Risk Factors by Fishnet

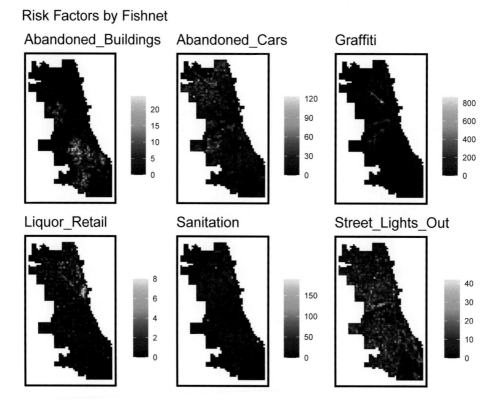

FIGURE 5.6 Aggregating risk factors to the fishnet.

5.3.1   Feature engineering - Nearest neighbor features

Grid cell counts impose a very rigid spatial scale of exposure. Our second feature engineering approach is to calculate average nearest neighbor distance (Section 3.2.2) to hypothesize a smoother exposure relationship across space. Here, the `nn_function` is used.

Average nearest neighbor features are created by converting `vars_net` grid cells to centroid points then measuring to k risk factor points. Note, the `nn_function` requires both input layers to be points. For demonstration purposes k is set to 3, but ideally, one would test different k definitions of scale. Two shortcut functions are created to make the code block less verbose.

```
st_c <- st_coordinates
st_coid <- st_centroid

vars_net <-
  vars_net %>%
    mutate(
      Abandoned_Buildings.nn =
        nn_function(st_c(st_coid(vars_net)),
                    st_c(abandonBuildings),3),
      Abandoned_Cars.nn =
        nn_function(st_c(st_coid(vars_net)),
```

```
                          st_c(abandonCars),3),
          Graffiti.nn =
            nn_function(st_c(st_coid(vars_net)),
                          st_c(graffiti),3),
          Liquor_Retail.nn =
            nn_function(st_c(st_coid(vars_net)),
                          st_c(liquorRetail),3),
          Street_Lights_Out.nn =
            nn_function(st_c(st_coid(vars_net)),
                          st_c(streetLightsOut),3),
          Sanitation.nn =
            nn_function(st_c(st_coid(vars_net)),
                          st_c(sanitation),3))
```

The nearest neighbor features are plotted in Figure 5.7. Note the use of `select` and `ends_with` to map only the nearest neighbor features.

```
vars_net.long.nn <-
  dplyr::select(vars_net, ends_with(".nn")) %>%
    gather(Variable, value, -geometry)

vars <- unique(vars_net.long.nn$Variable)
mapList <- list()

for(i in vars){
  mapList[[i]] <-
    ggplot() +
      geom_sf(data = filter(vars_net.long.nn, Variable == i),
              aes(fill=value), colour=NA) +
      scale_fill_viridis(name="") +
      labs(title=i) +
      mapTheme()}

do.call(grid.arrange,c(mapList, ncol = 3,
        top = "Nearest Neighbor risk Factors by Fishnet"))
```

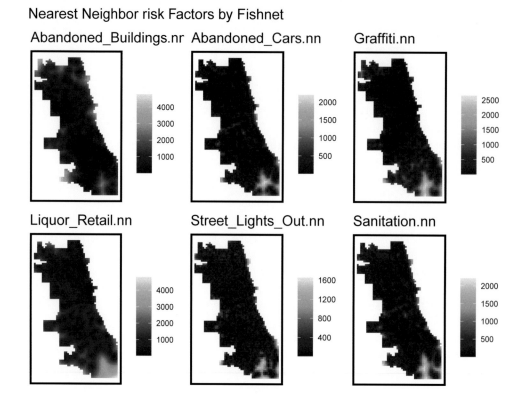

FIGURE 5.7 Aggregating nearest neighbor risk factors to the fishnet.

5.3.2   Feature Engineering - Measure distance to one point

It also may be reasonable to measure distance to a single point, like the centroid of the Loop - Chicago's central business district. This is done with `st_distance` and visualized in Figure 5.8.

```
loopPoint <-
  filter(neighborhoods, name == "Loop") %>%
  st_centroid()

vars_net$loopDistance =
  st_distance(st_centroid(vars_net), loopPoint) %>%
  as.numeric()
```

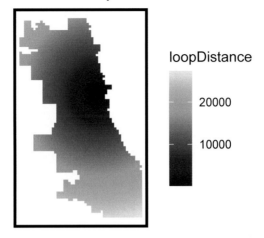

**Euclidean distance
to the Loop**

FIGURE 5.8 Measuring distance to the Loop.

5.3.3 Feature Engineering - Create the `final_net`

Next, the `crime_net` and `vars_net` layers are joined into one regression-ready, `final_net`.
In the following code block, the `left_join` is enabled by converting `vars_net` to a data
frame with `st_drop_geometry`.

```
final_net <-
  left_join(crime_net, st_drop_geometry(vars_net), by="uniqueID")
```

Neighborhood `name` and `policeDistrict` are spatially joined to the `final_net` using grid
cell centroids (Section 1.2.3). The `st_drop_geometry` and `left_join` operations then drop
the point centroid geometries, joining the result back to grid cell geometries and converting
again to `sf`. Some grid cell centroids do not fall into a neighborhood (returning `NA`) and are
removed with `na.omit`. Other neighborhoods are so small, they are only represented by one
grid cell. The results are shown in Figure 5.9.

```
final_net <-
  st_centroid(final_net) %>%
    st_join(dplyr::select(neighborhoods, name)) %>%
    st_join(dplyr::select(policeDistricts, District)) %>%
      st_drop_geometry() %>%
      left_join(dplyr::select(final_net, geometry, uniqueID)) %>%
      st_sf() %>%
  na.omit()
```

Police Districts   Neighborhoods

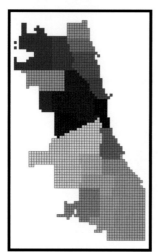 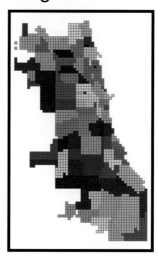

FIGURE 5.9 Visualizing the fishnet as Chicago neighborhoods and police districts.

5.4   Exploring the spatial process of burglary

In Section 4.2.1, 'Global' Moran's I was used to test for spatial autocorrelation (clustering) of home prices and model errors. This information provided insight into the spatial process of home prices, accounting for neighborhood scale clustering but not clustering at more local scales. Here, that local spatial process is explored.

To do so, a statistic called Local Moran's I is introduced. Here, the null hypothesis is that the burglary count at a given location is randomly distributed relative to its *immediate neighbors*.

Like its global cousin, a spatial weights matrix is used to relate a unit to its neighbors. In Section 4.2, a nearest neighbor weights matrix was used. Here, weights are calculated with 'polygon adjacency'. The following code block creates a neighbor list, `poly2nb`, and a spatial weights matrix, `final_net.weights` using `queen` contiguity. This means that every grid cell is related to its eight adjacent neighbors (think about how a queen moves on a chess board).

Figure 5.10 visualizes one grid cell and its queen neighbors. Any one grid cell's neighbors can be returned like so, `final_net.nb[[1457]]`.

```
final_net.nb <- poly2nb(as_Spatial(final_net), queen=TRUE)
final_net.weights <- nb2listw(final_net.nb, style="W",
                        zero.policy=TRUE)
```

'Queen' contiguity

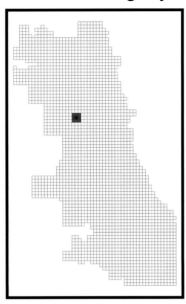

FIGURE 5.10 Visualizing the queen neighbors for one fishnet grid cell.

Figure 5.11 describes the *local* spatial process of burglary. `final_net.localMorans` is created by column binding `final_net` with the results of a `localmoran` test. The inputs to the `localmoran` test include `countBurglaries` and the spatial weights matrix. Several useful test statistics are output including I, the p-value, and `Significiant_Hotspots`, defined as those grid cells with higher local counts than what might otherwise be expected under randomness (p-values <= 0.05). The data frame is then converted to long form for mapping.

Another `grid.arrange` loop is used to create a small multiple map of the aforementioned indicators. The legend in Figure 5.11, shows that relatively high values of I represent strong and statistically significant evidence of local clustering. Further evidence of this can be seen in the p-value and significant hotspot maps. This test provides insight into the scale, location, and intensity of burglary hotspots.

```
final_net.localMorans <-
  cbind(
    as.data.frame(localmoran(final_net$countBurglaries,
                             final_net.weights)),
    as.data.frame(final_net)) %>%
    st_sf() %>%
      dplyr::select(Burglary_Count = countBurglaries,
                    Local_Morans_I = Ii,
                    P_Value = `Pr(z > 0)`) %>%
      mutate(Significant_Hotspots = ifelse(P_Value <=
                                          0.05, 1, 0)) %>%
      gather(Variable, Value, -geometry)

vars <- unique(final_net.localMorans$Variable)
```

```
varList <- list()

for(i in vars){
  varList[[i]] <-
    ggplot() +
      geom_sf(data = filter(final_net.localMorans, Variable==i),
              aes(fill = Value), colour=NA) +
      scale_fill_viridis(name="") +
      labs(title=i) +
      mapTheme() + theme(legend.position="bottom")}

do.call(grid.arrange,c(varList, ncol = 4,
        top = "Local Morans I statistics, Burglary"))
```

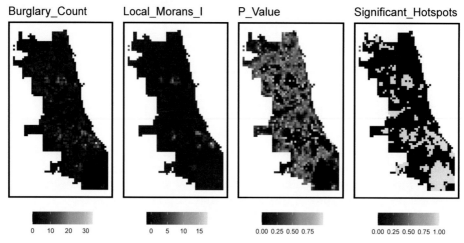

FIGURE 5.11 The right-most map shows the significant burglary hotspots in Chicago based on Moran's I results.

Why is this information useful? A generalizable model must predict equally as well in the hotspots as the coldspots. A model fit only to the coldspots, will underfit the hotspots and vice versa. Not only is this local insight useful exploratory analysis, it can also be engineered into powerful spatial features to control for the local spatial process.

What is the appropriate scale for this local spatial process? Figure 5.12 explores local hotspots by varying the p-value of the Local Moran's *I*. The smaller the p-value the more significant the clusters. 0.0000001 conforms to very strong and significant burglary hotspots.

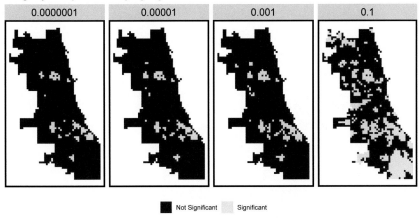

FIGURE 5.12 The extent of burglary hotspots changes when different signifiance levels are used.

The following code block creates a Local Moran's *I* feature in `final_net`. As before, a dummy variable, `burglary.isSig`, denotes a cell as part of a significant cluster (a p-value `<= 0.0000001`). `burglary.isSig.dist` then measures average nearest neighbor distance from each cell centroid to its nearest significant cluster and is mapped in Figure 5.13. We can now model important information on the local spatial process of burglaries.

```
final_net <-
  final_net %>%
  mutate(burglary.isSig =
          ifelse(localmoran(final_net$countBurglaries,
                          final_net.weights)[,5] <=
                 0.0000001, 1, 0)) %>%
  mutate(burglary.isSig.dist =
          nn_function(st_coordinates(st_centroid(final_net)),
                      st_coordinates(st_centroid(
                         filter(final_net, burglary.isSig ==
                                  1))), 1))
```

Distance to highly significant burglary hotspots

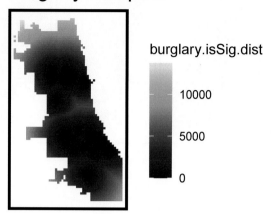

FIGURE 5.13 Visualizing the distance to burglary hotspots with a p-value <= 0.0000001.

5.4.1   Correlation tests

Correlation gives important context while also providing intuition on features that may predict `countBurglaries`. The following code block creates a small multiple scatterplot of `countBurglaries` as a function of the risk factors. `correlation.long` converts `final_net` to long form. `correlation.cor` groups by `Variable`, and calculates the Pearson R correlation, shown directly on the plot.

Figure 5.14 organizes count and nearest neighbor (`nn`) correlations side-by-side. While correlation for count features is a bit awkward, this approach can help with feature selection. For a given risk factor, avoid colinearity by selecting *either* the count or nearest neighbor feature. Just remember, when all features are entered into a multivariate regression, the correlations will change.

```
correlation.long <-
  st_drop_geometry(final_net) %>%
    dplyr::select(-uniqueID, -cvID, -loopDistance, -name,
                  -District) %>%
    gather(Variable, Value, -countBurglaries)

correlation.cor <-
  correlation.long %>%
    group_by(Variable) %>%
    summarize(correlation =
              cor(Value, countBurglaries, use = "complete.obs"))

ggplot(correlation.long, aes(Value, countBurglaries)) +
  geom_point(size = 0.1) +
  geom_text(data = correlation.cor,
            aes(label = paste("r =", round(correlation, 2))),
```

```
              x=-Inf, y=Inf, vjust = 1.5, hjust = -.1) +
   geom_smooth(method = "lm", se = FALSE, colour = "black") +
   facet_wrap(~Variable, ncol = 2, scales = "free") +
   labs(title = "Burglary count as a function of risk factors") +
   plotTheme()
```

5.5 Poisson Regression

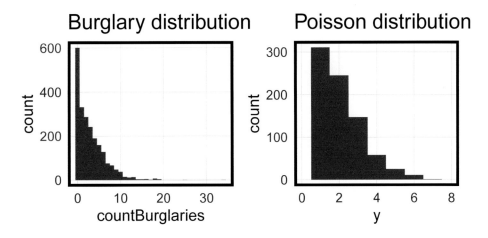

FIGURE 5.15 Poisson distribution: Burglary counts in the fishnet.

Take a look at the skewed distribution of `countBurglaries` in the left-most histogram of Figure 5.15. Given burglary is a relatively rare event, it is reasonable for most grid cells to contain no crime events. When data is distributed this way, an OLS regression is inappropriate. In this section, a Poisson regression is estimated which is uniquely suited to modeling a count outcome like `countBurglaries`.

There are many different approaches to modeling burglary counts. Here, a Poisson regression is used, which is based on a Poisson distribution, simulated in the right-most histogram of Figure 5.15. Does the observed and simulated distributions appear similar? There are many flavors of count-based regression, but the one used here is the most simple.[15]

---

[15]More advanced readers might consider negative binomial and its variants. Another option would be to model a 'binomial' outcome (Chapter 6) where crime counts are distilled to a 0 (no burglaries) and 1 (>0 burglaries). A prediction from this model would be interpreted as the 'probability of a burglary being committed here'. 73% of grid cells have at least 1 burglary, which would render most areas as having a high probability. Regressing on a count outcome is useful because it predicts a more continuous quantity of risk.

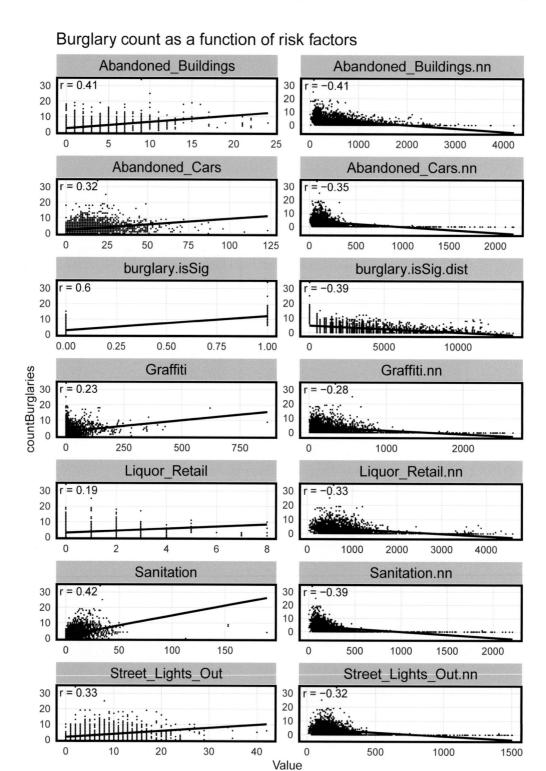

FIGURE 5.14 The relationship between count of burglaries and various risk factors.

5.5.1 Cross-validated Poisson regression

Recall, generalizability is important 1) to test model performance on new data and 2) on different (spatial) group contexts, like neighborhoods. In this section, both are addressed.

Unlike home prices, `final_net` is not split into training and test sets. Instead, we move directly to cross-validation, and because geospatial risk models are purely spatial, *spatial cross-validation* becomes an important option.

A well-generalized crime predictive model learns the crime risk 'experience' at both citywide and local spatial scales. The best way to test for this is to hold-out one local area, train the model on the remaining *n - 1* areas, predict for the hold-out, and record the goodness of fit. In this form of spatial cross-validation called 'leave-one-group-out' cross-validation (LOGO-CV), each neighborhood takes a turn as a hold-out.

Imagine one neighborhood has a particularly unique local experience. LOGO-CV assumes that the experience in other neighborhoods generalizes to this unique place - which is a pretty rigid assumption.

Three `final_net` fields can be used for cross-validation. A random generated `cvID` associated with each grid cell can be used for random k-fold cross-validation. Neighborhood `name` and police `District` can be used for spatial cross-validation.

Below, goodness of fit metrics are generated for four regressions - two including `Just Risk Factors` (`reg.vars`), and a second (`reg.ss.vars`) includes risk factors plus the Local Moran's I `Spatial Process` features created in Section 5.4.1. These features are relatively simple - can you improve on them?

```
reg.vars <-
  c("Abandoned_Buildings.nn", "Abandoned_Cars.nn", "Graffiti.nn",
    "Liquor_Retail.nn", "Street_Lights_Out.nn", "Sanitation.nn",
    "loopDistance")
```

```
reg.ss.vars <-
  c("Abandoned_Buildings.nn", "Abandoned_Cars.nn", "Graffiti.nn",
    "Liquor_Retail.nn", "Street_Lights_Out.nn", "Sanitation.nn",
    "loopDistance", "burglary.isSig", "burglary.isSig.dist")
```

The `crossValidate` function below is very simple and designed to take an input `dataset`; a cross-validation id; a `dependentVariable`; and a list of independent variables, `indVariables`. `cvID_list` is a list of unique `ids` which could be numbers or neighborhood `name`, for instance.

For a given neighborhood `name`, the function assigns each grid cell *not* in that neighborhood to the training set, `fold.train`, and each cell *in* that neighborhood to the test set, `fold.test`. A model is trained from the former and used to predict on the latter. The process is repeated until each neighborhood has a turn acting as a hold-out. **For now**, the countBurglaries variable is hardwired into the function, which you will **have to change** when using this function for future analyses. If you have read in the above `functions.r`, you can see the function by running `crossValidate`.

The following code block runs `crossValidate` to estimate four different regressions.

- `reg.cv` and `reg.ss.cv` perform random *k-fold* cross-validation using `Just Risk Factors` and the `Spatial Process` features, respectively.

- `reg.spatialCV` and `reg.ss.spatialCV` perform *LOGO-CV*, spatial cross-validation on neighborhood `name`, using the aforementioned two sets of features.

The function makes it easy to swap out different cross-validation group `id`'s. k-fold cross-validation uses the `cvID`. LOGO-CV uses the neighborhood `name`. You may also wish to explore results using the police `Districts`. Note, in the `select` operation at the end of the LOGO-CV models, the cross-validation `id` is standardized to `cvID`.

The result of each analysis is a `sf` layer with observed and predicted burglary counts.

```
reg.cv <- crossValidate(
  dataset = final_net,
  id = "cvID",
  dependentVariable = "countBurglaries",
  indVariables = reg.vars) %>%
    dplyr::select(
      cvID = cvID, countBurglaries, Prediction, geometry)

reg.ss.cv <- crossValidate(
  dataset = final_net,
  id = "cvID",
  dependentVariable = "countBurglaries",
  indVariables = reg.ss.vars) %>%
    dplyr::select(
      cvID = cvID, countBurglaries, Prediction, geometry)

reg.spatialCV <- crossValidate(
  dataset = final_net,
  id = "name",
  dependentVariable = "countBurglaries",
  indVariables = reg.vars) %>%
    dplyr::select(
      cvID = name, countBurglaries, Prediction, geometry)

reg.ss.spatialCV <- crossValidate(
  dataset = final_net,
  id = "name",
  dependentVariable = "countBurglaries",
  indVariables = reg.ss.vars) %>%
    dplyr::select(
      cvID = name, countBurglaries, Prediction, geometry)
```

5.5.2   Accuracy and generalzability

A host of goodness of fit metrics are calculated below with particular emphasis on generalizability across space. The following code block creates a long form `reg.summary`, that binds together observed/predicted counts and errors for each grid cell and for each `Regression`, along with the `cvID`, and the `geometry`.

```
reg.summary <-
  rbind(
    mutate(reg.cv,
           Error = Prediction - countBurglaries,
           Regression = "Random k-fold CV: Just Risk Factors"),

    mutate(reg.ss.cv,
           Error = Prediction - countBurglaries,
           Regression = "Random k-fold CV: Spatial Process"),

    mutate(reg.spatialCV,
           Error = Prediction - countBurglaries,
           Regression = "Spatial LOGO-CV: Just Risk Factors"),

    mutate(reg.ss.spatialCV,
           Error = Prediction - countBurglaries,
           Regression = "Spatial LOGO-CV: Spatial Process")) %>%
    st_sf()
```

In the next code block, `error_by_reg_and_fold` calculates and visualizes MAE for *each* fold across each regression. The `Spatial Process` features seem to reduce errors overall.

Recall, LOGO-CV assumes the local spatial process from all *other* neighborhoods generalizes to the hold-out. When the local spatial process is not accounted for (i.e., `Just Risk Factors`), some neighborhood hold-outs have MAEs greater than four burglaries. However, those large errors disappear when the `Spatial Process` features are added. The lesson is that there is a shared local burglary experience across Chicago, and accounting for it improves the model, particularly in the hotspots.

What more can you learn by plotting raw errors in the histogram format used in Figure 5.16?

```
error_by_reg_and_fold <-
  reg.summary %>%
    group_by(Regression, cvID) %>%
    summarize(Mean_Error = mean(Prediction - countBurglaries,
                                na.rm = T),
              MAE = mean(abs(Mean_Error), na.rm = T),
              SD_MAE = mean(abs(Mean_Error), na.rm = T)) %>%
  ungroup()

error_by_reg_and_fold %>%
  ggplot(aes(MAE)) +
    geom_histogram(bins = 30, colour="black", fill="#FDE725FF") +
    facet_wrap(~Regression) +
    geom_vline(xintercept = 0) + scale_x_continuous(
                                 breaks = seq(0, 8, by = 1)) +
    labs(title="Distribution of MAE",
         subtitle = "k-fold cross-validation vs. LOGO-CV",
         x="Mean Absolute Error", y="Count") +
    plotTheme()
```

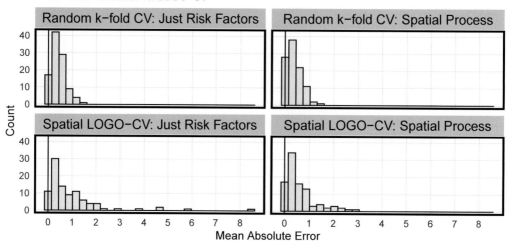

FIGURE 5.16 Results from LOGO-CV and k-fold cross-validation for both regressions.

Table 5.1 below builds on `error_by_reg_and_fold` to calculate the mean and standard deviation in errors by regression (note the additional `group_by`). The result confirms our conclusion that the `Spatial Process` features improve the model. The model appears slightly less robust for the spatial cross-validation because LOGO-CV is such a conservative assumption. For intuition on how severe these errors are, compare them to the observed mean `countBurglaries`.

```
st_drop_geometry(error_by_reg_and_fold) %>%
  group_by(Regression) %>%
    summarize(Mean_MAE = round(mean(MAE), 2),
              SD_MAE = round(sd(MAE), 2)) %>%
  kable() %>%
    kable_styling("striped", full_width = F) %>%
    row_spec(2, color = "black", background = "#FDE725FF") %>%
    row_spec(4, color = "black", background = "#FDE725FF")
```

Regression	Mean_MAE	SD_MAE
Random k-fold CV: Just Risk Factors	0.43	0.30
Random k-fold CV: Spatial Process	0.38	0.28
Spatial LOGO-CV: Just Risk Factors	0.98	1.27
Spatial LOGO-CV: Spatial Process	0.62	0.62

TABLE 5.1 The mean and standard deviation of errors by regression.

Figure 5.17 visualizes the LOGO-CV errors spatially. Note the use of `str_detect` in the `filter` operation to pull out just the LOGO-CV regression errors. These maps visualize where the higher errors occur when the local spatial process is not accounted for. Not surprisingly, the largest errors are in the hotspot locations.

```
error_by_reg_and_fold %>%
  filter(str_detect(Regression, "LOGO")) %>%
  ggplot() +
    geom_sf(aes(fill = MAE)) +
    facet_wrap(~Regression) +
    scale_fill_viridis() +
    labs(title = "Burglary errors by LOGO-CV Regression") +
    mapTheme() + theme(legend.position="bottom")
```

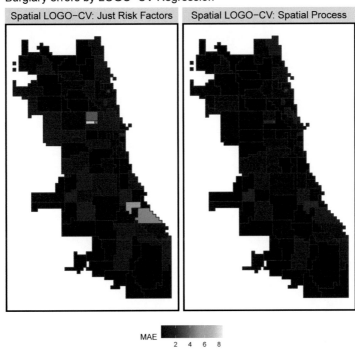

FIGURE 5.17 Visualizing LOGO-CV errors spatially.

As discussed in Chapter 4, accounting for the local spatial process should remove all spatial variation in `countBurglary`, which should leave little spatial autocorrelation in model errors. To test this, the following code block calculates a new `neighborhood.weights`, spatial weights matrix at the neighborhood instead of grid cell scale. Global Moran's I and p-values are then calculated for each LOGO-CV regression.

This provides more evidence that the `Spatial Process` features helped account for the spatial variation in burglary, although some still remains (Table 5.2). More risk *and* protective factor features would be the next step to improve this, followed perhaps by engineering improved spatial process features.

```
neighborhood.weights <-
  filter(error_by_reg_and_fold,
         Regression == "Spatial LOGO-CV: Spatial Process") %>%
    group_by(cvID) %>%
```

```
    poly2nb(as_Spatial(.), queen=TRUE) %>%
    nb2listw(., style="W", zero.policy=TRUE)

filter(error_by_reg_and_fold, str_detect(Regression, "LOGO")) %>%
    st_drop_geometry() %>%
    group_by(Regression) %>%
    summarize(Morans_I =
            moran.mc(abs(Mean_Error), neighborhood.weights,
                    nsim = 999, zero.policy = TRUE,
                    na.action=na.omit)[[1]],
        p_value =
            moran.mc(abs(Mean_Error), neighborhood.weights,
            nsim = 999, zero.policy = TRUE,
            na.action=na.omit)[[3]])
```

Regression	Morans_I	p_value
Spatial LOGO-CV: Just Risk Factors	0.2536938	0.001
Spatial LOGO-CV: Spatial Process	0.1489953	0.014

TABLE 5.2 Global Moran's I and p-values for LOGO-CV for both regressions.

On to model predictions. Figure 5.18 maps predictions for the LOGO-CV regressions. The `Spatial Process` features do a better job picking up the hotspots, as intended. Given the rigid assumptions of LOGO-CV, it is impressive that other local hotpots can generally predict hotspots in hold-out neighborhoods.

The spatial process features produce a more 'smooth' crime risk surface, relative to the observed counts. These predictions represent 'latent crime risk' - areas at risk even if a crime hasn't actually been observed. Accuracy is not as important as generalizability, nevertheless, of 6817 observed burglaries, `Spatial LOGO-CV: Spatial Process` predicted 6804 burglaries, citywide.

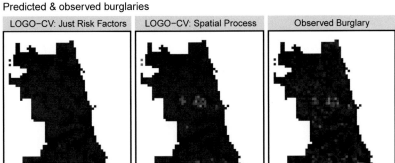

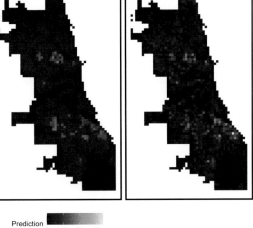

FIGURE 5.18 Predicted burglaries from each regression compared to observed burglaries.

Interestingly, Figure 5.19 shows that all models over-predict in low burglary areas and under-predict in hotspot areas. Over-predictions in lower burglary areas may highlight areas of latent risk. Under-prediction in higher burglary areas may reflect difficulty predicting the hotspots.

Let's now test for generalizability across racial-neighborhood context, as we did in Chapter 4.

```
st_drop_geometry(reg.summary) %>%
  group_by(Regression) %>%
    mutate(burglary_Decile = ntile(countBurglaries, 10)) %>%
  group_by(Regression, burglary_Decile) %>%
    summarize(meanObserved = mean(countBurglaries, na.rm=T),
              meanPrediction = mean(Prediction, na.rm=T)) %>%
    gather(Variable, Value, -Regression, -burglary_Decile) %>%
    ggplot(aes(burglary_Decile, Value, shape = Variable)) +
      geom_point(size = 2) +
      geom_path(aes(group = burglary_Decile), colour = "black") +
      scale_shape_manual(values = c(2, 17)) +
      facet_wrap(~Regression) + xlim(0,10) +
      labs(title = "Predicted and observed burglary by
                    observed burglary decile")  +
      plotTheme()
```

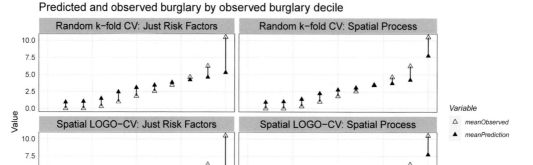

FIGURE 5.19 The models over-predict in low burglary areas and under-predict in hotspots.

5.5.3   Generalizability by neighborhood context

Does the algorithm generalize across different neighborhood contexts? To test this proposition, `tidycensus` is used to pull race data by census tract. `percentWhite` is calculated and tracts are split into two groups, `Majority_White` and `Majority_Non_White`. A spatial subset is used to get tracts within the study area. Like Boston, Chicago is a very segregated City, as the map in Figure 5.20 shows.

```
tracts18 <-
  get_acs(geography = "tract",
          variables = c("B01001_001E","B01001A_001E"),
          year = 2018, state=17, county=031, geometry=T) %>%
  st_transform('ESRI:102271') %>%
  dplyr::select(variable, estimate, GEOID) %>%
  spread(variable, estimate) %>%
  rename(TotalPop = B01001_001,
         NumberWhites = B01001A_001) %>%
  mutate(percentWhite = NumberWhites / TotalPop,
         raceContext = ifelse(percentWhite > .5,
           "Majority_White", "Majority_Non_White")) %>%
  .[neighborhoods,]
```

Race Context

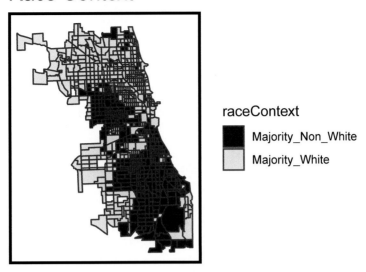

FIGURE 5.20 Racial delineations in Chicago at the census tract level.

As in Chapter 4, `Error` is calculated by subtracting the observed burglary count from the prediction. Thus, a positive difference represents an over-prediction. The least ideal result is a model that over-predicts risk in minority areas, and under-predicts in white areas. If reporting selection bias is an issue, such a model *may* unfairly allocate police resource disproportionately in black and brown communities. Table 5.3 compares average (non-absolute) errors for the LOGO-CV regressions by `raceContext`, by joining the fishnet grid cell centroids to tract boundaries.

The model on average, under-predicts in `Majority_Non_White` neighborhoods and over-predicts in `Majority_White` neighborhoods. The `Spatial Process` model not only reports lower errors overall, but a smaller difference in errors across neighborhood context.

It looks like this algorithm generalizes well with respect to race, right? We will return to this question in the conclusion. In the last stage of the analysis, the usefulness of this algorithm is judged relative to an alternative police allocation method.

```
reg.summary %>%
  filter(str_detect(Regression, "LOGO")) %>%
    st_centroid() %>%
    st_join(tracts18) %>%
    na.omit() %>%
      st_drop_geometry() %>%
      group_by(Regression, raceContext) %>%
      summarize(mean.Error = mean(Error, na.rm = T)) %>%
      spread(raceContext, mean.Error) %>%
      kable(caption =
              "Mean Error by neighborhood racial context") %>%
        kable_styling("striped", full_width = F)
```

Regression	Majority_Non_White	Majority_White
Spatial LOGO-CV: Just Risk Factors	-0.1135524	0.117997
Spatial LOGO-CV: Spatial Process	-0.0503718	0.039712

TABLE 5.3 Average errors for each model by racial context.

5.5.4 Does this model allocate better than traditional crime hotspots?

Police departments all over the world use hotspot policing to target police resources to the places where crime is most concentrated. In this section, we ask whether risk predictions outperform traditional 'kernel density' hotspot mapping.[16] To add an element of *across-time* generalizability, hotspot and risk predictions from these 2017 burglaries are used to predict the location of burglaries from *2018*.

Kernel density works by centering a smooth kernel, or curve, atop each crime point such that the curve is at its highest directly over the point and the lowest at the range of a circular search radius. The density in a particular place is the sum of all the kernels that underlie it. Thus, areas with many nearby points have relatively high densities. The key scale assumption in kernel density is the use of a global search radius parameter. Because of its reliance on nearby points, think of kernel density as one making 'predictions' based purely on spatial autocorrelation.

Figure 5.21 visualizes three kernel density maps at three different scales. Note the different burglary hotspot 'narratives' depending on the radius used.

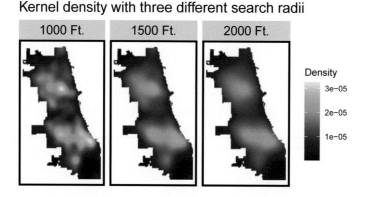

FIGURE 5.21 Burglary hotspots change depending on kernel density scale.

The following code block creates a kernel density map with a 1,000 foot search radius using the spatstat package. as.ppp converts burglary coordinates to a ppp class. The density function creates the Kernel density. To map, the ppp is converted to a data frame and then an sf layer. Points are spatially joined to the final_net, and the mean density is taken. In Figure 5.22 density is visualized with a sample_n of 1,500 points overlaid on top.

---

[16]This analytic is inspired by Daley, D., Bachmann, M., Bachmann, B. A., Pedigo, C., Bui, M. T., & Coffman, J. (2016). Risk terrain modeling predicts child maltreatment. Child abuse & neglect, 62, 29-38.

```
burg_ppp <- as.ppp(st_coordinates(burglaries),
                   W = st_bbox(final_net))
burg_KD <- spatstat::density.ppp(burg_ppp, 1000)

as.data.frame(burg_KD) %>%
  st_as_sf(coords = c("x", "y"), crs = st_crs(final_net)) %>%
  aggregate(., final_net, mean) %>%
  ggplot() +
    geom_sf(aes(fill=value)) +
    geom_sf(data = sample_n(burglaries, 1500), size = .5) +
    scale_fill_viridis(name = "Density") +
    labs(title = "Kernel density of 2017 burglaries") +
    mapTheme()
```

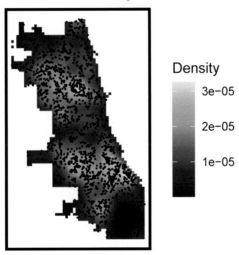

FIGURE 5.22 Density of burglaries in 2017 with a sample of points overlaid.

Next, a new goodness of fit indicator is created to illustrate whether the *2017* kernel density or risk predictions capture more of the *2018* burglaries. If the risk predictions capture more observed burglaries than the kernel density, then the risk prediction model provides a more robust targeting tool for allocating police resources. Here are the steps.

1. Download `burglaries18` from the Chicago open data site.
2. Compute the kernel density on 2017 `burglaries`.
3. Scale the kernel density values to run from 1-100 and then reclassify those values into five risk categories.
4. Spatial join the density to the fishnet.
5. Join to the fishnet, the count of burglaries *in 2018* for each grid cell.
6. Repeat for the risk predictions.
7. Take the rate of 2018 points by model type and risk category. Map and plot accordingly.

Step 1 downloads `burglaries18`.

```
burglaries18 <-
  read.socrata(
    paste0("https://data.cityofchicago.org/Public-Safety/",
           "Crimes-2018/3i3m-jwuy")) %>%
  filter(Primary.Type == "BURGLARY" &
         Description == "FORCIBLE ENTRY") %>%
  mutate(x = gsub("[()]", "", Location)) %>%
  separate(x,into= c("Y","X"), sep=",") %>%
  mutate(X = as.numeric(X),
         Y = as.numeric(Y)) %>%
  na.omit %>%
  st_as_sf(coords = c("X","Y"), crs=4326, agr="constant") %>%
  st_transform('ESRI:102271') %>%
  distinct() %>%
  .[fishnet,]
```

Next, kernel density is computed on the 2017 burglaries. `burg_KDE_sf` converts the density to an sf layer; spatial joins (`aggregate`) it to the fishnet; converts the density to 100 deciles (`ntile`); and again to four risk categories. Finally, one last spatial join adds the count of observed burglaries in 2018.

Check out `head(burg_KDE_sf)` to see the result.

```
burg_ppp <- as.ppp(st_coordinates(burglaries),
                   W = st_bbox(final_net))
burg_KD <- spatstat::density.ppp(burg_ppp, 1000)

burg_KDE_sf <- as.data.frame(burg_KD) %>%
  st_as_sf(coords = c("x", "y"), crs = st_crs(final_net)) %>%
  aggregate(., final_net, mean) %>%
  mutate(label = "Kernel Density",
    Risk_Category = ntile(value, 100),
    Risk_Category = case_when(
      Risk_Category >= 90 ~ "90% to 100%",
      Risk_Category >= 70 & Risk_Category <= 89 ~ "70% to 89%",
      Risk_Category >= 50 & Risk_Category <= 69 ~ "50% to 69%",
      Risk_Category >= 30 & Risk_Category <= 49 ~ "30% to 49%",
      Risk_Category >= 1 & Risk_Category <= 29 ~ "1% to 29%"))%>%
  cbind(
    aggregate(
      dplyr::select(burglaries18) %>%
        mutate(burgCount = 1), ., sum) %>%
      mutate(burgCount = replace_na(burgCount, 0))) %>%
  dplyr::select(label, Risk_Category, burgCount)
```

The same process is repeated for risk predictions. Note the prediction from the LOGO-CV with the spatial features is being used here.

```
burg_risk_sf <-
  filter(reg.summary,
         Regression == "Spatial LOGO-CV: Spatial Process") %>%
  mutate(label = "Risk Predictions",
    Risk_Category = ntile(Prediction, 100),
    Risk_Category = case_when(
      Risk_Category >= 90 ~ "90% to 100%",
      Risk_Category >= 70 & Risk_Category <= 89 ~ "70% to 89%",
      Risk_Category >= 50 & Risk_Category <= 69 ~ "50% to 69%",
      Risk_Category >= 30 & Risk_Category <= 49 ~ "30% to 49%",
      Risk_Category >= 1 & Risk_Category <= 29 ~ "1% to 29%"))%>%
  cbind(
    aggregate(
      dplyr::select(burglaries18) %>%
        mutate(burgCount = 1), ., sum) %>%
      mutate(burgCount = replace_na(burgCount, 0))) %>%
  dplyr::select(label,Risk_Category, burgCount)
```

For each grid cell and model type (density vs. risk prediction), there is now an associated risk category and 2018 burglary count. Figure 5.23 the risk categories for both model types with a sample of `burglary18` points overlaid. A strongly fit model should show that the highest risk category is uniquely targeted to places with a high density of burglary points.

Is this what we see? High-risk categories with few 2018 observed burglaries may suggest latent risk or a poorly fit model. This ambiguity is why accuracy for geospatial risk models is tough to judge. Nevertheless, more features/feature engineering would be helpful.

```
rbind(burg_KDE_sf, burg_risk_sf) %>%
  na.omit() %>%
  gather(Variable, Value, -label, -Risk_Category, -geometry) %>%
  ggplot() +
    geom_sf(aes(fill = Risk_Category), colour = NA) +
    geom_sf(data = sample_n(burglaries18, 3000), size = .1,
            colour = "black") +
    facet_wrap(~label, ) +
    scale_fill_viridis(discrete = TRUE) +
    labs(title="Comparison of Kernel Density & Risk Predictions",
         subtitle="2017 risk predictions; 2018 burglaries") +
    mapTheme()
```

Comparison of Kernel Density and Risk Predictions

2017 burglary risk predictions; 2018 burglaries

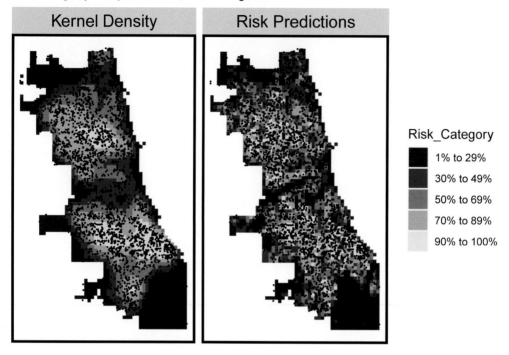

FIGURE 5.23 Visualizing predicted burglaries versus kernel density.

Finally, the following code block calculates the rate of 2018 burglary points by risk category and model type. A well-fit model should show that the risk predictions capture a greater share of 2018 burglaries *in the highest risk category* relative to the kernel density.

Figure 5.24 shows that the risk prediction model narrowly edges out the kernel density in the top two highest risk categories - suggesting this simple model has some value relative to the business-as-usual hotspot approach. Thus, we may have developed a tool to help target police resources, but is it a useful planning tool?

```
rbind(burg_KDE_sf, burg_risk_sf) %>%
  st_set_geometry(NULL) %>% na.omit() %>%
  gather(Variable, Value, -label, -Risk_Category) %>%
  group_by(label, Risk_Category) %>%
  summarize(countBurglaries = sum(Value)) %>%
  ungroup() %>%
  group_by(label) %>%
  mutate(Rate_of_test_set_crimes = countBurglaries /
                          sum(countBurglaries)) %>%
    ggplot(aes(Risk_Category,Rate_of_test_set_crimes)) +
      geom_bar(aes(fill=label), position="dodge",
```

```
                    stat="identity") +
    scale_fill_viridis(discrete = TRUE) +
    labs(title = "Risk prediction vs. Kernel density") +
    plotTheme() +
  theme(axis.text.x = element_text(angle = 45, vjust = 0.5))
```

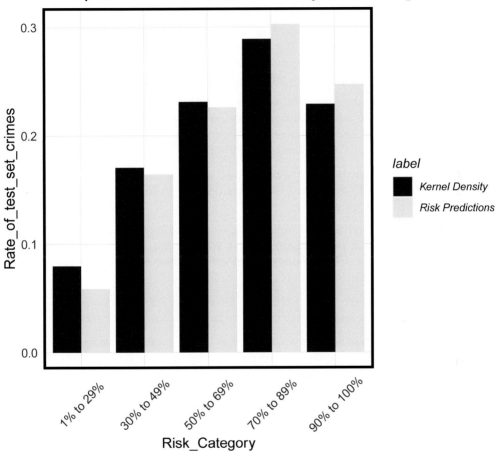

FIGURE 5.24 Comparing the performance of the predictive model to kernel density across five risk categories.

5.6   Conclusion - Bias but useful?

In this chapter, a geospatial risk prediction model borrows the burglary experience in places where it has been observed, and tests whether that experience generalizes to places where burglary risk may be high, despite few actual events. Should these tests hold, the resulting predictions can be thought of as 'latent risk' for burglary and can be used to allocate police response across space.

We introduced new and powerful feature engineering strategies to capture the local spatial process. Spatial cross-validation was also introduced as an important test of across-space generalizability.

Despite finding that the model generalizes well across different neighborhood contexts, we cannot be sure the model doesn't suffer from selection bias. As discussed in 5.1, if law enforcement systemtically over-polices certain communities, and this selection criteria goes unaccounted for in the model, then the model may be biased regardless of the above tests.

Nevertheless, we have demonstrated that even a simple risk prediction algorithm may outperform traditional hotspot analysis. By adding the element of time/seasonality (see Chapter 8) and deploying predictions in an intuitive user interface, this approach could easily compete with commercial predictive policing products. Should it?

Imagine if 'back-testing' the algorithm on historical data showed that its use would have predicted 20% more burglary than the current allocation process (either kernel density or otherwise). What if we could show Chicago officials that paying us $100k/year for a license to our algorithm would reduce property crime by $10 million - should they buy it?

Such a cost/benefit argument makes for a powerful sales pitch - and it is why data science is such a fast-growing industry. However, as I have mentioned, economic bottom lines are far from the only bottom lines in government.

What if the $10 million in savings lead police to increase enforcement and surveillance disproportionately in black and brown communities? Worse, what about feedback effects where steering police to these neighborhoods causes more reported crime, which then leads to increased predicted risk?

Stakeholders will either conclude, "but this tech reduces crime - this is a no-brainer!" or, "this technology perpetuates a legacy of systematic racism, fear, and disenfranchisement!"

Both opinions have merit, and the right approach is a function of community standards. Many big cities are currently at this point. Law enforcement sees machine learning as the next logical progression in the analytics they have been building for years. At the same time, critics and community stakeholders see these as tools of the surveillance state.

These two groups need a forum for communicating these views and for agreeing on the appropriate community standard. I refer to such a forum as one being part of the 'algorithmic governance' process, discussed in more detail in the book's Conclusion.

Finally, while these models may not be appropriate for crime prediction, there are a host of other planning outcomes that could benefit greatly. In the past I have built these models to predict risks for outcomes like fires and child maltreatment. I have also built them to predict where a company's next retail store should go. I urge readers to think about how these models could be used to predict 'opportunity', not just risk.

As always, this begins with an understanding of the use case and the current resource allocation process. The outcome of all this code should not be just a few maps and tables, but a strategic plan that converts these predictions into actionable intelligence.

5.7 Assignment - Predict risk

Your job is to build a version of this model **for a different outcome that likely suffers from more selection bias than burglary**. You can build this model in Chicago or any other city with sufficient open data resources. Please also add at least **two** new features not used in this chapter, and iteratively build models until you have landed on one that optimizes for accuracy and generalizability.

Your final deliverable should be **in R markdown** form **with code blocks**. Please provide the following materials with **brief annotations** (please don't forget this):

1. A map of your outcome of interest in point form, with some description of what, when, and why you think selection bias may be an issue.
2. A map of your outcome joined to the fishnet.
3. A small multiple map of your risk factors in the fishnet (counts, distance, and/or other feature engineering approaches).
4. Local Moran's I-related small multiple map of your outcome (see 4.1)
5. A small multiple scatterplot with correlations.
6. A histogram of your dependent variable.
7. A small multiple map of model errors by random k-fold and spatial cross-validation.
8. A table of MAE and standard deviation MAE by regression.
9. A table of raw errors by race context for a random k-fold vs. spatial cross-validation regression.
10. The map comparing kernel density to risk predictions for *the next year's crime.*
11. The bar plot making this comparison.
12. Two paragraphs on why or why not you would recommend your algorithm be put into production.

6

People-based ML Models

FIGURE 6.1 I'm a data scientist, not a graphic designer.

6.1 Bounce to work

Most organizations work on behalf of 'clients'. Government agencies provide services to firms and households; non-profits rely on donors to keep the lights on; businesses sell products and services to customers. At any point, a client may no longer wish to participate, donate, or purchase a good, which will affect the bottom line of the organization.

We have learned how data science can identify risk and opportunity in space, and not surprisingly, these methods can also be used to identify risk/opportunity for clients. In this chapter, we learn how to predict risk for individuals and use the resulting intelligence to develop cost/benefit analyses. Specifically, the goal is to predict 'churn' - the decision of a client not to re-subscribe to a product or service.

Imagine you are the head of sales and marketing for a pogo-transit start-up called 'Bounce to Work!'. Two years ago, Bounce to Work! rolled out 2,000 dockless, GPS-enabled pogo sticks around the city charging riders $3 per bounce or a membership of $30/month for unlimited bouncing. Bounce to Work!'s first year resulted in more bouncing then the company could have ever imagined, and to keep its customers engaged, the company is looking to embark on a membership drive.

DOI: 10.1201/9781003054658-6

Variable	Description
SeniorCitizen	Whether the customer is a senior citizen or not (1, 0)
WeekendBouncer	Does this customer bounce on the weekends or only on weekdays? (Yes, No)
avgBounceTime	Average length of a pogo trip in minutes
bounceInStreet	Does this customer tend to bounce on streets (Yes) or on sidewalks (No)?
phoneType	The operating system of the customer's phone (iPhone, Android, Unknown)
avgBounceDistance	Distance of a customer's average bounce as a categorical variable (<1 ft., 1-4 ft., 4+ ft.)
avgBounceHeight	Height of a customer's Average bounce as a categorical variable (<1 ft., 1-2 ft., 2+ ft.)
PaperlessBilling	Whether the customer has paperless billing or not (Yes, No)
monthlyDistanceBounced	The amount of distance in miles coverered last month
totalDistanceBounced	The amount of distance in miles coverered since becoming a member
Churn	Whether the customer churned or not (Churn or No_Churn)

TABLE 6.1 Data dictionary.

You have noticed that every month, between 20% and 25% of the roughly 30,000 members 'churn' or do not renew their membership at month's end. Not accounting for new members, that is a revenue loss of as much as $225,000 (7,500 members * $30 per membership) per month! This volatility is creating some uncertainty in the company's expansion efforts. They have asked you to put your data science skills to the test, by predicting for every member, the probability that they will churn, conditional on a host of bouncing data collected by the company. Those *predicted probabilities* will then be used to prioritize who gets a $2 marketing mailer that includes a 20% off membership coupon (an $8 expenditure, in total).

Predicting churn has all sorts of interesting cost/benefit implications for Bounce to Work!. If your algorithm predicts a customer will *not* churn and a mailer is not sent, but they do in fact churn (a *false negative*), then the company is out $30. If you predict a customer will churn and send them a mailer but they had no intention of churning, then you loose $8 (20% off a $30 membership plus a $2 mailer).

While Bounce to Work! is a slightly absurd premise for this chapter, data science can be most impactful (both positively and negatively) when used to target families and individuals for critical services. In this chapter, a classic churn-related dataset from IBM is used, although I have altered the variables names to make it more apropos.[1]

The next section performs exploratory analysis; Section 3 introduces logistic regression; Sections 4 and 5 focus on goodness of fit for these models as well as cross-validation. Section 6 delves into cost/benefit and 7 concludes. Table 6.1 is the data dictionary. Each row is a customer and the outcome of interest, `Churn`, consists of two levels, `Churn` and `No_Churn`. Our goal is to predict this 'binary' outcome using demographic and ridership-specific variables.

```
options(scipen=10000000)

library(tidyverse)
library(caret)
library(knitr)
library(pscl)
library(plotROC)
library(pROC)
library(scales)
```

---

[1] https://www.kaggle.com/blastchar/telco-customer-churn/home

```
root.dir =
  paste0("https://raw.githubusercontent.com/urbanSpatial",
         "/Public-Policy-Analytics-Landing/master/DATA/")
source(
  paste0("https://raw.githubusercontent.com/urbanSpatial/",
         "Public-Policy-Analytics-Landing/master/functions.r"))

palette5 <- c("#981FAC","#CB0F8B","#FF006A","#FE4C35","#FE9900")
palette4 <- c("#981FAC","#FF006A","#FE4C35","#FE9900")
palette2 <- c("#981FAC","#FF006A")

churn <-
  read.csv(file.path(root.dir,"/Chapter6/churnBounce.csv")) %>%
  mutate(churnNumeric =
           as.factor(ifelse(Churn == "Churn",1,0))) %>%
  na.omit()
```

Let's start by loading libraries and the data. In the previous code block, the outcome is recoded to a binary, 0 and 1 variable called `churnNumeric`. Any field with `NA` is removed from the data.

6.2 Exploratory analysis

Churn is defined as a customer not re-subscribing to a service. In this section, the data is explored by visualizing correlation between `churn` and the predictive features. Correlation for a continuous outcome like home price, can be visualized with a scatterplot. However, when the dependent variable is binary, with two possible outcomes, a different approach is needed. Useful features are those that exhibit *significant differences* across the `Churn` and `No_Churn` outcomes.

First, note that 1869 of 7032 customers in the dataset churned (27%).

Figure 6.2 plots the *mean* for three continuous features grouped by `Churn` or `No_Churn`. The interpretation is that the longer a customer bounces, both by trip and historically, the more likely, on average, a customer will re-up their membership (i.e., `No_Churn`).

```
churn %>%
  dplyr::select(Churn,avgBounceTime, totalDistanceBounced) %>%
  gather(Variable, value, -Churn) %>%
  ggplot(aes(Churn, value, fill=Churn)) +
    geom_bar(position ="dodge", stat ="summary", fun ="mean") +
    facet_wrap(~Variable, scales = "free") +
    scale_fill_manual(values = palette2) +
    labs(x="Churn", y="Mean",
      title ="Feature associations with the likelihood of churn",
      subtitle = "(Continous outcomes)") +
    plotTheme() + theme(legend.position = "none")
```

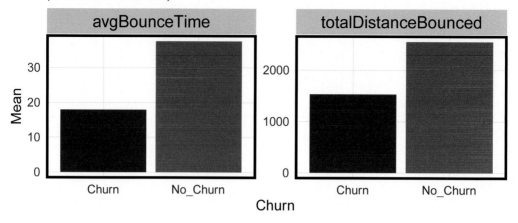

FIGURE 6.2 The relationship between customer churn and average bounce time and total distance bounced.

Not only is the dependent variable categorical, most of the features are as well. Figure 6.3 illustrate whether differences in customer factors associate with the likelihood that they will churn. The `count` function below calculates the total number of customers reported as 'Yes' for a given feature.

The interpretation is that more people who re-up their membership (`No_Churn`) tend to bounce in the street, pay by internet, and bounce on weekends.

```
churn %>%
  dplyr::select(Churn,SeniorCitizen, WeekendBouncer,
              bounceInStreet, PaperlessBilling) %>%
  gather(Variable, value, -Churn) %>%
  count(Variable, value, Churn) %>%
  filter(value == "Yes") %>%
    ggplot(aes(Churn, n, fill = Churn)) +
      geom_bar(position = "dodge", stat="identity") +
      facet_wrap(~Variable, scales = "free", ncol=4) +
      scale_fill_manual(values = palette2) +
      labs(x="Churn", y="Count",
      title = "Feature associations with the likelihood of churn",
        subtitle = "Two category features (Yes and No)") +
      plotTheme() + theme(legend.position = "none")
```

Finally, the folloiwng code block plots three category associations. Figure 6.4 suggests that a customer who bounces 4 feet at a time and upwards of 2 feet in the air, has a lower likelihood of `Churn`. Clearly, more experienced bouncers are more likely to continue their membership.

```
churn %>%
  dplyr::select(Churn, phoneType, avgBounceDistance, avgBounceHeight) %>%
  gather(Variable, value, -Churn) %>%
```

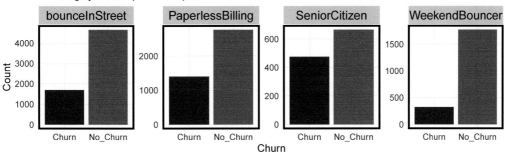

FIGURE 6.3 The relationship between customer churn and categorical variables.

```
count(Variable, value, Churn) %>%
ggplot(aes(value, n, fill = Churn)) +
  geom_bar(position = "dodge", stat="identity") +
  facet_wrap(~Variable, scales="free") +
  scale_fill_manual(values = palette2) +
  labs(x="Churn", y="Count",
    title = "Feature associations with the likelihood of churn",
    subtitle = "Three category features") +
  plotTheme() +
  theme(axis.text.x = element_text(angle = 45, hjust = 1))
```

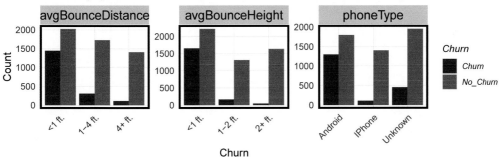

FIGURE 6.4 The relationship between customer churn and variables with multiple categories.

Churn has two possible outcomes, but imagine in Figure 6.5, if `churnNumeric` varied continuously as a function of `totalDistanceBounced`. The resulting scatterplot is awkward. OLS regression is not appropriate for binomial outcomes. Instead logistic regression is introduced below.

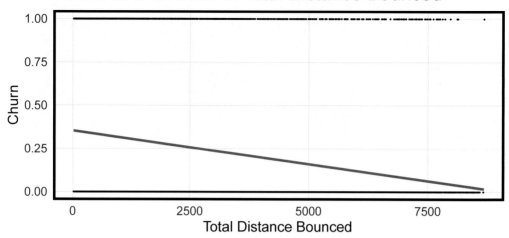

FIGURE 6.5 The relationship between customer churn and distanced bounced if churn was a continuous variable.

6.3   Logistic regression

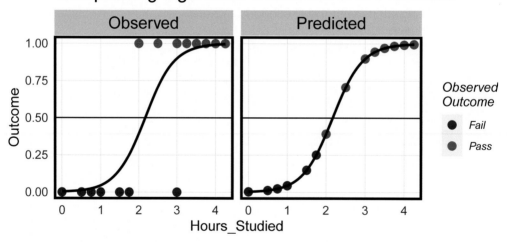

Figure 6.6 Fitting a logistic curve.

Logistic regression, in the generalized linear model (GLM) family, predicts the probability an observation is part of a group, like `Churn` or `Not_Churn`, conditional on the features of the model. OLS fits a linear line by minimizing the sum of squared errors, but model fitting in Logistic regression is based on a technique called maximum likelihood estimation. While the math is beyond the scope of this book, the idea is to iteratively fit regression coefficients to the model to maximize the probability of the observed data.

Logistic regression fits an S-shaped logistic curve like the one in Figure 6.6. For a simple illustration, imagine I trained an algorithm from the `Observed` test-taking experience of previous students, to estimate the `Predicted` probability that current students will pass an exam, conditional on one feature - hours spent studying. According to left-most panel in Figure 6.6, as `Observed` study hours increases so does the probability of passing.

The `Predicted` probabilities for the logistic model fall along the logistic curve and run from 0% probability of passing to 1, or 100% probability of passing. In the right-most panel in Figure 6.6, a model is fit, and the predicted probabilities are plotted along the fitted line colored by their observed Pass/Fail designation.

The predicted probabilities alone would be useful for the students, but I could also set a threshold above which a student would be 'classified' as `Pass`. Assume the threshold is 50%. The `Predicted` panel reveals one student who studied for just 2 hours but still passed the test. A threshold of 50% would incorrectly predict or classify that student as having failed the test - a *false negative*. As we'll learn, classification errors are useful for cost/benefit analysis.

6.3.1 Training/testing sets

Recall, a generalizable model 1) performs well on new data and 2) predicts with comparable accuracy across groups. Bounce to Work! doesn't collect race or geographic coordinates in the data, so groups will not be the focus. Thus, the focus will be on the first definition, which is critical, given that in a production setting, the model is only useful if it can predict for next month's churners.

In this section, training and test sets are created. `createDataPartition` is used to split the data. A 50% sample is used here to reduce processing time.

```
set.seed(3456)
trainIndex <- createDataPartition(churn$Churn, p = .50,
                                  list = FALSE,
                                  times = 1)
churnTrain <- churn[ trainIndex,]
churnTest  <- churn[-trainIndex,]
```

6.3.2 Estimate a churn model

Next, a logistic regression model is estimated as `churnreg1`. To keep things simple, the features are input as is, without any additional feature engineering or feature selection. As you now know, feature engineering is often the difference between a good and a great predictive model and is a critical part of the machine learning workflow.

Unlike an OLS regression, which is estimated with the `lm` function, the logistic regression is estimated with the `glm` function. Here, the `select` operation is piped directly into `glm` to remove two features that are marginally significant as well as the `Churn` feature encoded as a string.[2]

---

[2]These two features may be significant at the $p < 0.10$ level, depending on your random train/test split. Marginally significant features may be included in a model but are removed here to demonstrate the how `select` embedded in `glm` makes it easy to experiment with different feature selections.

```
churnreg1 <- glm(churnNumeric ~ .,
                 data=churnTrain %>%
                  dplyr::select(-SeniorCitizen, -WeekendBouncer,
                               -Churn),
                 family="binomial" (link="logit"))
```

```
summary(churnreg1)
```

OLS regression estimates coefficients on the scale of the dependent variable. Logistic regression coefficients are on the scale of 'log-odds'. Exponentiating (`exp()`) an estimate provides a coefficient as an 'odds ratio'. In Table 6.2, column 1 suggests, for example, that all else equal, bouncing in the street reduces the likelihood of churn by 45%.

Like OLS, logistic regression also provides p-value estimates of statistical significance. The missing coefficients may reflect colinearity or small variability across the three levels of `avgBounceDistance`. Perhaps the only signal in this feature that really matters is the `1-4 ft.` indicator. Thus, `avgBounceDistance` is recoded in `churnreg2` such that any value that does not equal `1-4 ft.` receives `Other`. New training/testing sets are generated, and the model is estimated once again.

Note there is no R^2 presented in the `summary`. Goodness of fit for logistic regression is not as straightforward as it is for OLS. In the next section, goodness of fit is judged in the context of classification errors.

```
churn <-
  mutate(churn, avgBounceDistance =
    ifelse(avgBounceDistance == "1-4 ft.", "1-4 ft.", "Other"))
```

```
set.seed(3456)
trainIndex <- createDataPartition(churn$Churn, p = .50,
                                  list = FALSE,
                                  times = 1)
churnTrain <- churn[ trainIndex,]
churnTest  <- churn[-trainIndex,]
```

```
churnreg2 <- glm(churnNumeric ~ .,
                 data=churnTrain %>%
                  dplyr::select(-SeniorCitizen,-WeekendBouncer,
                    -Churn),
                 family="binomial" (link="logit"))
```

```
summary(churnreg2)
```

| | churnNumeric | |
	Churn Regression 1	Churn Regression 2
	(1)	(2)
avgBounceTime	−0.059*** (0.009)	−0.059*** (0.009)
bounceInStreetYes	−0.807*** (0.207)	−0.807*** (0.207)
PaperlessBillingYes	0.494*** (0.103)	0.494*** (0.103)
monthlyDistanceBounced	0.012** (0.006)	0.012** (0.006)
totalDistanceBounced	0.0003*** (0.0001)	0.0003*** (0.0001)
phoneTypeIPhone	−1.211*** (0.380)	−1.211*** (0.380)
phoneTypeUnknown	−0.559*** (0.195)	−0.559*** (0.195)
avgBounceDistance1-4 ft.	−0.490*** (0.123)	
avgBounceDistance4+ ft.		
avgBounceDistanceOther		0.490*** (0.123)
avgBounceHeight1-2 ft.	−0.688*** (0.143)	−0.688*** (0.143)
avgBounceHeight2+ ft.	−1.608*** (0.259)	−1.608*** (0.259)
Constant	0.339 (0.417)	−0.151 (0.460)
N	3,517	3,517
Log Likelihood	−1,482.423	−1,482.423
AIC	2,986.847	2,986.847

*p < .1; **p < .05; ***p < .01

TABLE 6.2 Churn Regressions

6.4 Goodness of fit

For logistic regression, a robust model is one that can accurately predict instances of both `Churn` and `No_Churn`. In this section, several options are considered.

The first and weakest option is the 'psuedo R^2', which, unlike regular R^2, does not vary linearly from 0 to 1. It does not describe the proportion of the variance in the dependent variable explained by the model. However, it is useful for quickly comparing different model specifications, which may be helpful for feature selection. Below, the 'McFadden R^2' is demonstrated - the higher, the better.

```
pR2(churnreg2)[4]
```

```
## fitting null model for pseudo-r2
```

```
##   McFadden
## 0.2721287
```

A more useful approach to goodness of fit is to predict for `churnTest` then tally up the rate that `Churn` and `No_Churn` are predicted correctly. The first step is to create a data frame of test set probabilities, `testProbs`, which includes both the observed churn `Outcome` and predicted probabilities for each observation.

Setting `type="response"` in the `predict` function ensures the predictions are in the form of predicted probabilities. Thus, a probability of 0.75 means that customer has a 75% probability of churning.

```
testProbs <- data.frame(Outcome =
                        as.factor(churnTest$churnNumeric),
                    Probs = predict(churnreg2, churnTest,
                                    type= "response"))
head(testProbs)
```

```
##      Outcome      Probs
## 1          0 0.6429831
## 7          0 0.5832574
## 8          0 0.4089603
## 9          1 0.4943297
## 12         0 0.0195177
## 13         0 0.1369811
```

There are a number of interesting data visualizations that can be created by relating the predicted probabilities to the observed churn `Outcome`. Figure 6.7 shows the distribution of predicted probabilities (x-axis) for `Churn` and `No_Churn`, recoded as 1 and 0 (y-axis), respectively.

If `churnreg2` was very predictive, the 'hump' of predicted probabilities for `Churn` would cluster around 1 on the x-axis, while the predicted probabilities for `No_Churn` would cluster around 0. In reality, the humps are where we might expect them but with long tails.

```
ggplot(testProbs, aes(x = Probs, fill = as.factor(Outcome))) +
  geom_density() +
  facet_grid(Outcome ~ .) +
  scale_fill_manual(values = palette2) + xlim(0, 1) +
  labs(x = "Churn", y = "Density of probabilities",
       title = "Distribution of predicted
       probabilities by observed outcome") +
  plotTheme() + theme(strip.text.x = element_text(size = 18),
       legend.position = "none")
```

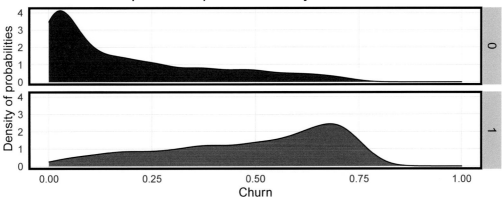

FIGURE 6.7 If the model performs well, there should be two distinct 'humps' clustering near the observed value for each outcome.

Next, a variable called `predOutcome` is created that classifies any predicted probability greater than 0.50 (or 50%) as a predicted `Churn` event. 50% seems like a reasonable threshold to start with, but one that we will explore in great detail in Section 6.6.1.

```
testProbs <-
  testProbs %>%
  mutate(
    predOutcome = as.factor(ifelse(testProbs$Probs > 0.5,1,0))
    )
```

```
head(testProbs)
```

```
##    Outcome     Probs predOutcome
## 1        0 0.6429831           1
## 2        0 0.5832574           1
## 3        0 0.4089603           0
## 4        1 0.4943297           0
## 5        0 0.0195177           0
## 6        0 0.1369811           0
```

Many interesting questions can now be asked. What is overall accuracy rate? Does the model do a better job predicting `Churn` or `No_Churn`? To answer these questions, the following code block outputs a 'confusion matrix'. A `positive` parameter is specified to let the function know that a value of 1 designates churn.

The table at the top of the output is the confusion matrix, which shows the number of 'Reference' or observed instances of churn that are predicted as such. Each entry in the matrix provides a different comparison between observed and predicted, given the 50% threshold.

There were 506 *true positives*, instances where observed `Churn` was correctly predicted as `Churn`. There were 428 *false positives*, instances where `Churn` was incorrectly predicted as `No_Churn`.

There were 2306 *true negatives*, instances where observed `No_Churn` was correctly predicted as `No_Churn`. Finally, there were 275 *false negatives*, instances where `No_Churn` was incorrectly predicted as `Churn`.

```
caret::confusionMatrix(testProbs$predOutcome, testProbs$Outcome,
                       positive = "1")
```

```
## Confusion Matrix and Statistics
##
##           Reference
## Prediction    0    1
##          0 2306  428
##          1  275  506
##
##                Accuracy : 0.8
##                  95% CI : (0.7864, 0.8131)
##     No Information Rate : 0.7343
##     P-Value [Acc > NIR] : < 0.00000000000000022
##
##                   Kappa : 0.4592
##
##  Mcnemar's Test P-Value : 0.000000009879
##
##             Sensitivity : 0.5418
##             Specificity : 0.8935
##          Pos Pred Value : 0.6479
##          Neg Pred Value : 0.8435
##              Prevalence : 0.2657
##          Detection Rate : 0.1440
##    Detection Prevalence : 0.2222
##       Balanced Accuracy : 0.7176
##
##        'Positive' Class : 1
##
```

The confusion matrix also calculates overall accuracy, defined as the number of true positives plus true negatives divided by the total number of observations. Here the accuracy is 80%. Is that good?

Two other metrics, 'sensitivity' and 'specificity', provide even more useful intelligence. The sensitivity of the model is the proportion of actual positives (1's) that were predicted to be positive. This is also known as the 'true positive rate'. The specificity of the model is the proportion of actual negatives (0's) that were predicted to be negatives. Also known as the 'true negative rate'.

The sensitivity and specificity of `churnreg2` is 54% and 89%, respectively. The interpretation is that the model is better at predicting those who are not going to churn than those who will. These metrics provide important intuition about *how useful our model is as a resource allocation tool*. It's not surprising that the model is better at predicting no churn given that 75% of the data has this outcome. However, given the business process at hand, we would prefer to do a bit better at predicting the churn outcome.

New features, better feature engineering, and a more powerful predictive algorithm would significantly improve this model. Another approach for improving the model is to search for an 'optimal' threshold that can limit the most costly errors (from a business standpoint). Most of the remainder of this chapter is devoted to this optimization, beginning with the 'ROC curve' in the next section, a common goodness of fit metric for binary classification models.

6.4.1 Roc curves

```
ggplot(testProbs, aes(d = as.numeric(testProbs$Outcome),
                      m = Probs)) +
  geom_roc(n.cuts = 50, labels = FALSE, colour = "#FE9900") +
  style_roc(theme = theme_grey) +
  geom_abline(slope = 1, intercept = 0, size = 1.5,
              color = 'grey') +
  labs(title = "ROC Curve - churnModel")
```

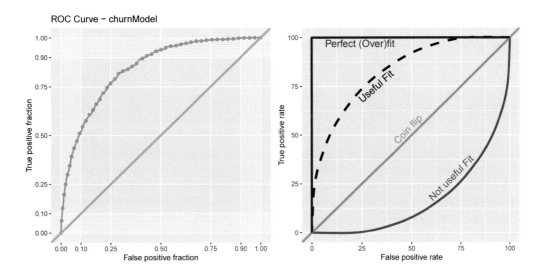

FIGURE 6.8 The ROC curve for the model and how to interpret.

Let's quickly revisit the business problem: The goal is to identify those customers at risk for churn, so we can offer them a 20% off membership coupon which costs Bounce to Work! $8.

Consider that at each predicted probability threshold, there is a different set of confusion metrics. A threshold of 10%, for instance, means that most predictions will be classified as churn, and most customers will receive a coupon. This may mean Bounce to Work! would ultimately lose money on the promotion. As we'll learn below, different confusion metrics have different costs and benefits, and searching for an optimal threshold, helps ensure we can stay in the black.

The Receiver Operating Characteristic Curve or ROC Curve is useful because it visualizes trade-offs for two important confusion metrics, while also providing a single goodness of fit indicator. The code block above uses the `plotROC` and `ggplot` packages to create a ROC Curve for the `churnreg2`.

The y-axis of the ROC curve (left-most, Figure 6.8) shows the rate of true positives (observed churn, predicted as churn) for each threshold from 0.01 to 1. The x-axis shows the rate of false positives (observed churn, predicted as no churn) for each threshold.

The notion of trade-offs is really important here. Follow the y-axis to 0.75 and then across to the orange curve. According to the ROC Curve, a threshold that predicts churn correctly 75% of the time, will predict `Churn` incorrectly >20% of the time. The critical question is whether this trade-off is appropriate given the cost/benefit of the business process?

What is really interesting about these trade-offs is that they come with diminishing returns. For every additional improvement in true positive rate, the model will make a greater proportion of false positive errors. Moving from a 75% to a 90% true positive rate dramatically increases the false positive rate.

To understand how the ROC curve doubles as a goodness of fit tool, it is helpful to start with the diagonal line in the right panel of Figure 6.8. Also known as the 'coin flip line', any true positive rate on this line has an equal corresponding false positive rate. Any classifier with an ROC curve along the diagonal line is no better than a coin flip. An ROC curve below the diagonal line represents a very poor fit. Consider along this line, a model that gets it right ~7% of the time, gets it wrong 50% of the time.

A 'perfect fit' may seem desirable, but it is actually indicative of an overfit model. A ROC curve like this yields 100% true positives and 0 false positives. If the model is so strongly fit to experiences in the training set, it will not likely generalize to experiences in new data. This is a really important point to remember. As before, we can test this model for its out-of-sample generalizability with cross-validation.

Another look at Figure 6.8 suggests that the usefulness of the algorithm can be judged by the proportion of the plotting area that is *under* the ROC curve. The 'area under the curve' metric or AUC for `churnreg2` is 0.8408635. AUC is another quick goodness of fit measure to guide feature selection across different models. 50% of the plotting area is under the coin flip line and 100% of the plotting area is underneath the perfect fit line. Thus, a reasonable AUC is between 0.5 and 1.

```
pROC::auc(testProbs$Outcome, testProbs$Probs)
```

```
## Area under the curve: 0.8409
```

6.5   Cross-validation

As a data scientist working at Bounce to Work!, your goal should be to train a predictive model that will be useful for many months to come, rather than re-training a model every month. Thus, the model is only as good as its ability to generalize to new data. This section performs cross-validation using the `caret::train` function as we saw in Chapter 3.

The `trainControl` parameter is set to run 100 k-folds and to output predicted probabilities, `classProbs`, for 'two classes', `Churn` and `No_Churn`. Additional parameters output AUC (the `train` function refers to this as 'ROC') and confusion metrics for each fold.

Importantly, the three metrics in the `cvFit` output are for *mean* AUC, sensitivity, and specificity across *all 100 folds*. Note that the dependent variable here is `Churn` not `churnNumeric`.

```
ctrl <- trainControl(method = "cv", number = 100,
                     classProbs=TRUE,
                     summaryFunction=twoClassSummary)


cvFit <- train(Churn ~ ., data = churn %>%
                                dplyr::select(
                                -SeniorCitizen,
                                -WeekendBouncer,
                                -churnNumeric),
               method="glm", family="binomial",
               metric="ROC", trControl = ctrl)


cvFit

## Generalized Linear Model
##
## 7032 samples
##    8 predictor
##    2 classes: 'Churn', 'No_Churn'
##
## No pre-processing
## Resampling: Cross-Validated (100 fold)
## Summary of sample sizes: 6961, 6961, 6961, 6962, 6961, 6962, ...
## Resampling results:
##
##   ROC        Sens       Spec
##   0.8407402  0.5333333  0.8949849
```

The means are not as important as the *across* fold goodness of fit. Figure 6.9 plots the distribution of AUC, sensitivity, and specificity across the 100 folds. `names(cvFit)` shows that `train` creates several outputs. `cvFit$resample` is a data frame with goodness of fit for each of the 100 folds. The following code block joins to this, the mean goodness of fit (`cvFit$results`), and plots the distributions as a small multiple plot.

The tighter each distribution is to its mean, the more generalizable the model. Our model generalizes well with respect to specificity - the rate it correctly predicts `No_Churn` (*the true negatives*). It does not generalize as well with respect to sensitivity - the rate it correctly predict `Churn` (*true positives*). Note that if the model was overfit with an AUC of 1, it would also not generalize well to new data.

It seems our would-be decision-making tool is inconsistent in how it predicts the business-relevant outcome, churn. That inconsistency could be systematic - perhaps it works better for younger bouncers or for more serious bouncers. Or the model could simply lack sufficient predictive power. Either way, this inconsistency will have a direct effect on the business process should this algorithm be put into production.

```
dplyr::select(cvFit$resample, -Resample) %>%
  gather(metric, value) %>%
  left_join(gather(cvFit$results[2:4], metric, mean)) %>%
  ggplot(aes(value)) +
    geom_histogram(bins=35, fill = "#FF006A") +
    facet_wrap(~metric) +
    geom_vline(aes(xintercept = mean), colour = "#981FAC",
               linetype = 3, size = 1.5) +
    scale_x_continuous(limits = c(0, 1)) +
    labs(x="Goodness of Fit", y="Count",
         title="CV Goodness of Fit Metrics",
         subtitle ="Across-fold mean reprented as dotted lines")+
    plotTheme()
```

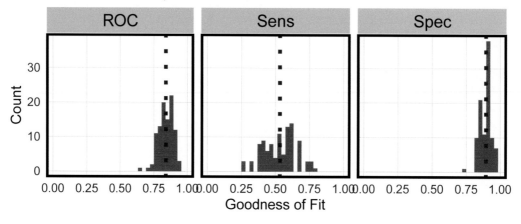

FIGURE 6.9 Cross-validation results.

6.6   Generating costs and benefits

Our goal again, is to target those at risk of churning with a 20% off coupon that hopefully convinces them to re-subscribe.

Let's assume the test set, `testProbs`, is the universe of potential customers, each paying $30 for the membership. The total revenue for the **previous month** would be $105,450 (`nrow(testProbs) * 30`). 27% of test set members churned, which equates to $28,020 of lost revenue this payment period, assuming no new customers sign up. Thus, the total revenue assuming this 'natural' churn, would be $77,430.

How could our predictive model help improve on this? Assuming the model successfully predicts churners, and assuming a 20% coupon was enough incentive to stay, can the algorithmic approach help optimize Bounce to Work!'s marketing campaign?

Let's make the following assumptions about the marketing campaign:

1. The membership costs $30.
2. Each mailer to a potential churn-er costs $8.00. It includes an offer for 20% off *this month's* subscription ($6 off) plus $2.00 for printing/postage.
3. Of those would-be churners who are sent a mailer, past campaigns show ~50% of recipients re-subscribe.

While there are many ways to approach a cost/benefit analysis, our approach will be to use the confusion matrix from `testProbs`. Next the cost/benefit for each outcome in our confusion matrix is calculated, like so[3]:

- **True negative revenue**: 'We predicted no churn, did not send a coupon, and the customer did not churn'. $30 - $0 = **$30**
- **True positive revenue**: 'We predicted churn and sent the mailer'. $30 - $8 = **$22** return for 50% of cases that re-subscribe. We lose $30 + $2 = **$-32** for 50% of cases who were sent the coupon but did not re-subscribe.
- **False negative revenue**: 'We predicted no churn, sent no coupon, and the customer churned'. $0 - 30 = **-$30**
- **False positive revenue**: 'We predicted churn and sent the mailer, the customer was not going churn but used the coupon anyway'. $30 - $8 = **$22**

For now, note that the greatest cost comes with 50% of the true positives where we offer a coupon but loose the customer anyway. The greatest marginal benefit is in maximizing the number of true negatives - customers who we correctly predict will not churn. To calculate the total cost/benefit, these confusion metrics are multiplied by their corresponding costs in the following code.

```
cost_benefit_table <-
  testProbs %>%
    count(predOutcome, Outcome) %>%
    summarize(
      True_Negative = sum(n[predOutcome==0 & Outcome==0]),
      True_Positive = sum(n[predOutcome==1 & Outcome==1]),
      False_Negative = sum(n[predOutcome==0 & Outcome==1]),
      False_Positive = sum(n[predOutcome==1 & Outcome==0])) %>%
    gather(Variable, Count) %>%
    mutate(Revenue =
     case_when(
      Variable == "True_Negative"  ~ Count * 30,
      Variable == "True_Positive"  ~ ((30 - 8) * (Count * .50))+
                                       (-32 * (Count * .50)),
      Variable == "False_Negative" ~ (-30) * Count,
      Variable == "False_Positive" ~ (30 - 8) * Count)) %>%
    bind_cols(data.frame(Description = c(
      "We predicted no churn and did not send a mailer",
```

---

[3]It may be reasonable to assume the false negative revenue is $0 rather than -$30. However, I choose to count these errors as a $30 loss because I want to penalize both the non-algorithm and algorithmic business process for actual instances of churn. This also provides an incentive to improve the model and thus reduce the marginal costs associated with false negatives.

```
    "We predicted churn and sent the mailer",
    "We predicted no churn and the customer churned",
    "We predicted churn and the customer did not churn")))
```

Variable	Count	Revenue	Description
True_Negative	2306	69180	We predicted no churn and did not send a mailer
True_Positive	506	-2530	We predicted churn and sent the mailer
False_Negative	428	-12840	We predicted no churn and the customer churned
False_Positive	275	6050	We predicted churn and the customer did not churn

TABLE 6.3 Cost/benefit calculations if the algorithm is used.

Assuming our algorithm was used, the total `Revenue` (column sum) in the Cost/Benefit Table 6.3 is $59,860. Assuming no algorithm was used and 934 customers churned (from `testProbs`), the cost/benefit would be (2,581 instances of no churn * $30 = $77,430) + (934 instances of churn * -30 = -$28,020), which leads to a net revenue of $49,410.

Thus, the algorithm would save Bounce to Work! $10,450. This savings is based on a 50% threshold, but maybe other thresholds can yield an even greater cost/benefit. Let's now try to optimize the threshold.

6.6.1   Optimizing the cost/benefit relationship

Recall, that a different confusion matrix, set of errors and cost/benefit calculation exists for each threshold. Ideally, the 'optimal' threshold is the one that returns the greatest cost/benefit. In this section, a function is created to iteratively loop through each threshold, calculate confusion metrics, and total the revenue for each. The results are then visualized for each threshold.

The `iterateThresholds` function (in the `functions.r` script) is based on a `while` loop. The threshold x, starts at 0.01 and while it is less than 1, a predicted classification, `predOutcome`, is `mutated` given x; confusion metrics are calculated; the cost benefit is performed and is appended to a data frame called `all_prediction`. Finally x is iterated by adding 0.01, and the process continues until $x = 1$.

`iterateThresholds` function is run in the next code block and includes a host of goodness of fit indicators, several of which are returned below. Recall, each row is a different `Threshold`.

```
whichThreshold <-
  iterateThresholds(
    data=testProbs, observedClass = Outcome,
      predictedProbs = Probs)


whichThreshold[1:5, 5:10]

## # A tibble: 5 x 6
##    Rate_TP Rate_FP Rate_FN Rate_TN Accuracy Threshold
##      <dbl>   <dbl>   <dbl>   <dbl>    <dbl>     <dbl>
```

```
## 1    0.995    0.864 0.00535    0.136    0.364    0.01
## 2    0.991    0.777 0.00857    0.223    0.427    0.02
## 3    0.988    0.730 0.0118     0.270    0.461    0.03
## 4    0.983    0.683 0.0171     0.317    0.494    0.04
## 5    0.978    0.650 0.0225     0.350    0.517    0.05
```

Next, the result is moved to long form and `Revenue` is calculated for each confusion metric at each threshold.

```
whichThreshold <-
  whichThreshold %>%
    dplyr::select(starts_with("Count"), Threshold) %>%
    gather(Variable, Count, -Threshold) %>%
    mutate(Revenue =
     case_when(
       Variable == "Count_TN"  ~ Count * 30,
       Variable == "Count_TP"  ~ ((30 - 8) * (Count * .50)) +
                                    (-32 * (Count * .50)),
       Variable == "Count_FN"  ~ (-30) * Count,
       Variable == "Count_FP"  ~ (30 - 8) * Count))
```

Figure 6.10 plots the `Revenue` for each confusion metric by threshold. This is a plot of trade-offs. Each is described below:

- **False negative revenue**: 'We predicted no churn and the customer churned'. As the threshold increases we see more customers churn that a mailer did not get sent to. As fewer mailers go out, the losses mount.
- **False positive revenue**: 'We predicted churn and sent the mailer, the customer did not churn but used the coupon anyway'. A low threshold assumes few customers are predicted to churn, which limits the revenue hit from those who used the coupon anyway, despite their intention to renew.
- **True negative revenue**: 'We predicted no churn, did not send a mailer, and the customer did not churn'. As the threshold goes up, the number of full-price paying customers goes up. At higher thresholds, the model assumes no churn, and the no revenue is lost to false negatives.
- **True positive revenue**: 'We predicted churn and sent the mailer'. Although the coupon convincing 50% of members to re-subscribe saves some revenue, the cost of actual churn leads to losses for most thresholds.

```
whichThreshold %>%
  ggplot(.,aes(Threshold, Revenue, colour = Variable)) +
  geom_point() +
  scale_colour_manual(values = palette5[c(5, 1:3)]) +
  labs(title = "Revenue by confusion matrix type and threshold",
       y = "Revenue") +
  plotTheme() +
  guides(colour=guide_legend(title = "Confusion Matrix"))
```

The next step of the cost/benefit analysis is to calculate the total `Revenue` across confusion metrics for each threshold.

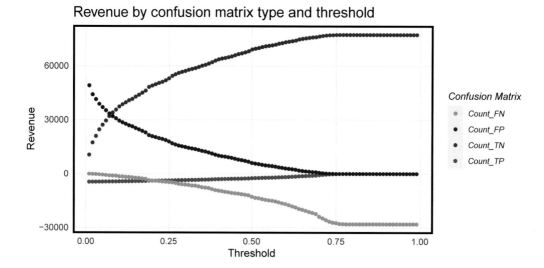

FIGURE 6.10 Optimizing different confusion metrics leads to varying revenue outcomes.

Below, `actualChurn` and `Actual_Churn_Rate` include 50% of the true positives (who were not swayed by the coupon) and all of the false negatives (those who never even received a coupon). `Actual_Churn_Revenue_Loss` is loss from this pay period, and `Revenue_Next_Period` is for the next, assuming no new customers are added.

Assuming `testProbs` is representative of Bounce to Work!'s customers, 934 (27%) of customers will churn resulting in a net loss of -$28,020 and a net revenue of $49,410. How do the other thresholds compare?

```
whichThreshold_revenue <-
  whichThreshold %>%
    mutate(actualChurn =
             ifelse(Variable == "Count_TP", (Count * .5),
             ifelse(Variable == "Count_FN", Count, 0))) %>%
    group_by(Threshold) %>%
    summarize(Revenue = sum(Revenue),
              Actual_Churn_Rate = sum(actualChurn) / sum(Count),
              Actual_Churn_Revenue_Loss =  sum(actualChurn * 30),
              Revenue_Next_Period =
                Revenue - Actual_Churn_Revenue_Loss)
```

A threshold of 26% is optimal and yields the greatest revenue at $62,499. After that mark, losses associated with False Negatives begin to mount (see Figure 6.10).

`Revenue` (this period) and `Revenue_Next_Period` are plotted in Figure 6.11 for each Threshold. Here we assume no new customers are added next pay period.

```
whichThreshold_revenue %>%
  dplyr::select(Threshold, Revenue, Revenue_Next_Period) %>%
  gather(Variable, Value, -Threshold) %>%
  ggplot(aes(Threshold, Value, colour = Variable)) +
    geom_point() +
```

```
geom_vline(xintercept = pull(arrange(whichThreshold_revenue,
                            -Revenue)[1,1])) +
scale_colour_manual(values = palette2) +
plotTheme() + ylim(0,70000)
```

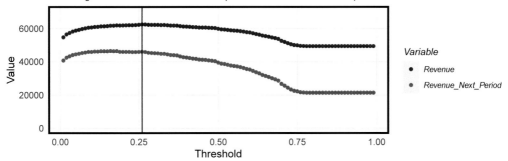

Revenue this pay period and the next by threshold
Assuming no new customers added next period. Vertical line denotes optimal threshold

FIGURE 6.11 The trends for revenue this period and revenue next period.

These cost/benefit functions are incredibly revealing. It's clear that Revenue (this_period) declines after the 26% threshold. The trend for Revenue_Next_Period is similar, but interestingly, the slope of the line is much steeper. Why do you think this is?

Table 6.4 shows the Revenue and the rate of churn for no model, the default 50% threshold and the optimal threshold. Not only does the optimal threshold maximize Revenue this pay period, but it also prevents fewer customers from actually churning in the next pay period, helping to maximize revenues in the long term as well.

Model	Revenue_This_Period	Lost_Customers_Next_Period
No predictive model	$49,410	27%
50% Threshold	$59,860	19%
26% Threshold	$62,499	16%

TABLE 6.4 Revenue and percent of customers lost for each scenario.

6.7 Conclusion - Churn

The goal of this chapter is to help pogo-transit company Bounce to Work! maximize revenues by reducing the number of customers who might not otherwise renew their membership (i.e., churn). A logistic regression model was estimated to predict Churn as a function of customer data and the relevant goodness of fit indicators were introduced. To demonstrate how machine learning can directly influence a business problem, these 'confusion metrics' were used to calculate the Revenue implications of the model relative to the business-as-usual approach, sans model. More experienced readers can swap out `glm` for more advanced machine learning algorithms, and notice an immediate improvement in predictive performance.

Unlike every other chapter in this book, this one focused on resource allocation for a for-profit company. It may not seem like 'cost/benefit' and 'customer' are terms that apply to government - but they absolutely do. Every taxpayer, household, child, parent, and senior is a client of government, and all deserve a government that works to their benefit.

The difference is in finding the 'optimal' resource allocation approach. This may be possible if the only bottom line is revenue, but it is largely impossible in government, which has many unquantifiable bottom lines like equity and social cohesion. Armed with the necessary domain expertise, however, government data scientists can still use these methods to improve service delivery.

There are no shortage of use cases in government that could benefit from these models. Which homelessness or drug treatment intervention might increase the probability for success? Which landlords are likely renting and evicting tenants illegally? Which buildings are at risk of falling down? Which gang member is at risk for gun crime? Which medicaid recipient might benefit from in-home nursing care? And the list goes on.

There are two ways to judge the usefulness of these models. First, does the data-driven approach improve outcomes relative to the business-as-usual approach? Chapter 4 compared the geospatial risk model to traditional hot spot mapping. Here, the business-as-usual approach may have just allowed churn; perhaps an employee had a method for choosing which customers receive a coupon; or maybe they pulled names from a hat. Consider that a confusion matrix is possible for each of these approaches.

The second way to judge usefulness is through the lens of 'fairness', which is the subject of the next chapter. Just because the model may improve cost/benefit, doesn't necessarily make for a more useful decision-making approach if it further disenfranchises one group or another. There are many ways to judge fairness, and our approach, not surprisingly, will be to analyze across-group generalizability.

Ultimately, an algorithm's usefulness should not be evaluated by an engineer alone, but by a team of engineers and domain experts who can evaluate models within the appropriate context.

6.8   Assignment - Target a subsidy

Emil City is considering a more proactive approach for targeting home owners who qualify for a home repair tax credit program. This tax credit program has been around for close to 20 years, and while the Department of Housing and Community Development (HCD) tries to proactively reach out to eligible homeowners ever year, the uptake of the credit is woefully inadequate. Typically only 11% of eligible homeowners they reach out to take the credit.

The consensus at HCD is that the low conversion rate is due to the fact that the agency reaches out to eligible homeowners at random. Unfortunately, we don't know the cost/benefit of previous campaigns, but we should assume it wasn't good. To move toward a more targeted campaign, HCD has recently hired you, their very first data scientist, to convert all the client-level data collected from previous campaigns into a decision-making analytic that can better target their limited outreach resources.

You have been given a random sample of records. Your goal is to train the best classifier you can and use the results to inform a cost/benefit analysis.

The data for this exercise has been adopted from Moro & Rita (2014).[4] Some variables have been changed to suit the current use case. The dependent variable is y, which is Yes to indicate the a homeowner took the credit and No to indicate they did not. There are many features related to this outcome described in Table 6.5.

Variable	Description	Class	Notes
age	Age of homeowner	Numeric	
job	Occupation indicator	Category	
marital	Marital Status	Category	
education	Educational attainment	Category	
taxLien	Is there a lien against the owner's property?	Category	
mortgage	Is the owner carrying a mortgage	Category	
taxbill_in_phl	Is the owner's full-time residence not in Philadelphia	Category	
contact	How have we previously contacted individual?	Category	
month	Month we last contacted individual	Category	
day_of_week	Day of the week we last contacted individual	Category	
campaign	# of contacts for this ind for this campaign	Category	
pdays	# days after ind. last contacted from a previous program	Category	999 = client not previously contacted
previous	# of contacts before this campaign for this ind.	Numeric	
poutcome	Outcome of the previous marketing campaign	Categorical	
unemploy_rate	Unemployment rate at time of campaign	Numeric	
cons.price.idx	Consumer Price Idex at campaign time	Numeric	
cons.conf.idx	Consumer confidence index at time of campaign	Numeric	
inflation_rate	US Inflation Rate	Numeric	daily indicator
spent_on_repairs	Amoung annually spent on home repairs	Numeric	
y	Indicates the individual took the credit	Category	Yes/No (but you may wish to recode to numeric)

TABLE 6.5 Data dictionary for Chapter 6 assignment.

After studying the credit program and related materials, you construct some stylized facts to help guide your cost/benefit analysis. If we predict that a household will take the credit, then HCD is willing to allocate **$2,850** per homeowner, which includes staff and resources to facilitate mailers, phone calls, and information/counseling sessions at the HCD offices. Given the new targeting algorithm, we should now assume 25% of contacted eligible homeowners take the credit. The remainder receive the marketing allocation but do not take the credit.

The credit costs **$5,000** per homeowner, which can be used toward home improvement. Academic researchers in Philadelphia evaluated, the program finding that houses that transacted after taking the credit, sold with a **$10,000** premium, on average. Homes surrounding the repaired home see an aggregate premium of **$56,000**, on average. Below is a run down of the costs and benefits for each potential outcome of the model you will build. This is a public-sector use case, so the cost/benefit is not as straightforward as Bounce to Work! If you feel that changing a constraint would be helpful, then please do so.

1. True Positive - Predicted correctly homeowner would take the credit; allocated the marketing resources, and 25% took the credit.
2. True Negative - Predicted correctly homeowner would not take the credit, no marketing resources were allocated, and no credit was allocated.
3. False Positive - Predicted incorrectly homeowner would take the credit; allocated marketing resources; no credit allocated.

---

[4]http://archive.ics.uci.edu/ml/datasets/Bank+Marketing

4. False Negative - Predicted incorrectly that a homeowner would not take the credit but they did. These are likely homeowners who signed up for reasons unrelated to the marketing campaign. Thus, we '0 out' this category, assuming the cost/benefit of this is $0.

Deliverables:

1. One paragraph on the motivation for the analysis.
2. Develop and interpret data visualizations that describe feature importance/correlation.
3. Split your data into a 65/35 training/test set.
4. The sensitivity (true positive rate) for a model with all the features is very low. **Engineer new features** that significantly increase the sensitivity.
   a. Interpret your new features in one paragraph.
   b. Show a regression summary for both the kitchen sink and your engineered regression.
   c. Cross-validate both models; compare and interpret two facetted plots of ROC, sensitivity and specificity.
5. Output an ROC curve for your new model and interpret it.
6. Develop a cost benefit analysis.
   a. Write out the cost/benefit equation for each confusion metric.
   b. Create the 'cost/benefit table' as seen above.
   c. Plot the confusion metric outcomes for each threshold.
   d. Create two small multiple plots that show `Threshold` as a function of `Total_Revenue` and `Total_Count_of_Credits`. Interpret this.
   e. Create a table of the `Total_Revenue` and `Total_Count_of_Credits` allocated for two categories. `50%_Threshold` and your `Optimal_Threshold`.
7. Conclude whether and why this model should or shouldn't be put into production. What could make the model better? What would you do to ensure that the marketing materials resulted in a better response rate?

7

People-based ML Models: Algorithmic Fairness

7.1 Introduction

The churn use case from Chapter 6 is one example of how machine learning algorithms increasingly make decisions in place of humans. Marketing campaigns, insurance, credit cards, bank loans, news, and shopping recommendations, are all now allocated with these methods. Bestsellers like Cathy O'Neil's, *Weapons of Math Destruction* and relentless news coverage of tech company data mining, suggests these algorithms can bring as much peril as they do promise.[1]

Government is still unsure how to regulate private-sector algorithms - their inner-workings cast as intellectual property and closed off from public scrutiny. In the public-sector however, there is an expectation that algorithms are open and transparent. While governments *today* are using algorithms to automate their decision-making, many lack the regulatory or planning wherewithal to ensure these models are fair.

In this chapter, we learn how to open the black box of these algorithms to better judge them for fairness and better understand the pertinent social costs. A person-based model is estimated to predict 'recidivism' - the term given to an offender released from prison, who then re-offends and must go back to prison. These algorithms have exploded in recent years - another example of the criminal justice system as an early adopter of machine learning.

A recidivism predictive model may be used by a judge to inform sentencing or parole decisions. It may also be used to prioritize who gets access to prisoner reentry programs like job training, for example.

If churn was the only context we had for the efficacy of these tools, we might think applying machine learning to recidivism is a no-brainer. This could not be further from the truth. Here, as was the case in predictive policing (Chapter 5), we will see that when human bias is baked into machine learning predictions, the result is a decision-making tool that is not useful.

As before, a model that is not useful is one that lacks generalizability across groups. With churn, generalizability was not considered, and the costs of getting it wrong is simply a loss of revenue. In geospatial predictive policing, the cost is racially discriminate police surveillance. With recidivism, the costs are the systematic and disproportional over-imprisonment of one race relative to another.

In other words, a biased business algorithm can cost money, but a biased government algorithm can cost lives and livelihoods. The associated social and economic costs could be massive, and we must learn to evaluate these models with these costs in mind.

---

[1] O'Neil, C. (2016). *Weapons of math destruction: How big data increases inequality and threatens democracy.* Broadway Books.

One example of bias in the recidivism use case is higher false positive rates for African American ex-offenders compared to Caucasians. A False Positive in this context means that the algorithm predicted an ex-offender would recidivate but they did not. If a judge uses a predicted recidivism 'risk score' to aid in his or her sentencing decision, and such a bias exists, then a disproportional number of African Americans may be incarcerated for longer than they otherwise deserve. Taken across tens of thousands of citizens in one metropolitan area, the social costs are unfathomable.

7.1.1   The specter of disparate impact

Social scientists are familiar with issues of fairness and discrimination, but identifying algorithmic discrimination is just as nuanced as would be in say, housing and labor markets. It is unlikely that a jurisdiction would create a discriminatory algorithm on purpose. Given the black box nature of these models, it is more likely they would create a decision-making tool that has a 'disparate impact' on members of a protected class. Disparate impact is a legal theory positing that although a policy or program may not be discriminatory *prima facie*, it still may have an adverse discriminatory effect, even if unintended.

Recall our need to ensure that *geospatial* predictive algorithms generalize from one urban context to the next. This same rationale applies with people-based models, but the concern is generalizability across different protected classes, like gender and race.

If an algorithm does not generalize to one group, its use for resource allocation may have a disparate impact on that group. The false positive example for African Americans relative to Caucasians is one such example. This may occur because the algorithm lacks appropriate features to accurately model the African American 'experience'. It may also be that the training data itself is biased, a critique discussed at length in Chapter 5.

As a reminder, systematic over-policing of historically disenfranchised communities creates a feedback loop where more reported crime leads to more cops on patrol, who then report more crimes, that ultimately lead to more convictions. In a predictive setting, if this *selection bias* goes unobserved, the systematic error will move into the error term and lead to bias and unintended social costs.

It is impossible to identify the effect of unobserved variables. As an alternative, researchers have very recently developed a series of fairness metrics that can be used to judge disparate impact.[2] A 2018 review by Verma & Rubin is particularly relevant for policymakers interested in learning more about fairness metrics.[3]

For example, in 2016, journalists from ProPublica released an evaluation of the COMPAS recidivism prediction algorithm built by a company called Northpointe, finding that while the algorithm had comparable *accuracy* rates across different racial groups, there were clear racial differences for *errors* that had high social costs.[4] This paradox lead ProPublica to ask a fascinating question - 'how could an algorithm simultaneously be fair and unfair?'[5] In

---

[2]Angwin, Julia & Larson, Jeff (2016) Bias in Criminal Risk Scores is Mathematically Inevitable, Researchers Say. ProPublica. https://www.propublica.org/article/bias-in-criminal-risk-scores-is-mathematically-inevitable-researchers-say

[3]Verma, S. and Rubin, J. (2018). Fairness definitions explained. In 2018 IEEE/ACM International Workshop on Software Fairness (FairWare) (pp. 1-7). IEEE.

[4]Larson et al. (2016). How We Analyzed the COMPAS Recidivism Algorithm. https://www.propublica.org/article/how-we-analyzed-the-compas-recidivism-algorithm.

[5]Ibid.

this chapter, we will make use of the COMPAS data ProPublica used for their analysis and develop fairness metrics that can help identify disparate impact.

7.1.2 Modeling judicial outcomes

In the criminal justice system, as in life, decisions are made by weighing risks. Among a host of federal sentencing guidelines, judges are to 'protect the public from further crimes of the defendant.'[6] Rhetorically, this sounds straightforward - identify the risk that an individual will cause the public harm and impose a sentence to reduce this risk. However, bias always plays a role in decision-making. We'd never ask the average citizen to weigh risks and punish accordingly because we do not believe the average citizen could act with impartiality. Although this is the standard we impose on judges, even they make systematic mistakes.[7]

And the use of these data-driven risk models in the criminal justice system is only increasing in recent years.[8] Algorithms are predicting risk for a host of use cases including bail hearings,[9] parole,[10] and to support sentencing decisions by assessing future criminal behavior.[11]

Can an algorithm help judges make better decisions? Recent research determined that even with much less data on hand, people without a criminal justice background make recidivism predictions as accurately as the COMPAS algorithm.[12] Very importantly, studies have also shown that introducing prediction into the decision-making process can reduce the odds of re-arrests.[13]

Collectively, this research suggests that there may be benefits for governments in adopting these tools - but do these benefits outweigh the social costs? No doubt, more research is needed on the social justice implications of these algorithms. However, the more timely need is for government to proactively explore biases in the models they are currently developing.

As was the case with churn, the confusion metrics are instrumental in communicating biases to non-technical decision-makers because they directly reflect the business process at hand.

7.1.3 Accuracy and generalizability in recidivism algorithms

Accuracy and generalizability continue to be the two yardsticks we use to measure the usefulness of our algorithms. The goal of a recidivism classifier is to predict two binary outcomes - `Recidivate` and `notRecidivate`. While the 'percent of correct predictions' is a

---

[6]18 U.S. Code § 3553. Imposition of a sentence. https://www.law.cornell.edu/uscode/text/18/3553

[7]Guthrie, C., Rachlinski, J. J., and Wistrich, A. J. (2000). Inside the judicial mind. Cornell L. Rev., 86, 777

[8]Barry-Jester, Anna Maria et al. (2020). The New Science of Sentencing

[9]Kleinberg, J., Lakkaraju, H., Leskovec, J., Ludwig, J., and Mullainathan, S. (2018). Human decisions and machine predictions. The quarterly journal of economics, 133(1), 237-293.

[10]Berk, R. (2017). An impact assessment of machine learning risk forecasts on parole board decisions and recidivism. Journal of Experimental Criminology, 13(2), 193-216.

[11]Silver, E., and Chow-Martin, L. (2002). A multiple models approach to assessing recidivism risk: Implications for judicial decision making. Criminal justice and behavior, 29(5), 538-568.

[12]Dressel, J. and Farid, H. (2018). The accuracy, fairness, and limits of predicting recidivism. Science advances, 4(1).

[13]Berk, R. (2017). An impact assessment of machine learning risk forecasts on parole board decisions and recidivism. Journal of Experimental Criminology, 13(2), 193-216

simple measure of accuracy, it lacks the nuance needed to detect disparate impact. As they were in Chapter 6, confusion metrics will continue to be key.

The basic premise of the recidivism model is to learn the recidivism experience of ex-offenders in the recent past and test the extent to which this experience generalizes to a population for which the propensity to recidivate is unknown. The prediction from the model is a 'risk score' running from 0 to 1, interpreted as 'the probability person i will recidivate'. The model can then be validated by comparing predicted classifications to observed classifications, giving a host of more nuanced errors including:

True Positive (Sensitivity) - 'The person was predicted to recidivate and actually recidivated'.
True Negative (Specificity) - 'The person was predicted not to recidivate and actually did not recidivate'.
False Positive - 'The person was predicted to recidivate and actually did not recidivate'.
False Negative - 'The person was predicted not to recidivate and actually did recidivate'.

7.2   Data and exploratory analysis

Begin by loading the necessary R packages, reading in the `plotTheme` with the source file, and some color palettes.

```
library(lubridate)
library(tidyverse)
library(caret)
library(kableExtra)
library(ModelMetrics)
library(plotROC)
library(knitr)
library(grid)
library(gridExtra)
library(QuantPsyc)

root.dir =
  paste0("https://raw.githubusercontent.com/urbanSpatial",
         "/Public-Policy-Analytics-Landing/master/DATA/")
source(
  paste0("https://raw.githubusercontent.com/urbanSpatial/",
         "Public-Policy-Analytics-Landing/master/functions.r"))

palette_9_colors <-
  c("#FF2AD4","#E53AD8","#CC4ADC","#996AE5",
    "#7F7BE9","#668BED","#33ABF6","#19BBFA","#00CCFF")
palette_3_colors <- c("#FF2AD4","#7F7BE9","#00CCFF")
palette_2_colors <- c("#FF2AD4", "#00CCFF")
palette_1_colors <- c("#00CCFF")
```

The data for this chapter comes directly from ProPublica's Github repository,[14] and was the impetus for a series of articles on bias in criminal justice algorithms.[15]

At the time of writing, no data dictionary had been posted, thus much of the feature engineering routines employed below were copied directly from ProPublica's IPython Notebook.[16] While this is not ideal, it is at times, the nature of working with open data. Table 7.1 shows each variable used in the analysis.

Variable	Description
sex	Categorical variables that indicates whether the ex-offender is male or female
age	The age of the person
age_cat	Variable that bins ex-offenders into three groups by age: Less than 25, 25 to 45, Greater than 45
race	The race of the person
priors_count	The number of prior crimes committed
two_year_recid	Numerical binary variable whether a person recidivated or not. 0 is not recidivate; 1 is recidivate
r_charge_desc	Description of the charge upon recidivating
c_charge_desc	Description of the original criminal charge
c_charge_degree	Degree of the original charge
r_charge_degree	Degree of the charge upon recidivating
juv_other_count	Categorical variable of the number of prior non-felony, juvenile convictions
length_of_stay	How long the person stayed in jail
Recidivated	Character binary variable whether the person recidivated (Recidivate) or not (notRecidivate)

TABLE 7.1 A description of each variable used in the analysis.

The cleaned dataset describes 6,162 ex-offenders screened by COMPAS in 2013 and 2014. There are 53 columns in the original data describing length of jail stays, type of charges, the degree of crimes committed, and criminal history. Many variables were added by Northpointe, the original author of the COMPAS algorithm, and are not relevant to the model building process. Also, noticeably absent, are economic and educational outcomes for these individuals. The model developed here is simplistic - it is not a replication of the existing Northpointe algorithm.

```
raw_data <- read.csv(file.path(root.dir,
                "Chapter7/compas-scores-two-years.csv"))

df <-
  raw_data %>%
  filter(days_b_screening_arrest <= 30) %>%
  filter(days_b_screening_arrest >= -30) %>%
  filter(is_recid != -1) %>%
  filter(c_charge_degree != "O") %>%
  filter(priors_count != "36") %>%
  filter(priors_count != "25") %>%
  mutate(
    length_of_stay = as.numeric(as.Date(c_jail_out) -
                          as.Date(c_jail_in)),
    priors_count = as.factor(priors_count),
```

[14]https://github.com/propublica/compas-analysis

[15]https://www.propublica.org/article/how-we-analyzed-the-compas-recidivism-algorithm

[16]https://github.com/propublica/compas-analysis/blob/master/Compas%20Analysis.ipynb

```
   Recidivated = as.factor(ifelse(two_year_recid == 1,
                           "Recidivate", "notRecidivate")),
   recidivatedNumeric= ifelse(Recidivated =="Recidivate", 1, 0),
   race2 = case_when(
            race == "Caucasian"         ~ "Caucasian",
            race == "African-American" ~ "African-American",
            TRUE                         ~ "Other")) %>%
 dplyr::select(
   sex,age,age_cat,race,race2,priors_count,two_year_recid,
   r_charge_desc,c_charge_desc,c_charge_degree,r_charge_degree,
   juv_other_count,length_of_stay,priors_count,Recidivated,
   recidivatedNumeric) %>%
 filter(priors_count != 38)
```

Figure 7.1 illustrates the most frequent initial charge. Crimes of varying severity are included in the dataset. Note the use of `reorder` and `FUN = max` in the `ggplot` call.

```
group_by(df, c_charge_desc) %>%
  summarize(count = n()) %>%
  mutate(rate = count / sum(count)) %>%
  arrange(-rate) %>% head(9) %>%
  ggplot(aes(reorder(c_charge_desc, rate, FUN = max),
            rate, fill = c_charge_desc)) +
   geom_col() + coord_flip() +
   scale_fill_manual(values = palette_9_colors) +
   labs(x = "Charge", y = "Rate",
       title= "Most frequent initial charges") +
   plotTheme() + theme(legend.position = "none")
```

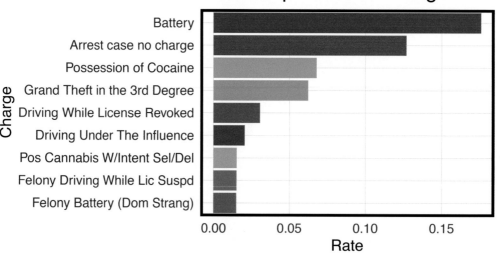

FIGURE 7.1 Initial charges with the highest frequency in the data.

Figure 7.2 visualizes the rate of recidivism by race. Note the rate of recidivism for African Americans is twice that (59%) of Caucasians (29%). If this reported rate is driven by reporting or other bias, then it may have important implications for the model's usefulness.

```
df %>%
  group_by(Recidivated, race) %>%
  summarize(n = n()) %>%
  mutate(freq = n / sum(n)) %>%
  filter(Recidivated == "Recidivate") %>%
  ggplot(aes(reorder(race, -freq), freq)) +
    geom_bar(stat = "identity", position = "dodge",
             fill = palette_2_colors[2]) +
    labs(title = "Recidivism rate by race",
         y = "Rate", x = "Race") +
    plotTheme() +
    theme(axis.text.x = element_text(angle = 45, hjust = 1))
```

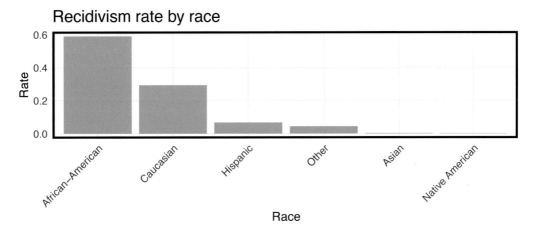

FIGURE 7.2 Rate of recidivism for racial/ethnic groups.

7.3   Estimate two recidivism models

"You mustn't include race in the model because that will ensure resource allocation decisions will, in part, be guided by race". I've heard this line countless times in my career. But as we'll learn, the bottom line is that if racial bias is baked into the training data, then controlling explicitly for race, is not likely to remove it. This section tests this theory by estimating a logistic regression with race and one without.

The dependent variable is Recidivated, which is coded as 1 for inmates who experienced a recidivism event and 0 for those that did not. Aside from race, the following two models include sex, age, the number of 'other' convictions as a juvenile, the count of prior adult convictions, and the length of stay in prison.

The data is split into a 75% training set and a 25% test set using a simple `dplyr` approach.

```
train <- df %>% dplyr::sample_frac(.75)
train_index <- as.numeric(rownames(train))
test <- df[-train_index, ]
```

`reg.noRace` and `reg.withRace` are estimated in the following code block. `summary(reg.noRace)` shows that all features are statistically significant and their signs reasonable. For example, as age increases, the probability of recidivism decreases. Conversely, the longer `length_of_stay` in the prison system, the greater the likelihood that an individual recidivates.

Note that `priors_count` is input as a factor. If it were input as a continuous feature, the interpretation would be 'a one unit increase in priors leads to a corresponding increase in the propensity to recidivate'. By converting to factor, the interpretation is that there is a statistically significant difference between 0 and n priors. Most of these fixed effects are significant.

```
reg.noRace <- glm(Recidivated ~ ., data = train %>%
                       dplyr::select(sex, age, age_cat,
                         juv_other_count, length_of_stay,
                         priors_count, Recidivated),
                 family = "binomial"(link = "logit"))

reg.withRace <- glm(Recidivated ~ ., data = train %>%
                       dplyr::select(
                         sex, age, age_cat, race,
                         juv_other_count, length_of_stay,
                         priors_count, Recidivated),
                 family = "binomial"(link = "logit"))
```

The summary of `reg.withRace` is quite revealing. You may try two specifications with both the current 6-category `race` feature or an alternative `race2` feature including categories for just `Caucasian`, `African-American`, and `sOther`. In both instances the race variables are largely insignificant suggesting that differences in race are not driving propensity to recidivate.

How can that be given the differences illustrated in Figure 7.2 above? To explore further, try to estimate another regression, the same as `reg.withRace`, but with `race2` (instead of `race`) and without `priors_count`.

Why is race significant when `priors_count` is removed? Figure 7.3 shows the mean `priors_count` by race. African Americans are reported to have far higher prior rates than other races. Thus, `race` and `priors_count` are colinear, or correlated with one another, rendering `race` insignificant when both are included in the model.

As race plays no role in the usefulness of our model, `reg.noRace` is used for the remainder of the analysis.

```
group_by(df, race2) %>%
  summarize(averagePriors = mean(as.numeric(priors_count))) %>%
  ggplot(aes(race2, averagePriors, fill = race2)) +
    geom_bar(stat="identity", position = "dodge") +
    labs(title="Mean priors by race", y = "Mean Priors",
        x = "Race") +
    scale_fill_manual(values = palette_3_colors,
                      name = "Recidivism") +
    plotTheme() + theme(legend.position = "none")
```

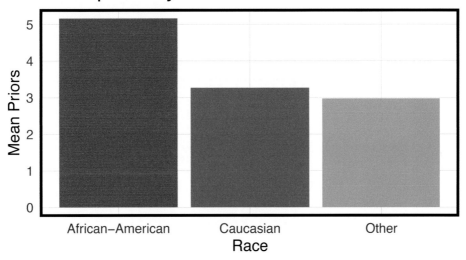

FIGURE 7.3 The average number of priors by racial group.

7.3.1 Accuracy and generalizability

Both accuracy and the confusion metrics are discussed here with emphasis on generalizability across race. To begin, the following code calculates a predicted recidivism class, `predClass`, for any predicted probability over 0.50.

```
testProbs <-
  data.frame(class = test$recidivatedNumeric,
             probs = predict(reg.noRace, test, type="response"),
             Race = test$race2)
```

The first cause for concern comes in Figure 7.4 which contrasts observed and predicted recidivism rates given the 50% threshold. About 45% of ex-offenders are observed to recidivate across all races, but only 40% are predicted to do so. This underprediction is far more pronouced for Caucasians and other races, relative to African Americans.

```
mutate(testProbs, predClass = ifelse(probs >= .5, 1, 0)) %>%
  group_by(Race) %>%
  summarize(Observed.recidivism = sum(class) / n(),
            Predicted.recidivism = sum(predClass) / n()) %>%
  gather(Variable, Value, -Race) %>%
  ggplot(aes(Race, Value)) +
    geom_bar(aes(fill = Race),
             position="dodge", stat="identity") +
    scale_fill_manual(values = palette_3_colors) +
    facet_wrap(~Variable) +
    plotTheme() +
    theme(axis.text.x = element_text(angle = 45, hjust = 1))
```

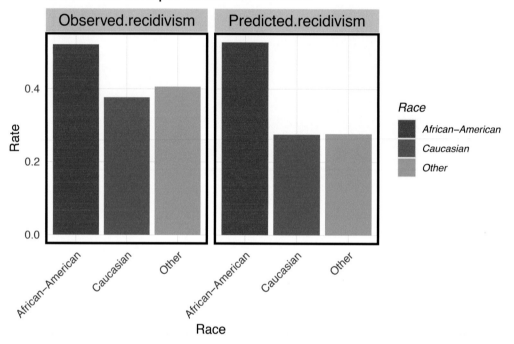

FIGURE 7.4 The observed rate of recidivism by race compared to the predicted rate of recidivism.

Let's delve a bit deeper by visualizing confusion metrics by race. Northpointe, the company that markets decision-making tools based on these data, has argued that the algorithm is fair because of the comparable across-race accuracy rates.[17] Table 7.2 confirms this claim - but that is far from the entire story.

Despite equal accuracy rates, the issue is in the disparities for each confusion metric. The `iterateThreshold` function, first used in Chapter 6 (`functions.r`), will be used again to calculate confusion metrics for each threshold by race.

---

[17]Dieterich et al. (2016). COMPAS Risk Scales: Demonstrating Accuracy Equity and Predict Parity. http://go.volarisgroup.com/rs/430-MBX-989/images/ProPublica_Commentary_Final_070616.pdf

The function takes several inputs including the `data` frame of predicted probabilities; an `observedClass`; a column of predicted probabilities, `predictedProbs`, and an optional `group` parameter that provides confusion metrics by race.

Next, the function is run and the results are filtered for just the 50% threshold. Accuracy and the confusion metrics as rates are selected out, converted to long form and then plotted as a grouped bar plot. Let's interpret each metric in the context of social cost.

```
testProbs.thresholds <-
  iterateThresholds(data=testProbs, observedClass = class,
                    predictedProbs = probs, group = Race)

filter(testProbs.thresholds, Threshold == .5)  %>%
  dplyr::select(Accuracy, Race, starts_with("Rate")) %>%
  gather(Variable, Value, -Race) %>%
  ggplot(aes(Variable, Value, fill = Race)) +
    geom_bar(aes(fill = Race), position = "dodge",
             stat = "identity") +
    scale_fill_manual(values = palette_3_colors) +
    labs(title="Confusion matrix rates by race",
         subtitle ="50% threshold", x ="Outcome",y = "Rate") +
    plotTheme() +
    theme(axis.text.x = element_text(angle = 45, hjust = 1))
```

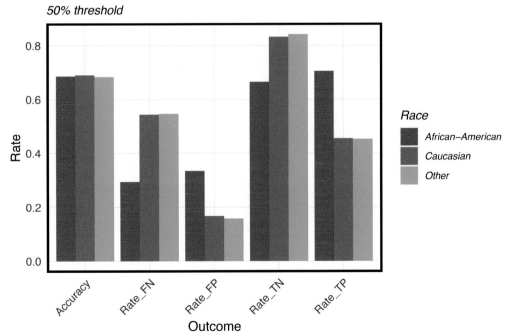

FIGURE 7.5 Confusion metrics by race using a 0.5 threshold.

- **False Negatives** - The rate at which African Americans are incorrectly predicted *not* to recidivate is noticeably lower than for other races. A judge granting parole errant in this way, means an individual is incorrectly released from prison only to commit another crime. Here, the social cost is on society not the ex-offender. In the context of disparate impact, Caucasians will be incorrectly released at greater rates than African Americans.

- **False Positives** - The rate at which African Americans are incorrectly predicted to recidivate is noticeably higher than for other races. A judge faced with a parole decision when this error comes into play will incorrectly prevent a prisoner from being released. Here, the social cost is most certainly with the ex-offender, with a much greater disparate impact for African Americans.

These two metrics alone suggest that the use of this algorithm may have a disparate impact on African Americans. Thus, we should be weary of how useful this algorithm is for making criminal justice decisions.

7.4   What about the threshold?

As we learned in the previous chapter, the threshold at which an individual outcome is classified to be true can make all the difference. The same is true in this use case, but can finding an optimal threshold help to erase the disparate impact? Let's explore some metrics related to the threshold, beginning with an across race ROC curve.

The ROC curve measures trade-offs in true positive and false positive rates for each threshold. Recall from Figure 6.8 (the 'football plot') that the diagonal 'coin flip line' suggests a classifier that gets it right 50% of the time, but also gets it wrong 50% of the time. Anything classified on or below the coin flip line is not useful.

```
aucTable <-
  testProbs %>%
  group_by(Race) %>%
  summarize(AUC = auc(class,probs)) %>%
  mutate(AUC = as.character(round(AUC, 3)))

mutate(testProbs.thresholds,
       pointSize = ifelse(Threshold == .48, 24, 16)) %>%
  ggplot(aes(Rate_FP, Rate_TP, colour=Race)) +
  geom_point(aes(shape = pointSize)) + geom_line() +
    scale_shape_identity() +
  scale_color_manual(values = palette_3_colors) +
  geom_abline(slope = 1, intercept = 0, size = 1.5,
              color = 'grey') +
  annotation_custom(tableGrob(aucTable, rows = NULL),
    xmin = .65, xmax = 1, ymin = 0, ymax = .25) +
  labs(title="ROC Curves by race", x="False Positive Rate",
       y="True Positive Rate") +
  plotTheme()
```

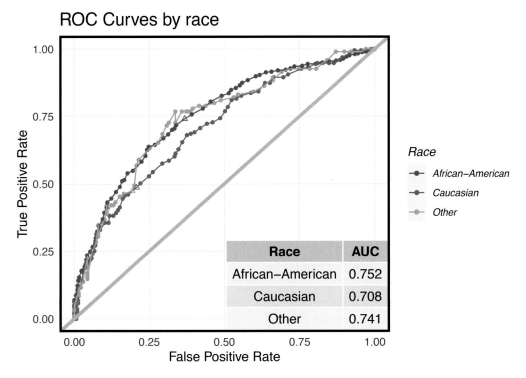

FIGURE 7.6 Testing model performance with an ROC curve by race.

In Figure 7.6, the ROC curve is generated for each race and shows there are really three different curves. `testProbs.thresholds` shows that a threshold that gives an African American true positive rate of roughly 74% of the time, gives one for Caucasians 49% of the time. At that same threshold, however, the model makes more False Positives for African Americans (37%) than it does for Caucasians (21%).

To see evidence of these disparities, note the triangles in Figure 7.6 above or try `filter(testProbs.thresholds, Threshold == 0.48)`.

What is the appropriate risk score threshold at which we should conclude an ex-offender will recidivate? The ROC curves suggest a threshold suitable for one race may not be robust for another. It stands to reason then that perhaps a different threshold for each race may help to equalize some of these confusion metric differences.

7.5 Optimizing 'equitable' thresholds

If a given predicted threshold leads to a disparate impact for one race, then it is inequitable. Let's explore the possibility of reducing disparate impact by searching for an equitable threshold for each race. I was first exposed to the idea of equitable thresholds through the work of colleagues at Oregon's State Department of Child Protective Services, who develop machine learning models to predict child welfare outcomes and allocate limited social worker resources. Fairness is a key concern for the development team who published a paper on their approach for 'fairness correction.'[18] In this section, I replicate a more simple version of that work.

Consider a simple measure of disparity that argues for a comparable absolute difference in false positive (`Rate_FP`) and false negative (`Rate_FN`) rates across both races. Table 7.2 shows what that disparity looks like at the 50% threshold. We see a comparable `Difference` in accuracy, but diverging error rates across races.

Var	African-American	Caucasian	Difference
Accuracy	0.6858573	0.6903353	0.0044780
Rate_FN	0.2949640	0.5445026	0.2495386
Rate_FP	0.3350785	0.1677215	0.1673570

TABLE 7.2 Disparities in across-race confusion metrics (0.5 threshold)

Let's try to achieve equitable thresholds that:

1. Exhibit little difference in across-race false positive and negative rates; while ensuring both rates are relatively low.
2. Exhibit little difference in across-race Accuracy rates; while ensuring these rates are relatively high.

To create this optimization, across-race confusion metrics and accuracies are calculated for each possible threshold combination. Here, to keep it simple, thresholds are analyzed at 10% intervals and only for two races. Doing so creates the results in Figure 7.7.

Here, the x-axis runs from 0 (no difference in across-race confusion metrics) and 1 (perfect accuracy). The y-axis shows each threshold pair. Shades of purple represent accuracy rates - which we hope are close to 1 and comparable, across races. Shades of blue represent differences in across-rate confusion metrics, which should be close to 0 and comparable. False error rates in shades of green are shown for only African Americans, given the associated social costs.

The plot is sorted in a way that maximizes the (euclidean) distance between accuracies and differences, such that a distance of 1 would mean both differences are 0 and both accuracies are 1.

When the `0.5, 0.5` threshold (in red) is visualized this way, it is clear that a 50% default is far from ideal. There are some interesting candidates here for most equitable - but tradeoffs exist. `0.6, 0.5` has high and comparable accuracy rates; differences in false positives close to 0; but an overall high false negative rate for African Americans. Consider how this contrasts with `0.5, 0.4`, which lowers the threshold for Caucasians instead of increasing it for African Americans. What more can you say about the seemingly most equitable threshold pair, 0.7, 0.6?

Note that these results are likely influenced by the results of the training/test split. Iteratively sampling or 'bootstrapping' many splits, and calculating equitable thresholds for each, would be a better approach. In addition, estimating results using thresholds at the hundredths of a percent may be more robust than at the tenths of a percent.

---

[18]Purdy & Glass (2020). The Pursuit of Algorithmic Fairness: On "Correcting" Algorithmic Unfairness in a Child Welfare Reunification Success Classifier. https://arxiv.org/abs/2010.12089

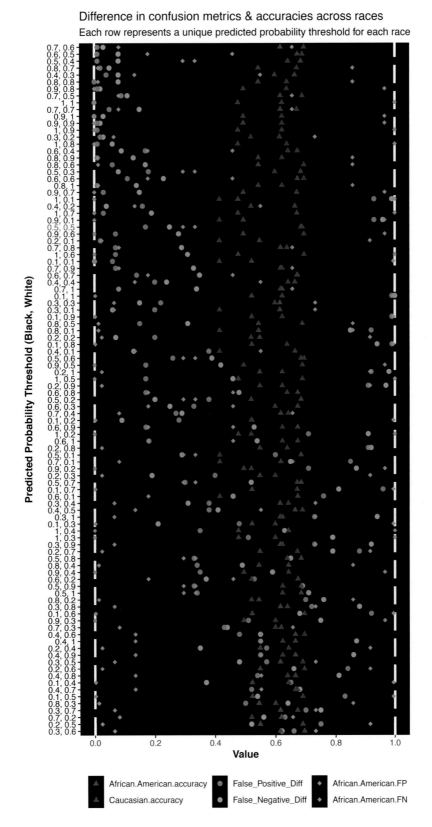

FIGURE 7.7 Optimizing equitable thresholds

Does engineering equitable thresholds help reduce disparate impact? Perhaps, but like many interesting social science phenomena, trade-offs must be made and no threshold is perfect. Consider how such an outcome relates to the across-race selection bias in these data. In this chapter, the focus is has been on social costs - which is just one of many potential decision-making bottom lines in government.

While it is often difficult to qualitatively or quantitatively judge the social costs and benefits of algorithms, I urge you to try. The results may not communicate neatly with dollar signs. Instead, careful discussion is needed on the decision-making process, the business-as-usual approach, the underlying data and all the many trade-offs. More so, terms like 'false positive', ROC curves, etc., will likely be lost on the police chief, mayor, or other non-technical decisions-makers.

That's fine. The police chief has enough domain expertise to understand how the trade-offs effect the efficiency and effectiveness of her agency - so long as you or a member of your team can communicate well. Keep in mind, that these decision are already being made by human beings, and you can create a confusion matrix for the business-as-usual decision-making.

By now, it is clear that these methods are imperfect. Algorithms make mistakes, as do humans and even judges. The question is are these methods useful?

Judging a useful algorithm thus requires far more than data science prowess. For use cases with potentially significant social costs, proper governance is key. We return to the role of 'algorithmic governance' next, in the book's conclusion.

7.6   Assignment - Memo to the mayor

Let's see how good you are at communicating these very nuanced data science results to non-technical domain experts. Assume you are a data scientist working for the Department of Prisons, and you are to *make recommendations* to your city's mayor about whether or not she should adopt a new recidivism algorithm into how the city allocates an ex-offender job training program. Some in the administration have expressed their concern that expanding the city's limited job training resources on ex-offenders who recidivate shortly after their release is not good policy. What do you think?

Begin by sketching out the basics of the job training program, quantifying the program costs. Although our concern is social costs, research the financial costs to individuals and society related to imprisonment. Calculate costs and benefits using this research as well as your own sensible assumptions; choose a threshold from `testProbs.thresholds`, and use it to develop a qualitative and quantitative cost/benefit analysis.

In your memo, no shorter than 600 words and no longer than 800 words, **you must argue for the use of the algorithm**, including the following information:

1. Explain the job training program, why the city is considering an algorithm to allocate the program and how the algorithm works, in brief.
2. Acknowledge and explain to the mayor why she should be concerned with algorithmic fairness.

3. Present your cost/benefit analysis for your equitable threshold of choice **including** an across-race grouped bar plot of each confusion metric the 0.5, 0.5 threshold and your optimal threshold.

4. Interpret the trade-off between accuracy and generalizability as it relates to *the use* of this algorithm in prioritizing a job training program and advocate that the mayor adopt the algorithm.

Remember, if your memo is too technical, you will lose the mayor's attention. If you are disingenuous about disparate impact, the press and other advocates will eventually get hold of your memo and use it to hurt the mayor politically. If you are too strong about the implications for fairness, the mayor will not agree to use the algorithm and your boss, may fire you. The best hint I can give you is to focus your memo on the use case at hand - but don't forget, politics are an important consideration.

8

Predicting Rideshare Demand

8.1 Introduction - Rideshare

This last chapter returns to spatial problem solving to predict space/time demand for rideshare in Chicago. Companies like Uber and Lyft generate and analyze tremendous amounts of data to incentivize rideshare use; to employ dynamic or 'surge' pricing; to solve routing problems; and to forecast rideshare demand to minimize driver response times. This last use case is the focus of this chapter.

The model developed here is similar to the other geospatial machine learning models built thus far, with two exceptions. First, this chapter focuses on time effects, adding additional complexity to our models, and two, social costs are less important here than they have been in previous chapters.

We have dealt with time once previously. Recall the predictive policing algorithm was trained on 2017 burglaries and validated on 2018 (Section 5.5.4). Here, time was not an explicit parameter in the model. Instead, it was assumed that the 2017 burglary experience generalized to 2018.

Time must be accounted for explicitly to forecast rideshare. Conceptually, modeling time is not all that different from modeling space. Spatial autocorrelation posits that values *here* are, in part, a function of nearby values. In the case of temporal or 'serial correlation', a similar hypothesis can be posited - that the value *now* is, in part, a function of values in the past.

There are many examples of serial correlation. Gas prices today are related to gas prices yesterday. Same with stock prices, traffic, and daily temperatures. Just as an understanding of the underlying spatial process is the key to a strong spatial model, the key to a strong time series model is an understanding of the underlying temporal process.

Uber describes its Marketplace Algorithm as one that, 'enables us to predict user supply and demand in a spatio-temporal fine granular fashion to direct driver-partners to high demand areas before they arise, thereby increasing their trip count and earnings.'[1] They go on to remark, 'Spatio-temporal forecasts are still an open research area'.

In a word, this is a dispatch problem, and there are two general approaches to consider. The more naive is to route drivers in response to space/time demand spikes as they emerge in real time. The problem with this approach is that by the time drivers reach a hot spot, the spike may have ended. Not only might this improperly allocate vehicles in the short run, but feedback effects may increase response times to other parts of the city in the long run.

---

[1] Bell, Franziska & Smyl, Slawek (2018). Forecasting at Uber: An Introduction. https://eng.uber.com/for ecasting-introduction/

The second approach is to generalize from recent rideshare experiences to predict demand in the near future. Take rush hour for example - demand occurs in the same locations at the same times, Monday through Friday. Thus, rush hour demand on Tuesday can be used to predict rush hour demand on Wednesday.

An actual rideshare forecast would likely predict trip demand or `Trip_Count` for very high resolution space/time intervals, like for every 5 minutes for every 100 by 100 ft fishnet grid cell. Our model will take a low resolution approach, reducing millions of Chicago rideshare trips from November through December, 2018, into a 20% subsample and aggregating to hourly intervals and a subset of Chicago Census tracts.

We will learn new approaches for manipulating temporal data and creating time-based features using the `lubridate` package. We also learn the `purrr` family of functions to loop through the validation of many different regressions. Data is wrangled in the next section. Exploratory analysis then analyzes space/time patterns in the data. The final section trains and validates a space/time forecast.

8.2   Data wrangling - Rideshare

Begin by loading the required libraries and functions. The rideshare data is then read in and wrangled along with weather data. Rideshare trip data is then wrangled into a complete 'panel' of observations that include every possible space/time combination.

```
library(tidyverse)
library(sf)
library(lubridate)
library(tigris)
library(gganimate)
library(riem)
library(gridExtra)
library(knitr)
library(kableExtra)

options(tigris_class = "sf")

root.dir =
  paste0("https://raw.githubusercontent.com/urbanSpatial",
         "/Public-Policy-Analytics-Landing/master/DATA/")
source(
  paste0("https://raw.githubusercontent.com/urbanSpatial/",
         "Public-Policy-Analytics-Landing/master/functions.r"))

palette5 <- c("#eff3ff","#bdd7e7","#6baed6","#3182bd","#08519c")
palette4 <- c("#D2FBD4","#92BCAB","#527D82","#123F5A")
palette2 <- c("#6baed6","#08519c")
```

The rideshare data for November and December 2018 is read in. These data exist on the Chicago Open Data portal, but because they are so large, querying with the API can take a very long time.[2] Instead, the data below is a ~20% sample (n = ~1.793 million rows) of the original data.

```
ride <- read.csv(file.path(root.dir,
                paste0("Chapter8/chicago_rideshare_trips_",
                "nov_dec_18_clean_sample.csv")))
```

To keep the data size manageable, only three pertinent fields are included in the data and defined in Table 8.1.

Variable_Name	Description
Trip.Start.Timestamp	Date/time trip started
Pickup.Census.Tract	Census Tract origin
Dropoff.Census.Tract	Census Tract destination

TABLE 8.1 Variables selected for Chapter 8 data.

8.2.1 Lubridate

Next, temporal data wrangling is performed using the fantastically simple `lubridate` package. One of the more powerful features of `lubridate` is its ability to standardize date/time stamps. In the code following block, a list contains my birthday written four different ways. Subjecting that list to the `ymd` function miraculously standardizes three of the four items.

```
ymd(c("1982-09-06", "1982-Sep-6", "1982-Sept-06",
      "1982-Sept-six"))
```

```
## [1] "1982-09-06" "1982-09-06" "1982-09-06" NA
```

`ymd` is a one of several components of the `parse_date_time` function. As below, these functions standardize the `Trip.Start.Timestamp` field (when a trip departed) into the 60-minute and 15-minute intervals needed for our analysis. Functions like `week`, `wkday`, and `hour` convert the data/time stamp into week of the year, day of the week, and hour of the day, respectively.

Two `Pickup.Census.Tract` units for Chicago's O'Hare International Airport are dropped. Surely rideshare companies forecast airport demand, but they likely employ additional features/models that account for takeoff and landing patterns.

```
ride2 <-
  ride %>%
  mutate(
    interval60 = floor_date(mdy_hms(Trip.Start.Timestamp),
```

---

[2]Chicago Data Portal. (2020). Transportation Network Providers - Trips. https://data.cityofchicago.org /Transportation/Transportation-Network-Providers-Trips/m6dm-c72p

```
                               unit = "hour"),
        interval15 = floor_date(mdy_hms(Trip.Start.Timestamp),
                               unit = "15 mins"),
        week = week(interval60),
        dotw = wday(interval60, label=TRUE),
        Pickup.Census.Tract = as.character(Pickup.Census.Tract),
        Dropoff.Census.Tract = as.character(Dropoff.Census.Tract))%>%
    filter(Pickup.Census.Tract != "17031980000" &
           Pickup.Census.Tract != "17031770602")
```

```
ride2[1:3, c(1,4,6,7)]
```

```
##      Trip.Start.Timestamp          interval60 week dotw
## 1 12/07/2018 04:30:00 PM 2018-12-07 16:00:00   49  Fri
## 2 12/30/2018 06:00:00 PM 2018-12-30 18:00:00   52  Sun
## 3 11/24/2018 07:45:00 AM 2018-11-24 07:00:00   47  Sat
```

8.2.2   Weather data

One might reasonably assume that inclement weather in the Windy City would incentivize rideshare. There once were a host of open weather data APIs available to the rstats community, but that changed when IBM bought Weather Company and Weather Underground, two giant aggregators of weather data. Recently, the good people at the Iowa Environment Mesonet released the `riem` package,[3] which provides free space/time weather data.

The `riem_measures` function downloads `weather.Data` for O'Hare Airport between November 1, 2018 and January 1, 2019. Note that the O'Hare weather station sufficiently provides temporal weather for all of Chicago.

```
weather.Data <-
  riem_measures(station = "ORD", date_start = "2018-11-01",
                date_end = "2019-01-01")
```

In this chapter, several 'panel' datasets are created. A panel is long form data, typically giving repeat observations for particular items. An example would be a dataset tracking student grades over time. Here, each row would represent a student/year pair. Every twelve rows would represent one student's grades across twelve years of schooling.

In the next code block, a `weather.Panel` is generated to summarize temperature, precipitation, and wind speed for every hour between November and December. In the code block, `mutate_if` and `replace_na` converts any character or numeric field with `NA` to 0. The first `mutate` function creates `interval60` by converting the date/time stamp, `valid`, from 5-minute intervals to 60-minute intervals. Note what `?substr` does. Then `group_by` each hour (`interval60`) to `summarize` a final set of hourly weather indicators.

The weather data is plotted in Figure 8.1 as a time series using `grid.arrange`.

---

[3]Maëlle Salmon (2016). riem: Accesses Weather Data from the Iowa Environment Mesonet. R package version 0.1.1. https://CRAN.R-project.org/package=riem

```
weather.Panel <-
  weather.Data %>%
    mutate_if(is.character,
              list(~replace(as.character(.), is.na(.), "0"))) %>%
    replace(is.na(.), 0) %>%
    mutate(interval60 = ymd_h(substr(valid, 1, 13))) %>%
    mutate(week = week(interval60),
           dotw = wday(interval60, label=TRUE)) %>%
    group_by(interval60) %>%
    summarize(Temp = max(tmpf),
              Percip = sum(p01i),
              Wind = max(sknt)) %>%
    mutate(Temp = ifelse(Temp == 0, 42, Temp))

grid.arrange(top = "Weather Data - Chicago - Nov. & Dec., 2018",
  ggplot(weather.Panel, aes(interval60,Percip)) + geom_line(),
  ggplot(weather.Panel, aes(interval60,Wind)) + geom_line(),
  ggplot(weather.Panel, aes(interval60,Temp)) + geom_line())
```

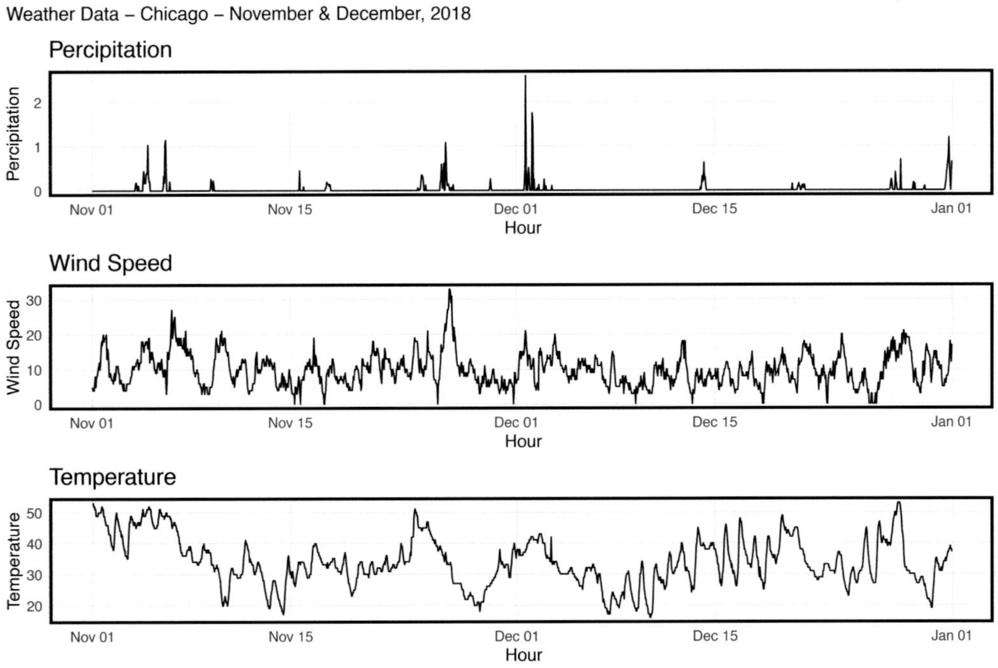

FIGURE 8.1 Percipitation, wind speed, and temperature data for November through December, 2018.

8.2.3 Subset a study area using neighborhoods

A rideshare forecast for every Cook County tract, for every hour, for 8 weeks, would yield a time/space panel (data frame) consisting of `nrow(chicagoTracts) * 24 * 7 * 8 =`

1,771,392 rows. A regression that size will melt your laptop. Instead, 201 census tracts are subset across Chicago's downtown, the Loop, up through Wrigleyville and Lincoln Square.

The following code block pulls all tract geometries from the `tigris` package, loads a neighborhood geojson and subsets those found in a `neighborhoodList`. `st_intersection` then finds `studyArea.tracts`. Figure 8.2 maps `studyArea.tracts` relative to `chicagoTracts`.

```
chicagoTracts <-
  tigris::tracts(state = "Illinois", county = "Cook") %>%
  dplyr::select(GEOID) %>% filter(GEOID != 17031990000)

neighborhoodList <-
  c("Grant Park","Printers Row","Loop","Millenium Park",
    "West Loop","United Center","West Town","East Village",
    "Ukranian Village","Wicker Park","River North",
    "Rush & Division","Streeterville","Gold Coast","Old Town",
    "Bucktown","Lincoln Park","Sheffield & DePaul","Lake View",
    "Boystown","Wrigleyville","North Center","Uptown",
    "Lincoln Square","Little Italy, UIC")

nhoods <-
  st_read(
    paste0("https://data.cityofchicago.org/api/geospatial/",
           "bbvz-uum9?method=export&format=GeoJSON")) %>%
  st_transform(st_crs(chicagoTracts)) %>%
  filter(pri_neigh %in% neighborhoodList)

studyArea.tracts <-
  st_intersection(chicagoTracts, st_union(nhoods))
```

Study Area Tracts

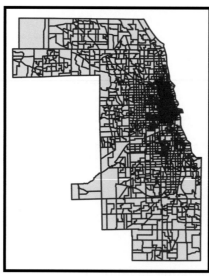

FIGURE 8.2 Tracts located near Chicago's downtown are selected to be in the study.

8.2.4 Create the final space/time panel

The dataset for this analysis must be a complete panel with an observation for every possible space/time combination. The `ride2` data frame is incomplete as some space/time intervals saw no trips. In the following code blocks, the panel is completed by finding all unique space/time intervals and inserting 0 trips where necessary. Additional feature engineering is also performed.

The complete `study.panel` includes 8 weeks of rideshare trips. How many total space/time combinations exist over 8 weeks? 24 hours a day * 7 days a week * 8 weeks = 1,344 possible time units. That multiplied by 201 tracts in `studyArea.tracts` = 270,144 unique space/time units. Thus, the final data frame must also have precisely this many rows.

The first step is `ride.template` which `filters` for the 8 weeks of interest and uses `semi_join` to return only those trips in the `studyArea.tracts`. A quick calculation shows `ride.template` captures all the needed `unique` space/time units.

```
ride.template <-
  filter(ride2, week %in% c(45:52)) %>%
  semi_join(st_drop_geometry(studyArea.tracts),
            by = c("Pickup.Census.Tract" = "GEOID"))

length(unique(ride.template$interval60)) *
  length(unique(ride.template$Pickup.Census.Tract))
```

```
## [1] 270144
```

An empty data frame, `study.panel`, is then created with the complete space/time panel. This is done using the `expand.grid` function and `unique`. `nrow` shows that the space/time count is still correct.

```
study.panel <-
  expand.grid(
    interval60 = unique(ride.template$interval60),
    Pickup.Census.Tract =
      unique(ride.template$Pickup.Census.Tract))

nrow(study.panel)
```

```
## [1] 270144
```

The final `ride.panel` is created by merging space/time intervals from actual trips in `ride.template` with intervals that saw no trips in `study.panel`.

A `Trip_Counter` is created in `ride.template` giving 1 for each trip. `right_join` then returns *non-trip* space/time intervals from `study.panel`. If a trip occurred at a given interval, `Trip_Counter` returns 1, otherwise `NA`. Trips are then grouped by each space/time interval and `Trip_Count` is set equal to the `sum` of `Trip_Counter`. `na.rm = T` prevents `sum` from returning `NA`.

Next, the `weather.Panel` and `studyArea.tracts` are joined to provide weather and geometry information, respectively. Finally, features denoting week and day of the week are created with `lubridate`.

The output is a complete panel. Note that `nrow(ride.template) ==` `sum(ride.panel$Trip_Count) == TRUE`.

```
ride.panel <-
  ride.template %>%
    mutate(Trip_Counter = 1) %>%
    right_join(study.panel) %>%
      group_by(interval60, Pickup.Census.Tract) %>%
      summarize(Trip_Count = sum(Trip_Counter, na.rm=T)) %>%
      left_join(weather.Panel, by = "interval60") %>%
        left_join(studyArea.tracts,
                    by = c("Pickup.Census.Tract" = "GEOID")) %>%
          mutate(week = week(interval60),
                  dotw = wday(interval60, label = TRUE)) %>%
            st_sf()
```

To test for serial (temporal) correlation, additional feature engineering creates time lags. `arrange` sorts the data by space then time; `group_by` groups by tract, and `lag` returns the Trip-Count for the previous *nth* time period.

```
ride.panel <-
  ride.panel %>%
    arrange(Pickup.Census.Tract, interval60) %>%
    group_by(Pickup.Census.Tract) %>%
    mutate(lagHour = dplyr::lag(Trip_Count,1),
            lag2Hours = dplyr::lag(Trip_Count,2),
            lag3Hours = dplyr::lag(Trip_Count,3),
            lag4Hours = dplyr::lag(Trip_Count,4),
            lag12Hours = dplyr::lag(Trip_Count,12),
            lag1day = dplyr::lag(Trip_Count,24)) %>%
  ungroup()

as.data.frame(filter(
    ride.panel, Pickup.Census.Tract ==
      "17031831900"))[1:6, c(1,3,10:11)]
```

```
##               interval60 Trip_Count lagHour lag2Hours
## 1 2018-11-05 00:00:00           2      NA        NA
## 2 2018-11-05 01:00:00           2       2        NA
## 3 2018-11-05 02:00:00           0       2         2
## 4 2018-11-05 03:00:00           0       0         2
## 5 2018-11-05 04:00:00           0       0         0
## 6 2018-11-05 05:00:00           3       0         0
```

8.2.5   Split training and test

How might generalizability be tested for in this use case? Random k-fold cross-validation or spatial cross-validation (Section 5.5.1) both seem reasonable. LOGO-CV could even be used to cross-validate in time, across hours, days, or days of the week.

Here, a time series approach is taken, training on 5 weeks of data, weeks 45-49, and testing on the following 3 weeks, 50-52. If the time/space experience is generalizable, it can be used to project into the near future. The next code block splits the data by `week`.

```
ride.Train <- filter(ride.panel, week < 50)
ride.Test <- filter(ride.panel, week >= 50)
```

8.2.6   What about distance features?

Why not measure exposure or distance to points of interest, as we have in previous chapters? It seems reasonable for instance, that rideshare trips would decline as distance to subway stations decline, as riders trade-off car trips for transit. Why not account for this? Check out Table 8.2.

time	tract	Distance_to_subway	Trip_Count
1	1	200	10
2	1	200	13
3	1	200	18
4	1	200	22
5	1	200	24
1	2	1890	45
2	2	1890	62
3	2	1890	89
4	2	1890	91
5	2	1890	100

TABLE 8.2 Number of trips by distance and tract over time.

The first two columns in the table are examples of a short, 2 space/time interval panel. Note the similarity between `Distance_to_subway` and `tract` and note the coefficient on `Distance_to_subway` when it is included in a regression with `time` and `tract`.

The missing coefficient reflects the fact that `Distance_to_Subway` is perfectly colinear with `tract`. The lesson is that these exposure variables are not needed for panel data, when `Pickup.Census.Tract` is controlled for directly. It may be hard to conceptualize, but controlling for tract-level variation in part, controls exposure to points of interest.

8.3   Exploratory Analysis - Rideshare

In this section, the rideshare data is explored for time, space, weather, and demographic relationships. Sections 8.3.1 and 8.3.2 illustrate temporal and spatial trends, respectively, while Section 8.3.3 creates a space/time animation. Finally, Section 8.3.4 explores correlations with weather.

	Trip_Count
time	8.800*** (2.248)
tract	60.000*** (6.359)
Distance_to_subway	
Constant	−69.000*** (12.107)
N	10
R^2	0.937
Adjusted R^2	0.919
Residual Std. Error	10.054 (df = 7)
F Statistic	52.178*** (df = 2; 7)

*p < .1; **p < .05; ***p < .01

TABLE 8.3 Colinear Regression

8.3.1 Trip_Count serial autocorrelation

Should `Trip_Count` exhibit serial (temporal) correlation, then the time lag features will lead to better predictions. Several tests are conducted below, beginning with a time series visualization (Figure 8.3). `geom_vline` is used to visualize `mondays` as well as Thanksgiving and Christmas (dotted lines).

There are some interesting trends to note. Most weeks exhibit remarkably comparable time series patterns with consistent peaks and troughs. This suggests the presence of serial correlation. Weeks surrounding Thanksgiving and Christmas appear as clear outliers, however.

```
mondays <-
  mutate(ride.panel,
         monday = ifelse(dotw == "Mon" & hour(interval60) == 1,
                         interval60, 0)) %>%
  filter(monday != 0)

tg   <- as.POSIXct("2018-11-22 01:00:00 UTC")
xmas <- as.POSIXct("2018-12-24 01:00:00 UTC")

st_drop_geometry(rbind(
  mutate(ride.Train, Legend = "Training"),
  mutate(ride.Test, Legend = "Testing"))) %>%
  group_by(Legend, interval60) %>%
  summarize(Trip_Count = sum(Trip_Count)) %>%
  ungroup() %>%
    ggplot(aes(interval60, Trip_Count, colour = Legend)) +
      geom_line() +
      scale_colour_manual(values = palette2) +
      geom_vline(xintercept = tg, linetype = "dotted") +
      geom_vline(xintercept = xmas, linetype = "dotted") +
      geom_vline(data = mondays, aes(xintercept = monday)) +
      labs(
        title="Rideshare trips by week: November-December",
        subtitle="Dotted lines for Thanksgiving & Christmas",
```

```
        x="Day", y="Trip Count") +
    plotTheme() + theme(panel.grid.major = element_blank())
```

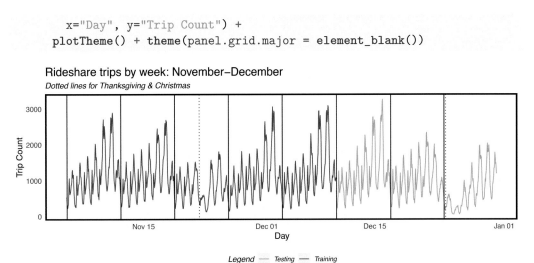

FIGURE 8.3 How rideshare trips fluctuate over the week for an 8-week period.

Next, the time `lag` features are tested for correlation with `Trip_Count`. `plotData.lag` returns the `Trip_Count` and time lag features for week 45. `fct_relevel` reorders the lag levels. Omit that line and try `levels(plotData.lag$Variable)`.

Pearson correlation is then calculated for each `Variable` in `correlation.lag`.

```
plotData.lag <-
  filter(as.data.frame(ride.panel), week == 45) %>%
  dplyr::select(starts_with("lag"), Trip_Count) %>%
  gather(Variable, Value, -Trip_Count) %>%
  mutate(Variable = fct_relevel(Variable,
          "lagHour","lag2Hours","lag3Hours",
          "lag4Hours","lag12Hours","lag1day"))
correlation.lag <-
  group_by(plotData.lag, Variable) %>%
    summarize(correlation = round(cor(Value, Trip_Count,
                                use = "complete.obs"), 2))
```

The very strong `Trip_Count` correlations are visualized in Figure 8.4. Note that the correlation decreases with each additional lag hour, but predictive power returns with the 1-day lag. These features should be strong predictors in a model. See Section 5.4.1 to overlay correlation coefficients in a `ggplot`.

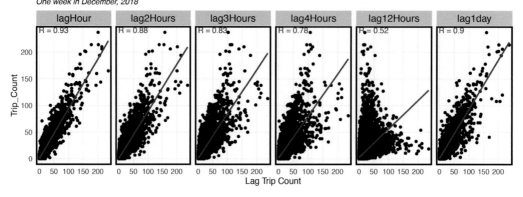

FIGURE 8.4 The relationship between number of rideshare trips and time lags.

8.3.2 `Trip_Count` spatial autocorrelation

rideshare exhibits strong temporal correlation, but how about spatial autocorrelation? Figures 8.5 and 8.6 map tract `Trip_Count` sums by week and by day of the week, respectively. Sum is chosen over mean here to avoid tract/time pairs with 0 counts. Even during the holidays, the spatial pattern appears consistent, with trips concentrated in Chicago's central business district, The Loop (southeastern portion of the study area).

Note the `q5` function is used to map quintile breaks, but a list of `labels` are fed to `scale_fill_manual`. Set the data wrangling portion of the next code block to a `temp.df` and run `qBr(temp.df, "Sum_Trip_Count")` to get the breaks.

```
group_by(ride.panel, week, Pickup.Census.Tract) %>%
  summarize(Sum_Trip_Count = sum(Trip_Count)) %>%
  ungroup() %>%
  ggplot() + geom_sf(aes(fill = q5(Sum_Trip_Count))) +
    facet_wrap(~week, ncol = 8) +
    scale_fill_manual(
      values = palette5,
      labels = c("16", "140", "304", "530", "958"),
      name = "Trip_Count") +
    labs(title="Sum of rideshare trips by tract and week") +
    mapTheme() + theme(legend.position = "bottom")
```

Sum of rideshare trips by tract and week

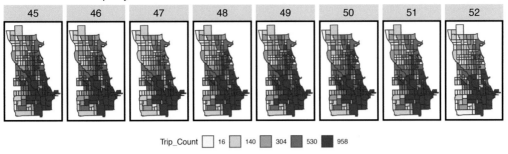

FIGURE 8.5 The number of rideshare trips in study area tracts for each week in the study time period.

Sum of rideshare trips by tract and day of the week

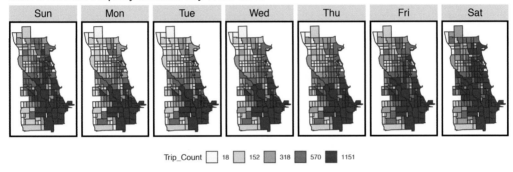

FIGURE 8.6 The number of rideshare trips in study area tracts for each day of the week.

Finally, spatial autocorrelation is tested for by visualizing spatial lag correlations (Section 4.2) in Figure 8.7. A queen contiguity spatial weights matrix (Section 5.4) relates tract t to adjacent tracts. 'First order contiguity' refers to those tracts that touch tract t. 'Second order' refers to the tracts that touch those tracts, etc.

This code is a bit verbose and thus withheld. These features will not be used in the model, but the resulting plot does show that there is strong spatial autocorrelation in rideshare.

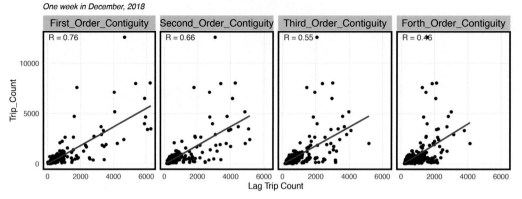

FIGURE 8.7 The relationship between number of rideshare trips and spatial lags for one week in December 2018.

8.3.3   Space/time correlation?

Rideshare in Chicago exhibits very strong space/time dependencies, so why not visualize both together? The `gganimate` package is used to build an animated gif map of rideshare trips over space and time. Here, the 15 minute intervals, `interval15`, are used from a single Monday in `week45.panel`. Tract geometries are pulled from `ride2`.

```
week45 <-
  filter(ride2 , week == 45 & dotw == "Mon")

week45.panel <-
  expand.grid(
    interval15 = unique(week45$interval15),
    Pickup.Census.Tract = unique(ride2$Pickup.Census.Tract))
```

A `ride.animation.data` panel is created following the same routine as Section 8.2.4 above. Recall, we are using a 20% sample of the data, so the actual number of trips is much higher. Nevertheless, the space/time pattern emanating outward from the Loop is apparent. Note again, the use of `fct_relevel`.

```
ride.animation.data <-
  mutate(week45, Trip_Counter = 1) %>%
  right_join(week45.panel) %>%
  group_by(interval15, Pickup.Census.Tract) %>%
  summarize(Trip_Count = sum(Trip_Counter, na.rm=T)) %>%
    ungroup() %>%
    left_join(chicagoTracts,
              by=c("Pickup.Census.Tract" = "GEOID")) %>%
    st_sf() %>%
    mutate(Trips =
      case_when(
        Trip_Count == 0 ~ "0 trips",
        Trip_Count > 0 & Trip_Count <= 3 ~ "1-3 trips",
        Trip_Count > 3 & Trip_Count <= 6 ~ "4-6 trips",
        Trip_Count > 6 & Trip_Count <= 10 ~ "7-10 trips",
```

```
        Trip_Count > 10 ~ "11+ trips")) %>%
  mutate(Trips = fct_relevel(Trips,
                  "0 trips","1-3 trips","4-6 trips",
                  "7-10 trips","10+ trips"))
```

The animation object is created next. Install and load the `gifski` package. `transition_manual` is set to `interval15` to suggest a new map be generated for each 15-minute interval. `animate` creates the gif, setting `duration` to ensure that the entire animation lasts only 20 seconds.

```
rideshare_animation <-
  ggplot() +
    geom_sf(data = ride.animation.data, aes(fill = Trips)) +
    scale_fill_manual(values = palette5) +
    labs(title ="Rideshare pickups for one day in November 2018",
         subtitle = "15 minute intervals: {current_frame}") +
    transition_manual(interval15) +
    mapTheme()
```

The animation can then be created with the following code block.

```
animate(rideshare_animation, duration=20,
        renderer = gifski_renderer())
```

One can also use this code to write the animated gif to the local machine.

```
anim_save("rideshare_local", rideshare_animation, duration=20,
          renderer = gifski_renderer())
```

8.3.4   Weather

`ride.panel` includes three weather-related variables. Figure 8.8 removes the spatial variation and creates a dummy variable, `isPercip`, to ask whether precipitation effects mean `Trip_Count`. There appears to be little effect.

```
st_drop_geometry(ride.panel) %>%
  group_by(interval60) %>%
  summarize(Trip_Count = mean(Trip_Count),
            Percipitation = first(Percipitation)) %>%
  mutate(isPercip = ifelse(Percipitation > 0,
                           "Rain/Snow", "None")) %>%
  group_by(isPercip) %>%
  summarize(Mean_Trip_Count = mean(Trip_Count)) %>%
    ggplot(aes(isPercip, Mean_Trip_Count)) +
      geom_bar(stat = "identity") +
      labs(title="Does ridership vary with percipitation?",
           x="Percipitation", y="Mean Trip Count") +
      plotTheme()
```

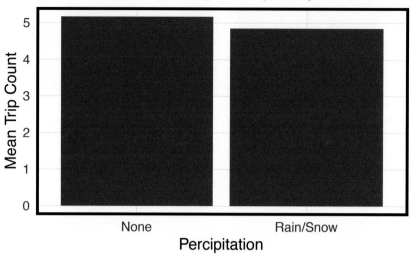

FIGURE 8.8 Percipitation appears to have little effect on rideshare trips.

Do more people take rideshare when it is colder? In Figure 8.9, `Trip_Count` is plotted as a function of `Temp` by `week`. These plots suggest the opposite - that in most weeks, rideshare increases as temps warm. If that sounds strange for November and December, it is because this correlation is 'spurious'.

A key relationship has been omitted - namely that both temperature and rideshare increase with the hour of the day. Temperature may still be an important predictor, but only when time is controlled for. A couple of quick regressions can illustrate this point. Regressing `Trip_Count` as a function of `Temp`, estimates that a 1 degree increase in temps leads to a 5.54 increase in trips.

When hourly fixed effects are added to the regression, the model suggests a 1 degree increase in temps leads to a -7.47 *decrease* in `Trip_Count`. This is what we'd expect - that all else equal, as temperature increases, travelers are less likely to take rideshare versus, say walking.

```
st_drop_geometry(ride.panel) %>%
  group_by(interval60) %>%
  summarize(Trip_Count = mean(Trip_Count),
            Temp = first(Temp)) %>%
  mutate(week = week(interval60)) %>%
  ggplot(aes(Temp, Trip_Count)) +
    geom_point() + geom_smooth(method = "lm", se= FALSE) +
    facet_wrap(~week, ncol=8) +
    labs(title="Trip Count as a fuction of Temperature by week",
        x="Temperature", y="Mean Trip Count") +
    plotTheme()
```

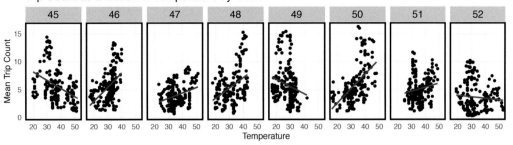

FIGURE 8.9 The relationship between temperature and rideshare trips.

8.4 Modeling and validation using `purrr::map`

In this section, models are estimated from `ride.Train` and tested on `ride.Test` to gauge how well the space/time features forecast rideshare demand. The `purrr` family of functions will be used to loop through a set of 'nested' data frames to efficiently compare across different model specifications. This functionality is very powerful, and programmatically, is a step up from the `tidy` used thus far.

8.4.1 A short primer on nested `tibbles`

Let's return to the example space/time panel created above, `colinear_df`, by re-engineering this data frame as a nested `tibble`. A `tibble` is a like a data frame with more bells and whistles. In the following code block, `colinear_df` is converted `as.tibble`. `nest` then embeds 5 separate tibbles in `colinear_nested`, delineated by `time`. This gives a tibble of tibbles.

```
colinear_nested <- nest(as.tibble(colinear_df), -time)
colinear_nested
```

```
## # A tibble: 5 x 2
##    time data
##   <dbl> <list>
## 1     1 <tibble [2 x 3]>
## 2     2 <tibble [2 x 3]>
## 3     3 <tibble [2 x 3]>
## 4     4 <tibble [2 x 3]>
## 5     5 <tibble [2 x 3]>
```

Nesting allows one to split and wrangle data in all sorts of interesting ways. Any nested `tibble` can be `unnested` with:

```
unnest(colinear_nested[1,2])
```

```
## # A tibble: 2 x 3
##    tract Distance_to_subway Trip_Count
##    <dbl>              <dbl>      <dbl>
## 1      1                200         10
## 2      2               1890         45
```

8.4.2   Estimate a rideshare forecast

In this section, four different Linear regressions are estimated on `ride.Train`, each with different fixed effects:

1. `reg1` focuses on just time, including hour fixed effects, day of the week, and `Temp`.
2. `reg2` focuses on just space effects with the `Pickup.Census.Tract` fixed effects.
3. `reg3` includes both time and space fixed effects.
4. `reg4` adds the time `lag` features.

Time features like `hour` could be modeled as either a continuous or categorical feature. As a continuous feature, the interpretation is that a 1 `hour` increase is associated with an estimated change in `Trip_Count`. As a factor, the interpretation is that there are significant differences in `Trip_Count` by hour. Both options can be explored, but in the next code block, the latter is chosen.

Spatial fixed effects for `Pickup.Census.Tract` are also included to account for the across-tract differences, like amenities, access to transit, distance to the Loop, etc.

Ordinary least squares (OLS) is chosen, despite `Trip_Count` being a count variable. Poisson is an option, but the counts are sufficiently large to feel at ease with OLS. Not surprisingly, the best choice of algorithm is that which leads to the most accurate and generalizable model.

```
reg1 <- lm(Trip_Count ~
             hour(interval60) + dotw + Temp,
             data=ride.Train)

reg2 <- lm(Trip_Count ~
             Pickup.Census.Tract + dotw + Temp,
             data=ride.Train)

reg3 <- lm(Trip_Count ~
             Pickup.Census.Tract + hour(interval60) + dotw +
             Temp, data=ride.Train)

reg4 <- lm(Trip_Count ~
             Pickup.Census.Tract +  hour(interval60) + dotw +
             Temp + lagHour + lag2Hours + lag3Hours +
             lag12Hours + lag1day,
             data=ride.Train)
```

8.4.3   Validate test set by time

In this section, mean absolute error (MAE) is calculated on `ride.Test` for each model. `ride.Test` includes three weeks and is highly influenced by the Christmas holiday. To understand if models generalize to the holiday and non-holiday weeks, `ride.Test.weekNest` nests `ride.Test` by week. Note that the `data` field contains three sf tibbles (with geometries), and `unnest(ride.Test.weekNest[1,2])` returns one week's worth of simple features data.

```
ride.Test.weekNest <-
  as.data.frame(ride.Test) %>%
  nest(-week)
```

```
ride.Test.weekNest
```

```
## # A tibble: 3 x 2
##     week data
##    <dbl> <list>
## 1     50 <tibble [33,768 x 14]>
## 2     51 <tibble [33,768 x 14]>
## 3     52 <tibble [33,768 x 14]>
```

Next, a small function is created that takes a tibble, `dat` and a regression model, `fit` as its inputs, and outputs predictions as `pred`. This function is used to predict for each week in `ride.Trest.weekNest`.

```
model_pred <- function(dat, fit){
   pred <- predict(fit, newdata = dat)}
```

The nested format allows one to loop through each model for each week and `mutate` summary statistics. In the following code block, `week_predictions` are calculated for each week in `ride.Test`. The `map` function applies the `model_pred` function to each nested tibble.

Look at `mutate` in the next code block, for example. A new column, `Time_FE`, includes predictions for `reg1` - the time fixed effects model. The predictions are created by `mapping` the function, `model_pred`, to each row of `data`, parameterizing `fit` as the `reg1` model.

```
week_predictions <-
  ride.Test.weekNest %>%
    mutate(
      A_Time_FE = map(.x = data, fit = reg1, .f = model_pred),
      B_Space_FE = map(.x = data, fit = reg2, .f = model_pred),
      C_Space_Time_FE = map(.x = data, fit = reg3,
                            .f = model_pred),
      D_Space_Time_Lags = map(.x = data, fit = reg4,
                              .f = model_pred))
```

```
week_predictions[1:3, 1:4]
```

```
## # A tibble: 3 x 4
##    week data                     A_Time_FE      B_Space_FE
##    <dbl> <list>                  <list>         <list>
## 1     50 <tibble [33,768 x 14]> <dbl [33,768]> <dbl [33,768]>
## 2     51 <tibble [33,768 x 14]> <dbl [33,768]> <dbl [33,768]>
## 3     52 <tibble [33,768 x 14]> <dbl [33,768]> <dbl [33,768]>
```

The output shows that each new column is a `list` of predictions for each model by week. Once columns are moved to long form with `gather`, four new columns are generated in the next code block.

`Observed` is the actual space/time `Trip_Count` for that week, created by looping through (map) each nested tibble in the `data` field and pulling `Trip_Count`. `Absolute_Error` is created with `map2`, which maps over two inputs. In this case, `Observed` and `Prediction` are fed into a function (~) that calculates the absolute value of their difference.

To calculate MAE, `map_dbl`, a variant of `map`, is used to loop through `Absolute_Error`, calculating the `mean`. The same function calculates the standard deviation of absolute error, `sd_AE`, which is a useful measure of generalizability.

```
week_predictions <- week_predictions %>%
    gather(Regression, Prediction, -data, -week) %>%
    mutate(Observed = map(data, pull, Trip_Count),
           Absolute_Error = map2(Observed, Prediction,
                                 ~ abs(.x - .y)),
           MAE = map_dbl(Absolute_Error, mean),
           sd_AE = map_dbl(Absolute_Error, sd))
```

The resulting data frame shows goodness of fit by week and model. The MAE for the time effects model (`reg1`) in week 50 is comparable to the mean observed `Trip_Count` of 5.86. However, with increasing sophistication, the model becomes more accurate and more generalizable.

This nested framework makes it easy to plot MAE by model by week, as follows Both the spatial fixed effects and time lags add significant predictive power.

```
week_predictions %>%
  dplyr::select(week, Regression, MAE) %>%
  gather(Variable, MAE, -Regression, -week) %>%
  ggplot(aes(week, MAE)) +
    geom_bar(aes(fill = Regression),
             position = "dodge", stat="identity") +
    scale_fill_manual(values = palette5) +
    labs(title = "Mean Absolute Errors by model and week") +
  plotTheme()
```

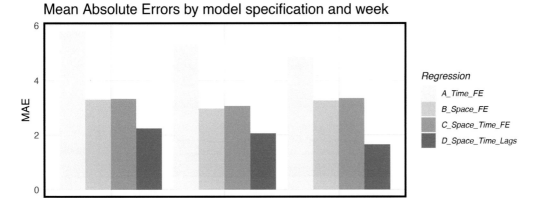

FIGURE 8.10 Model errors for each model, for each week.

For each model, predicted and observed `Trip_Count` is taken out of the spatial context and their means plotted in time series form in Figure 8.11. Models `A` and `C` appear to have the same time trend because again, the spatial context has been removed.

With more sophistication comes the ability to predict for the highest peaks, and the time lags help make this happen. The time series does show that the model over-predicts trips for some of the days around Christmas. This may be because the training data suggests more trips should otherwise occur during those times.

```
week_predictions %>%
  mutate(interval60 = map(data, pull, interval60),
         Pickup.Census.Tract =
           map(data, pull, Pickup.Census.Tract)) %>%
  dplyr::select(interval60, Pickup.Census.Tract,
                Observed, Prediction, Regression) %>%
  unnest() %>%
  gather(Variable, Value, -Regression, -interval60,
         -Pickup.Census.Tract) %>%
    group_by(Regression, Variable, interval60) %>%
    summarize(Value = mean(Value)) %>%
    ggplot(aes(interval60, Value, colour=Variable)) +
      geom_line(size = 1.1) +
      facet_wrap(~Regression, ncol=1) +
      scale_colour_manual(values = palette2) +
      labs(
        title = "Mean Predicted/Observed rideshare by hour",
        x = "Hour", y= "Rideshare Trips") +
      plotTheme()
```

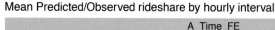

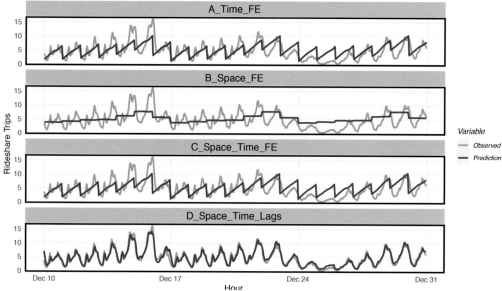

FIGURE 8.11 Average number of predicted versus observed rideshare trips per hour over 3 weeks.

8.4.4   Validate test set by space

```
error.byWeek <-
  filter(week_predictions, Regression == "D_Space_Time_Lags") %>%
  unnest() %>% st_sf() %>%
  dplyr::select(Pickup.Census.Tract, Absolute_Error,
                week, geometry) %>%
  gather(Variable, Value, -Pickup.Census.Tract,
         -week, -geometry) %>%
    group_by(Variable, Pickup.Census.Tract, week) %>%
    summarize(MAE = mean(Value))
```

MAE by tract by week

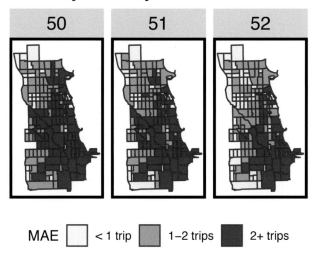

FIGURE 8.12 Average errors by census track for each week.

MAE for `reg4` is mapped in Figure 8.12, by `unnesting` it from `week_predictions`. Errors for all time periods are averaged by `Pickup.Census.Tract` and `week`. The highest errors are in the Loop where more trips occur, and there are some interesting error patterns along arterial routes running west and north from downtown.

MAE is then mapped by hour for Monday of the 50th week in Figure 8.13. Errors cluster in the Loop but are otherwise distributed throughout. Each map in Figure 8.13 could be tested for spatial autocorrelation, which may suggest the addition of new features. Given the use case, however, is there an incentive to have a really generalizable model?

We have been weary of geospatial machine learning models with errors that vary systematically across space. In other uses cases, the concern was that these differences could drive disparate impact. Do rideshare companies have an incentive to be fair in the communities they serve? Could errors in this model be driven by selection bias in the training data?

It is possible that rideshare drivers select in to neighborhoods based on passenger perception but what incentive do rideshare companies have to ensure that everyone who wants a ride gets one?

```
error.byHour <-
  filter(week_predictions, Regression == "D_Space_Time_Lags") %>%
    unnest() %>%
    st_sf() %>%
    dplyr::select(Pickup.Census.Tract, Absolute_Error,
                  geometry, interval60) %>%
    gather(Variable, Value, -interval60,
           -Pickup.Census.Tract, -geometry) %>%
    filter(wday(interval60, label = TRUE) == "Mon" &
             week(interval60) == 50) %>%
    group_by(hour = hour(interval60), Pickup.Census.Tract) %>%
    summarize(MAE = mean(Value))
```

Mean absolute trip count error by tract and hour
For the Monday of Week 50

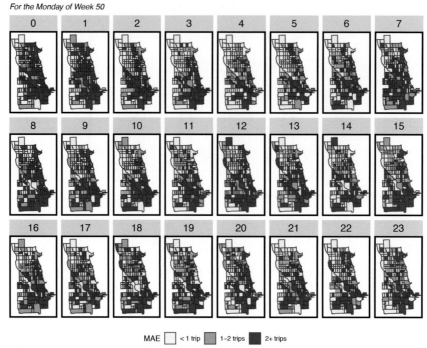

FIGURE 8.13 Trip count error by census tract for every hour on the Monday of week 50.

8.5   Conclusion - Dispatch

Why does our model predict so well?

It is rare that linear models have such small errors, but in this case, the time lag features are very strong predictors. These very high-resolution time lags can reasonably be included because the dispatch use case allows for near real time predictions - like the next hour. Many temporal forecasts have much longer time horizons.

Unlike previous chapters, no cross-validation was performed, and thus, it is possible that our model is not actually as useful as the results suggest. Random k-fold or spatial cross-validation are options. One might also cross-validate by hour, day of the week or some other time unit to understand how well our model generalizes across time. Space/time cross-validation is also possible.

A dispatch algorithm

Uber's Marketplace Algorithm is an example of how Uber uses space/time forecasting to reduce response times, save mone,y and maybe even lower automobile congestion. How can Uber be sure that a given algorithm is optimized for these bottom lines?

Rideshare companies take many thousands of trips every day. To find the optimal approach, imagine randomly allocating two or more dispatch algorithms across 1000 Chicago drivers over the course of a week. Such a randomized control trial, or what tech companies sometimes call 'A/B testing', could help reveal the most optimal algorithm.

What about the public sector use of this algorithm?

What space/time prediction problems might public sector data scientists wrestle with? Any public or private entity that needs to 'rebalance' an asset, like bike share bikes or personal scooters, would benefit from understanding near future demand. Public parking authorities could maximize parking ticket revenues by allocating patrols to time/space units predicted to have illegal parkers. Emergency management offices can use metrics like this to strategically place ambulances to reduce response times. Finally, this is an obvious extension to the predictive policing use case discussed in Chapter 5, which would allocate police cruisers in space and time.

8.6 Assignment - Predict bike share trips

One of the most difficult operational problems for urban bike share systems is the need to 're-balance' bicycles across the network. Bike share is not useful if a dock has no bikes to pick up, nor if there are no open docking spaces to deposit a bike. Re-balancing is the practice of anticipating (or predicting) bike share demand for all docks at all times and manually redistributing bikes to ensure a bike or a docking place is available when needed.

In this assignment, you will pick a city with a bike share open data feed and forecast space/time demand for bike share pickups. Most bike share data has fields for origin, destination, and date/time.

Envision a bike re-balancing plan and design an algorithm to inform such a plan. The deliverables include:

1. Two to three paragraphs that introduce the reader to bike share and the need for re-balancing. How will re-balancing occur? Perhaps you will manage a small fleet of trucks to move bikes from here to there or perhaps you will offer rewards, discounts, or other incentives for riders to move a bike from place to place. *Keep in mind*, your plan will inform the appropriate time lag features you can use. How far forward do you wish to predict for at any given time?

2. Your unit of analysis here is the bike share station, not census tract. Engineer features to account for weather and time effects and experiment with some amenity/exposure features as well. Develop two different training/test sets including 1) a 3-week training set and a 2-week test set of all the stations and 2) a complete 5-week panel for cross-validation.

3. Develop exploratory analysis plots that describe the space/time dependencies in the data and create an animated map. Interpret your findings in the context of the re-balancing plan.

4. Use `purrr` to train and validate several models for comparison on the latter 2-week test set. Perform either random k-fold cross-validation or LOGO-CV on the 5-week panel. You may choose to cross validate by time or space. Interpret your findings in the context of accuracy and generalizability.

5. Conclude with how useful your algorithm is for the bike re-balancing plan.

Conclusion - Algorithmic Governance

In these last few pages, I would like to conclude by considering how some of the key themes of this book pertain to the future of public-sector data science.

The most critical is the importance of evidenced-based decision-making in government. While the evidenced-based approach is now celebrated far and wide, most of its support comes from the program evaluation community. Evaluation is absolutely critical and can actually compliment prediction, but at times, some researchers get defensive at the role of machine learning in this movement.

Their beef typically reflects one of two concerns. First, that the data scientist with little domain expertise should not attempt meaningful policy prescriptions from hastily prepared maps or regressions. Second, that machine learning is useless because it is not driven by theory.

To the first point - I too am weary of computer scientists, physicists, and other engineers who are drawn to complex urban systems but may lack domain expertise. There are some use cases where an engineer can have an impact - like counting cars from satellite imagery or forecasting ride-share demand, even. However, when social costs and benefits are present, more public policy context is required.

Having said that, data science is a new and exciting field and many young people are eager to learn how these skills can be used to have impact. If this is you, it is with great enthusiasm that I urge you to experiment, learn, and have fun.

The world is full of gatekeepers - forget them. Be curious, make mistakes and problem solve - just know that most problems are more complex than the solution from your weekend hackathon project. Go talk to a domain expert or a policy maker; learn about the business-as-usual approach; and consider the relevant costs and benefits.

To the second point on machine learning driven not by theory: In 2008, *Wired Magazine* published, 'The End of Theory: The Data Deluge Makes the Scientific Method Obsolete,'[4] claiming:

> This is a world where massive amounts of data and applied mathematics replace every other tool that might be brought to bear. Out with every theory of human behavior, from linguistics to sociology. Forget taxonomy, ontology, and psychology. Who knows why people do what they do? The point is they do it, and we can track and measure it with unprecedented fidelity. With enough data, the numbers speak for themselves.

Rightfully, this idea generated tremendous backlash from academics who generate evidence by testing theory. One critique was that machine learning models are based on correlation not causation, and while the latter requires theory, the former does not.

---

[4] Anderson, Chris (2008). The End of Theory: The Data Deluge Makes the Scientific Method Obsolete. Wired Magazine. https://www.wired.com/2008/06/pb-theory/

A bad causal model suffers from selection bias and sample bias and is ultimately just as useless as a bad machine learning model. A machine learning model is based on correlation, but if it leads to a better cost/benefit and allocates resources without disparate impact, then it may be useful.

This book has taught you how to develop and evaluate algorithms with these outcomes in mind. The *theory* that we have learned here is not statistical theory, but decision theory. Hence the first sentence of the book, which reads, 'At its core, this book is about public-sector decision-making'. I hope you agree that machine learning has a role to play in evidence-based policy.

Why has government been slow to adopt data science relative to the private sector? It could be that policymakers fear disparate impact, or that the technology is too intimidating, and the bureaucratic hurdles too great. While these are valid issues, consider that algorithms force agencies to look inward on their own business-as-usual decision-making. Government may be worried that shining this light will reveal programs that are currently ineffective.

An algorithm will not make a bad program effective, but it may improve a good one at the margins. Developing strong programs complemented by useful algorithms requires a comprehensive planning approach. It requires what I call, 'algorithmic governance'.

In 2017, New York City established a first of its kind, Automated Decision Systems Task Force, to examine how city agencies were using algorithms to allocate resources.[5] By the spring of 2019, the task force began publicly complaining that not a single NYC agency had to date, been transparent about their algorithms.[6]

In the fall of 2020, the task force issued a watered-down final report with half of its 36 pages dedicated to member bios, thank-yous, and other info besides policy recommendations.[7] The effort was largely a failure, and it took the George Floyd protests to force meaningful reform, for at least one agency. The POST act, now requires the New York City Police Department (NYPD) to publish surveillance technology usage policies and give communities and City Council the opportunity for comment.[8]

What incentives might NYPD have for not being transparent by default, about their algorithms? Of all the reasons listed above, let's again consider the possibility that the programs informed by those algorithms may not be effective crime deterrents to begin with.

Algorithmic governance starts with the evaluation of an existing program to understand its efficacy, as well as its costs and benefits. Next, communities are engaged on the program, its objectives, its value, as judged by the evaluation, and are also engaged in a a proposal for using data and algorithms to make the program more effective. This includes information on whether the algorithm will be created in-house or procured from a private vendo; where the training data comes from; tests for fairness and more.

Community engagement is the foundation of algorithmic governance. It is how governments and their citizens agree to 'community standards', as discussed at the end of Chapter 5. It gives them the opportunity to understand the value of trading off automation with better

[5] Kirchner, Lauren (2017). New York City Moves to Create Accountability for Algorithms. ProPublica. https://www.propublica.org/article/new-york-city-moves-to-create-accountability-for-algorithms

[6] Lecher, Colin (2019). New York City's algorithm task force is fracturing. The Verge. https://www.theverge.com/2019/4/15/18309437/new-york-city-accountability-task-force-law-algorithm-transparency-automation

[7] Fox Cahn, Albert (2020). The first effort to regulate AI was a spectacular failure. Fast Company.https://www.fastcompany.com/90436012/the-first-effort-to-regulate-ai-was-a-spectacular-failure

[8] Sheard, Nathan (2020). Victory! New York city council Passes the POST Act. Electronic Frontier Foundation. https://www.eff.org/deeplinks/2020/06/victory-new-yorks-city-council-passes-post-act)

government. Without engagement, communities will be fearful of third-party software, data privacy, and increased surveillance.

Following the evaluation and engagement phases, an algorithm is created and deployed, and a randomized control trial evaluation compares outcomes for the business-as-usual decision-making approach to those from the algorithm. A second round of community engagement asks stakeholders to judge whether the use of data and algorithms was worth the benefit for both participants and taxpayers.

Algorithmic governance is based on the idea that algorithmic decision-making is just a new take on the traditional Planning approach governments use to create programs. I do not know of a government anywhere that has engaged in such a comprehensive process around algorithms. It is far easier for an agency to procure a soup-to-nuts private-sector algorithm, even if little is known about the black box or its utility.

The 'procure first and ask questions later strategy' is the Mark Zuckerberg approach to algorithmic governance. Zuckerberg's famous mantra, 'Move fast and break things', landed Facebook in hot water, much the way that police departments, early adopters of machine learning, are now on the defensive about their use of algorithmic surveillance.

A more deliberate planning approach will likely lead to better programs, better outcomes, and more social cohesion among stakeholders. This is not to say that a more transparent approach will deliver political cover to government agencies. Ultimately, it is up to mayors and agency officials to lead - but without transparency, innovation will suffer.

To end on this note, I hope I have succeeded in convincing you that data science and Planning are intertwined. Data science cannot replace more participatory forms of Planning, but it does have an emerging role to play in both Planning education and Planning practice.

Assuming you made it through this book (or my class that uses this book), how can you keep learning? I direct the Master of Urban Spatial Analytics program at the University of Pennsylvania - a graduate program that teaches at the intersection of data science and public policy. A couple years back a prospective student at an open house asked me this: "My professor told me there is no way I could come here and become a data scientist in one year - what do you say to that?"

My response was, "your professor sounds like a great mentor - he or she is absolutely correct." The data scientist is a tradesperson - a problem is revealed, the right tool is found, and a solution implemented. Becoming a data scientist takes humility, team spirit, legwork, and lots of trial and error. Above all, it takes years of experience. Here are some suggestions for furthering your data science skills:

1. Start a portfolio where you can showcase your work. Assume no one will read a single use case for more than 6-8 minutes so lead with data visualization and focus on the business process.
2. Start learning and practicing more complicated machine learning algorithms and use cases.
3. Your first job will likely be as a 'data analyst', where you will be cleaning data and performing other menial tasks. Remember that if the ball is dropped in the data wrangling phase, then all the fancy analytical work to follow is wasted. Perform these tasks with a smile on your face.
4. Find yourself a strong mentor who will respectfully shred your work but offer two quick nuggets of wisdom before sending you on your way. You know someone is a good mentor if you leave their office like, "so and so doesn't know what they're

talking about," before realizing they were totally correct after you implement the change.

Finally, challenge yourself; stay curious and rely on your creativity to solve problems that you find impactful. I hope you found this book useful.

Index